DIETRICH BONHOEFFER WORKS, VOLUME 2

Act and Being

This series is a translation of
DIETRICH BONHOEFFER WERKE
Edited by
Eberhard Bethge, Ernst Feil,
Christian Gremmels, Wolfgang Huber,
Hans Pfeifer, Albrecht Schönherr,
Heinz Eduard Tödt†, Ilse Tödt

DIETRICH BONHOEFFER WORKS

General Editor
Wayne Whitson Floyd, Jr.

DIETRICH BONHOEFFER

Act and Being

Transcendental Philosophy and Ontology in Systematic Theology

Translated from the German Edition
Edited by
HANS-RICHARD REUTER

English Edition
Edited by
WAYNE WHITSON FLOYD, JR.

Translated by
H. MARTIN RUMSCHEIDT

FORTRESS PRESS   MINNEAPOLIS

Funding for this volume has come from the National Endowment for the Humanities, the Anderson-Paffard Foundation, the Bowen H. and Janice Arthur McCoy Charitable Foundation, the John N. Bergstrom Endowment Fund, the Lusk-Damen Charitable Gift Fund, and the Wisconsin Conference of the United Church of Christ.

DIETRICH BONHOEFFER WORKS, Volume 2
Act and Being

New English-language translation with new supplementary material published by Fortress Press in 1996 as part of *Dietrich Bonhoeffer Works*.

Original English-language edition of *Act and Being* copyright © 1961 William Collins Sons & Co., Ltd., and Harper and Row Publishers, Inc. Published in German as *Akt und Sein* by Gütersloher Verlag in 1931 and by Christian Kaiser Verlag in 1956.

Dietrich Bonhoeffer Works, Volume 2

First English-language edition of *Dietrich Bonhoeffer Works, Volume 2,* published by Fortress Press in 1996. Originally published in German as *Dietrich Bonhoeffer Werke, Band 2,* by Christian Kaiser Verlag in 1988.

Dietrich Bonhoeffer Works, Volume 2, copyright © 1996 Augsburg Fortress. All rights reserved.

Jacket design: Cheryl Watson
Internal design: The HK Scriptorium, Inc.

Library of Congress has catalogued this series as follows:

Bonhoeffer, Dietrich, 1906–1945.
    [Works. English. 1996]
    Dietrich Bonhoeffer works / [general editor, Wayne Whitson Floyd,
Jr.]. — 1st English-language ed. with new supplementary material.
       p.   cm.
    Translation of: Dietrich Bonhoeffer Werke.
    Includes bibliographical references and index.
    Contents: — v. 5. Life together; Prayerbook of the Bible
    ISBN 0-8006-8305-6 (v. 5 : alk. paper)
    1. Theology. I. Floyd, Wayne W. II. Title.
BR45.B6513   1996
230'.044—dc20   95-38988
                                        CIP

The paper used in this publication meets the minimum requirements of American National Standard for Information Sciences—Permanence of Paper for Printed Library Materials, ANSI Z329.48-1984.

ISBN 0-8006-8302-1
Manufactured in the U.S.A.   AF 1-8302

CONTENTS

GENERAL EDITOR'S FOREWORD TO DIETRICH BONHOEFFER WORKS

Since the time that the writings of Dietrich Bonhoeffer (1906–1945) first began to be available in English after World War II, they have been eagerly read both by scholars and by a wide general audience. The story of his life is compelling, set in the midst of historic events that shaped a century.

Bonhoeffer's leadership in the anti-Nazi Confessing Church and his participation in the *Abwehr* resistance circle make his works a unique source for understanding the interaction of religion, politics, and culture among those few Christians who actively opposed National Socialism. His writings provide not only an example of intellectual preparation for the reconstruction of German culture after the war but also a rare insight into the vanishing world of the old social and academic elites. Because of his participation in the resistance against the Nazi regime, Dietrich Bonhoeffer was hanged in the concentration camp at Flossenbürg on April 9, 1945.

Yet Bonhoeffer's enduring contribution is not just his moral example but his theology. As a student in Tübingen, Berlin, and at Union Theological Seminary in New York — where he also was associated for a time with the Abyssinian Baptist Church in Harlem — and as a participant in the European ecumenical movement, Bonhoeffer became known as one of the few figures of the 1930s with a comprehensive and nuanced grasp of both German- and English-language theology. His thought resonates with a prescience, subtlety, and maturity that continually belies the youth of the thinker.

In 1986 the Christian Kaiser Verlag, now part of Gütersloher Verlagshaus, marked the eightieth anniversary of Bonhoeffer's birth by issuing the first of the sixteen volumes of the definitive German edition of his writings, the *Dietrich Bonhoeffer Werke*. Preliminary discussions about an English translation began even as the German series was beginning to emerge. As a consequence, the International Bonhoeffer Society, English Language Section, formed an editorial board, initially chaired by Robin Lovin, assisted by Mark Brocker, to undertake this project. Since 1993 the *Dietrich Bonhoeffer Works* translation project has been located in the Krauth Memorial Library of the Lutheran Theological Seminary at Philadelphia, under the leadership of its general editor — Wayne Whitson Floyd, Jr., the director of the seminary's Dietrich Bonhoeffer Center — and its executive director — Clifford J. Green of Hartford Seminary.

Dietrich Bonhoeffer Works provides the English-speaking world with an entirely new, complete, and unabridged translation of the written legacy of one of the twentieth century's most notable theologians; it includes a large amount of material appearing in English for the first time. Key terms are translated consistently throughout the corpus, with special attention being paid to accepted English equivalents of technical theological and philosophical concepts.

The *Dietrich Bonhoeffer Works* strives, above all, to be true to the language, style, and — most importantly — the theology of Bonhoeffer's writings. Translators have sought, nonetheless, to present Bonhoeffer's words in a manner that is sensitive to issues of language and gender. Consequently, accurate translation has removed sexist formulations that had been introduced inadvertently or unnecessarily into earlier English versions of his works. In addition, translators and editors generally have employed gender-inclusive language, so far as this was possible without distorting Bonhoeffer's meaning or dissociating him from his own time.

At times Bonhoeffer's theology sounds fresh and modern, not because the translators have made it so, but because his language still speaks with a hardy contemporaneity even after more than half a century. In other instances, Bonhoeffer sounds more remote, a product of another era, not due to any lack of facility by the translators and editors, but because his concerns and his rhetoric are, in certain ways, bound to a time that is past.

Volumes include introductions written by the editors of the English edition, footnotes provided by Bonhoeffer, editorial notes added by the

German and English editors, and afterwords composed by the editors of the German edition. In addition, volumes provide tables of abbreviations used in the editorial apparatus, as well as bibliographies which list sources used by Bonhoeffer, literature consulted by the editors, and other works related to each particular volume. Finally, volumes contain pertinent chronologies, charts, and indexes of scriptural references, names, and subjects.

The layout of the English edition has retained Bonhoeffer's original paragraphing, as well as his manner of dividing works into chapters and sections. The pagination of the German critical edition, the *Dietrich Bonhoeffer Werke,* is indicated in the outer margins of the pages of the translated text. At times, for the sake of precision and clarity of translation, a word or phrase that has been translated is provided in its original language, in normal type, set within square brackets at the appropriate point in the text. All biblical citations come from the New Revised Standard Version, unless otherwise noted. Where versification of the Bible used by Bonhoeffer differs from the NRSV, the verse number in the latter is noted in the text in square brackets.

Bonhoeffer's own footnotes — which are indicated by plain, superscripted numbers — are reproduced as they appear in the German critical edition, complete with his idiosyncrasies of documentation. In these, as in the accompanying editorial notes, existing English translations of books and articles have been substituted for their counterparts in other languages whenever available. When non–English titles are not listed individually in the bibliographies (along with an English translation of those titles), a translation of those titles has been provided within the footnote or editorial note in which they are cited.

The editorial notes — which are indicated by superscripted numbers in square brackets, except in volume five where they are indicated by plain, superscripted numbers — provide information on the intellectual, ecclesiastical, social, and political context of Bonhoeffer's pursuits during the first half of the twentieth century. These are based on the scholarship of the German critical edition; they have been supplemented by the contributions of the editors of the English edition. Where the editors or translators of the English edition have substantially added to or revised a German editor's note, the initials of the person making the change(s) appear at the note's conclusion. When any previously translated material is quoted within an editorial note in an altered form, such changes should be assumed to be the responsibility of the translators.

Bibliographies at the end of each volume provide the complete information for each source that Bonhoeffer or the various editors have mentioned in their work. References to the archives, collections, and personal library of materials that had belonged to Bonhoeffer and that survived the war — as cataloged in the *Nachlaß Dietrich Bonhoeffer* — are indicated within the *Dietrich Bonhoeffer Works* by the initials NL followed by the appropriate reference code within that published index.

The production of any individual volume of the *Dietrich Bonhoeffer Works* requires the assistance of numerous individuals and organizations, whose support is duly noted in the respective editor's introduction. A special note of gratitude, however, is owed to all those prior translators, editors, and publishers of various portions of Bonhoeffer's literary legacy who heretofore have made available to the English-speaking world the writings of this remarkable theologian.

This English edition depends especially upon the careful scholarship of all those who labored to produce the critical German edition from which these translations have been made. Their work has been overseen by a board of general editors — responsible for both the concept and the content of the German edition — composed of Eberhard Bethge, Ernst Feil, Christian Gremmels, Wolfgang Huber, Hans Pfeifer, Albrecht Schönherr, Heinz Eduard Tödt†, and Ilse Tödt.

The present English edition would have been impossible without the creative and untiring dedication of the members of the editorial board of the *Dietrich Bonhoeffer Works:* Mark Brocker, James H. Burtness, Keith W. Clements, Clifford J. Green, Barbara Green, John W. de Gruchy, James Patrick Kelley, Geffrey B. Kelly, Reinhard Krauss, Robin W. Lovin, Michael Lukens, Nancy Lukens, Paul Matheny, Mary Nebelsick, and H. Martin Rumscheidt.

The deepest thanks for their support of this undertaking is owed, as well, to all the various members, friends, and benefactors of the International Bonhoeffer Society; to the National Endowment for the Humanities, which supported this project during its inception; to the Lutheran Theological Seminary at Philadelphia and its Auxiliary who established and help support the Dietrich Bonhoeffer Center on its campus specifically for the purpose of facilitating these publications; and to our publisher, Fortress Press, as represented with uncommon patience and *Gemütlichkeit* by Marshall Johnson, Rachel Riensche, Pam McClana-han, and Lois Torvik. Such a collaboration as this is fitting testimony to the spirit of Dietrich Bonhoeffer, who was himself always so attentive to the creative mystery of community and that ever-deepening collegiality that is engendered by our social nature as human beings.

Wayne Whitson Floyd, Jr. , General Editor
January 27, 1995
The Fiftieth Anniversary of the Liberation of Auschwitz

ABBREVIATIONS

AB	*Act and Being*
CC	*Christ the Center* (U.K. title *Christology*)
CD	*The Cost of Discipleship*
CF/T	*Creation and Fall/Temptation*
CS	*The Communion of Saints* (U.K. title *Sanctorum Communio*)
DBW	*Dietrich Bonhoeffer Werke*—German Edition
DBWE	*Dietrich Bonhoeffer Works*—English Edition
E	*Ethics*
GS	*Gesammelte Schriften* (Collected Works)
ILTP	*I Loved This People*
LPP	*Letters and Papers from Prison,* 4th ed.
LT	*Life Together*
LW	[Martin] *Luther's Works,* American Edition
MW	*Meditating on the Word*
NL	*Nachlaß Dietrich Bonhoeffer*
NRS	*No Rusty Swords*
PB	*The Prayerbook of the Bible*
PP	*Prayers from Prison*
PTB	*Preface to Bonhoeffer*
SPC	*Spiritual Care*
TF	*A Testament to Freedom*
TP	*True Patriotism*
WA	*Werke: Kritische Gesamtausgabe* (Martin Luther, Weimar Ausgabe)
WF	*The Way to Freedom*
WP	*Worldly Preaching*

WAYNE WHITSON FLOYD, JR.

EDITOR'S INTRODUCTION TO THE ENGLISH EDITION

Dietrich Bonhoeffer's name was introduced to the English-speaking world through the appreciative reception that was given to certain of his writings in the generation following the second world war. Titles such as *The Cost of Discipleship, Life Together, Ethics,* and *Letters and Papers from Prison* summoned an image of a courageous pastor and thoughtful theologian who rose above the confusion and inaction of his age not only to speak prophetic words of clarity but also to take costly actions of resistance against the horrors of National Socialism. His provocative words became a staple among those themselves searching for an adequate response to a 'world come of age' in the 1950s and 1960s. He evoked a fearless openness to the challenges of modernity, a way to be Christian without succumbing to mere religiosity, a spiritual path that led into the midst of this world, evoking a compassionate and redemptive embrace of both life's gifts and its deep wounds and needs.

Far less well known and read, however, were the works that come from the first half of Bonhoeffer's adult life — the writings from the time of his academic preparation for an anticipated professional life as a university professor, as well as those that were the first fruits of his academic vocation. To be ignorant, however, of his first dissertation *Sanctorum Communio*,[1] or the university lectures later published as *Creation and*

[1.] *Sanctorum Communio* was Bonhoeffer's doctoral dissertation, the first of two theses that were required of a candidate wishing to receive a doctorate and to teach in a German university.

1

Fall and *Christ the Center*,[2] not to mention *Act and Being*,[3] is both to disregard the very foundations of the better-known works that followed and, almost invariably, to misunderstand them.

Dietrich Bonhoeffer's academic theological career was distinguished, despite its brevity. It began with the year he spent (1923–24) studying theology at the University of Tübingen. This was followed, beginning in June 1924, with a three-year program at the University of Berlin, culminating in the acceptance of his doctoral dissertation *Sanctorum Communio* in 1927. In February 1928, Bonhoeffer left Berlin to become curate of a German-speaking congregation in Barcelona.

In 1929–30 Bonhoeffer was back in Berlin working as an assistant to Wilhelm Lütgert, a specialist in German idealism. His qualifying thesis or *Habilitationsschrift*, *Act and Being*, was accepted in 1930, and in July of that year Bonhoeffer presented his inaugural lecture, "Humanity in Contemporary Philosophy and Theology," at the University of Berlin. Bonhoeffer then spent the academic year 1930–31 as a postgraduate student at Union Theological Seminary in New York. On his return to Germany, Bonhoeffer taught at Berlin from mid–1931 to 1933.

In the summer of that year Bonhoeffer's formal academic career came to an end with his final lectures at Berlin on "Christology" and his seminar on "Hegel."[4] That autumn he accepted a call to serve two German congregations in London, where he entered a self-imposed quasi-exile, increasingly convinced that Christianity in Germany faced in its new leader, Adolf Hitler, a crisis — a *status confessionis* — such as it had not known since the Protestant Reformation.

The Writing of *Act and Being*

On a summer day exactly sixteen years before the fateful day of July 20, 1944 — when the failed attempt to assassinate Adolf Hitler finally

---

[2.] The lectures subsequently published as *Creation and Fall* were delivered at the University of Berlin during the winter semester, 1932–33. Those subsequently published as *Christ the Center* were delivered at Berlin during the summer semester, 1933.

[3.] *Act and Being* was Bonhoeffer's second thesis, the *Habilitationsschrift* that qualified him to teach at the University of Berlin.

[4.] The former lectures, although the manuscript is incomplete, formed the basis for the publication of *Christ the Center*. The text of the latter has been lost; a reconstruction of the student notes of Ferenc Lehel from that seminar has been edited by Ilse Tödt and published as *Dietrich Bonhoeffers Hegel-Seminar*.

sealed Bonhoeffer's fate as a conspirator in that plot — Dietrich had written to his doctoral adviser, the Berlin systematic theologian and church historian Reinhold Seeberg, saying that he had chosen as the topic of his second doctoral thesis "not a historical one, but rather a systematic one. It connects to the question of consciousness and conscience in theology and to several Luther citations from the major Galatians commentary." The exploration of this question of consciousness, Bonhoeffer wrote, ought to "be not a psychological but rather a theological investigation."[5]

In deference to Seeberg, who was facing retirement in the near future, Bonhoeffer previously had agreed to write his first dissertation, *Sanctorum Communio*, on a topic "that is half-historical and half systematic."[6] But now he wanted to turn to theology per se, and to do so with a writing project that would be the entree to a serious academic career, not just a stepping stone to ecclesiastical life. To his friend Helmut Rößler, Bonhoeffer later wrote that he was planning "in connection with the problem of consciousness" to write a thesis with a somewhat surprising goal, the treatment of the "problem of the child in theology."[7] Neither friend nor teacher could have imagined how the ambitious student of theology could deliver on both promises — a theology of consciousness and a theology of the child — in a single philosophical-theological volume such as *Act and Being*.[8]

[5.] Bonhoeffer's letter to Reinhold Seeberg (July 20, 1928), *GS* 6:142f. Also see Eberhard Bethge, *Dietrich Bonhoeffer*, 87–89. Although the present work consistently endeavors to use gender-inclusive language, quotations from others remain as published.

[6.] Bonhoeffer's letter to his parents (September 21, 1925), *DBW* 9:156.

[7.] Bonhoeffer's letter to Helmut Rößler (August 7, 1928), *NRS* 38–39 (*GS* 1:53).

[8.] Cf. Reinhold Seeberg's letter to Bonhoeffer, in which his mentor wrote of his quite different expectations for his student: "I am in suspense about the topic you yourself will choose. Perhaps it would be advisable now to seek out something historically or biblically oriented, in order independently to get used to the line of questioning and methods of these fields as well. How would it be, for example, with the consideration of the question of why in the Scholasticism of the twelfth century the ethical problems recede so strongly, and of how to judge the presentation in John of Salisbury's *Metalogicus*. But this is only an example and if you have something of greater personal interest to you, then it is naturally better. But the history of ethics, and still more of morality, is an area on which a young man today could focus himself, with the goal of something like an ethical history of dogma from the Sermon on the Mount to our own days" (October 19, 1928), *NRS* 36, trans. altered (*GS* 3:17).

Bonhoeffer wrote *Act and Being* during the summer semester of 1929 and the winter semester of 1929–30 at Berlin, facing a February 1930 deadline. While writing this second thesis, he held the position of *Voluntärassistent* or training assistant with Wilhelm Lütgert, who had just been called to the Berlin theological faculty as Reinhold Seeberg's successor.[9] Lütgert considered his inherited postdoctoral student to be a Heideggerian, on whose philosophy Lütgert — had he not just "taken over" Bonhoeffer — "would have surely exercised some more pressure."[10] Bonhoeffer himself described the period of the writing of *Act and Being* in words that bring to mind the labors of many a thesis writer facing a deadline: "I plunged myself into my work in a very unchristian and arrogant manner. A crazy ambition, which many observed in me, made life difficult for me. . . . Back then I was frightfully alone and abandoned to myself. It was very bad."[11]

The following summer semester Bonhoeffer underwent both the oral *Habilitation* examinations in the theological faculty and a required examination with the Berlin church. He completed the latter from July 5th to July 8th, 1930,[12] having been granted permission by the Protestant superior church council not to attend the normally mandatory preaching seminar, since he "has shown now once again through his *Habilitationsschrift*, which has been recognized by the theological faculty as a good achievement, that his scholarly preparation is a good one."[13] Approximately one week later the postdoctoral student presented his examination lecture.[14] At the beginning of August 1930, the dean, Erich Seeberg, communicated to the Prussian minister for Science, Art and National Education, under the diary number 730, "that on the 12th of July 1930 Mr. Lic. *Bonhoeffer* has qualified for the postdoctoral degree

---

[9.] Bonhoeffer's fear that his new mentor, identified as a specialist in idealism, "[will] have even less understanding than Seeberg . . . for my work," did not appear to interfere with his research. See Bonhoeffer's letter to his parents (February 6, 1929), *GS* 6:163.

[10.] Bethge, *Dietrich Bonhoeffer*, 94.

[11.] Letter of January 1936, *GS* 6:367.

[12.] Bethge, *Dietrich Bonhoeffer*, page 178 of the German edition.

[13.] Writing of the Protestant Consistory from May 22, 1930, as well as the written response of the Protestant superior church council from May 31, 1930 (*GS* 6:173f.).

[14.] Cf. letter to Helmut Rößler (June 24, 1930), *NL* A 20, 4.5. The topic of the examination lecture is not known.

in systematic theology in the theological faculty," adding that "the *Habilitationsschrift*, which is not yet printed, shall be handed in later."[15]

Publication and Reception

Bonhoeffer's first attempt to publish *Act and Being* was with Christian Kaiser Verlag, the publisher of Karl Barth and of 'dialectical theology'. Paul Althaus offered to try to find a place for Bonhoeffer's *Habilitationsschrift* in the series he edited at Christian Kaiser along with Karl Barth and Karl Heim, *Forschungen zur Geschichte und Lehre des Protestantismus* (Studies in the history and teachings of Protestantism), but this could not be arranged without a significant delay. Bonhoeffer's next option, to have *Act and Being* appear as a supplementary issue to *Zwischen den Zeiten*, also published by Kaiser Verlag, also was unsuccessful, due to Bonhoeffer's desire for a timely publication. Finally, through the mediation of Lütgert[16] and Althaus,[17] the work was accepted by C. Bertelsmann publishers for their series *Beiträge zur Förderung christlicher Theologie* (Contributions to the advancement of Christian theology).

Althaus wrote to Bonhoeffer's new publisher that "I consider the work to be an exceedingly significant achievement which must be printed as soon as possible."[18] The book appeared in September 1931 as the second issue in the thirty-fourth volume of the Gütersloh series, copies of which were sent by the author to Althaus,[19] Erwin Sutz,[20] and Rößler.[21] To his sponsor Paul Althaus he sent the printed version of his dissertation, *Sanctorum Communio*, too, writing that "There remain for me, however, essential material connections as well between both works, connections that pertain in principle precisely to the church."[22]

[15.] *NL* D 4. Bethge's *Dietrich Bonhoeffer* incorrectly dates the *Habilitation* as July 18, 1930.

[16.] Cf. Lütgert's letter to Bonhoeffer (January 18, 1931), *GS* 3:20.

[17.] Cf. letter to Althaus (January 28, 1931), *NL* Appendix A 10.

[18.] Letter from Althaus to Karl Bonhoeffer (March 4, 1931), cited from Bethge, *Dietrich Bonhoeffer*, 100, trans. altered [MR]. After the death of Lütgert and Schlatter, Althaus became the sole editor of the *Beiträge zur Förderung christlicher Theologie*.

[19.] Letter to Althaus (September 16, 1931), *NL* Appendix A 10.

[20.] Letter to Erwin Sutz (October 8, 1931), *NRS* 123 (*GS* 1:22).

[21.] Letter to Rößler (October 8, 1931), *GS* 1:62.

[22.] See above, editorial note 19.

In the two years after its initial publication, reviews and discussions of *Act and Being* appeared by Heinz Eisenhuth in the *Theologischen Literaturzeitung* and by Hinrich Knittermeyer in *Zwischen den Zeiten*.[23] Earlier Emil Brunner, made cognizant of the newcomer no doubt through Sutz, referred in a note on his *Ethics* to this "instructional writing."[24]

A quarter-century later in 1956, through the efforts of Ernst Wolf, a new edition allowed *Act and Being* to appear at last under the imprint of Christian Kaiser, volume five of the *Theologische Bücherei* (Theological Library). Translations of this appeared in 1961 and 1962 in English, in 1968 in Japanese, in 1970 in selections in French, and in 1985 in Italian.

Beyond his own lifetime Bonhoeffer's notoriety clearly originated with the publication and clamorous reception of his *Letters and Papers from Prison*, followed by the growing awareness of other examples of his writings, particularly those from during the church struggle. And the fragmentary character of many of these works seemed to eclipse Bonhoeffer's own attempts in *Sanctorum Communio* and *Act and Being* to articulate the conditions of the possibility of a coherent theological methodology. Moreover, the level of difficulty of the work itself made *Act and Being* seem at odds with the portrait drawn by Bonhoeffer's early interpreters of a rhetorically inspiring, yet antispeculative, nonmetaphysical — that is to say, not academic — writer.

The perception of *Act and Being* as an uncharacteristically dense and opaque tome has been, however, a two-edged sword. It has contributed, to be sure, to the regrettable neglect of this work, especially among Bonhoeffer's English readership who were at times hampered merely by the limits of the available translation. Yet, for those who have attempted to undertake a close study of Bernard Noble's earlier English version, these very characteristics of *Act and Being* often have had the beneficial effect of helping to turn the "eminently quotable" Bonhoeffer of the *Ethics, The Cost of Discipleship,* and the *Letters and Papers from Prison* back into a genuinely scholarly explorer of theology's deepest methodological needs. Bonhoeffer's writing here is an example of what Theodor Adorno once called a "substantive thought — a thought of whose movement the thinker becomes aware only as [one] performs it."[25] *Act and*

[23.] See below, Bibliography to *Act and Being*, 204, 205.
[24.] Emil Brunner, *The Divine Imperative*, 606.
[25.] Theodor W. Adorno, *Negative Dialectics*, xix.

Being undertakes such a form of thought whose movement the reader can comprehend only when one thinks along with Bonhoeffer. It resists facile summation, demanding disciplined theological engagement.

Cultural, Theological, and Philosophical Context

Act and Being evidences Bonhoeffer's emerging practical concern to find for theology a methodology adequate and proper to its unique subject matter — and to the challenging terrain of its cultural and historical location. Despite its seemingly abstract philosophical cast, this work begs to be interpreted within the concrete, historical context of the cultural crisis in Germany between the world wars, which eventuated in the National Socialist rise to power in 1933. For, as Robin Lovin has insightfully noted, "unlike Barth and Brunner, Bonhoeffer experienced the dislocations in European society after 1914 as the background of his life, and not as a strange intrusion that called his theology into question."[26]

Bonhoeffer stringently refused to join in the growing antimodernist, neo-Romantic, *völkisch* worldview that was then threatening theology's best attempts at rational thinking.[27] But neither was his theology merely a 'modern theology', drawing all of its inspiration from — and speaking all of its conclusions to — the theological and philosophical traditions from the nineteenth century that tried to sustain a naive confidence in human rationality and moral perfectibility even in the face of the recent horrors of World War I.[28] Bonhoeffer wished theology to speak with all the resources of modern thought, yet with its own distinctive voice, including the prophetic tone of the critique of idolatry.

Bonhoeffer therefore approached his chosen topic for *Act and Being*, a theology of consciousness, from within the perspective of the Reformation tradition's insights about the origin of human sinfulness in the *cor curvum in se* — the heart turned in upon itself and thus open neither to the revelation of God, nor to the encounter with the neighbor.[29] Bon-

---

[26.] Robin Lovin, *Christian Faith and Public Choices*, 126.

[27.] See Wayne Whitson Floyd, Jr., "The Search for an Ethical Sacrament: From Bonhoeffer to Critical Social Theory."

[28.] See Wolfgang Huber, "Bonhoeffer and Modernity," N.B. 10ff.

[29.] One of the surprising discoveries of a careful reading of *Act and Being* may be the discovery of the extent to which the central philosophical sections of the book are deeply indebted to theological insights from Martin Luther, especially his *Lectures on Galatians*.

hoeffer wished to analyze consciousness, that is to say, as itself inherently moral. Epistemology was to be understood in terms of the dynamics of power — humanity's desire to have the power to make itself over in its own image, rather than God's, and humanity's concomitant resistance to any encounter with genuine Otherness that threatens the central, sovereign position of the human subject, the "I."[30] What is needed, Bonhoeffer is proposing in *Act and Being*, is a theological epistemology, or philosophy of knowledge, capable of articulating an alternative vision of divine and human community that transcends the desire of the knower to grasp and control the object of knowledge, whether God or another human being. "The concept of revelation," Bonhoeffer wrote in *Act and Being*, "must . . . yield an epistemology of its own."[31]

It was this need for a conceptuality adequate to the theological category of revelation that initially attracted Bonhoeffer to the circle of the early dialectical theologies of Karl Barth, Emil Brunner, Paul Tillich, Friedrich Gogarten, and Eberhard Grisebach. In this task Bonhoeffer clearly took his cue from Karl Barth's problematic relationship to Immanuel Kant: the inescapability of confronting the similarities and differences between transcendental philosophy's and dialectical theology's treatments of Otherness.[32]

When one tries to understand Bonhoeffer's unique contributions to this crucial subject, it is not so much that the philosophical influences on Bonhoeffer's early work have been misrepresented as that they have not yet been reconstructed in anything approaching a comprehensive manner.[33] Yet there are hints throughout the existing biographical material that philosophy, particularly the problematic relationship between the Kant of *The Critique of Pure Reason* and the ensuing Hegelian and post-Hegelian idealism, was an early and consistent influ-

---

[30.] Cf. the lectures on Genesis (summer 1933), published as *CF*, N.B. 40, 69–76.

[31.] See page 31 below.

[32.] For a full treatment of the theological voices in chorus with whom Bonhoeffer is writing here, see below the Afterword by Hans-Richard Reuter, pages 162–83. On the Bonhoeffer-Barth question in particular, see Andreas Pangritz, *Karl Barth in der Theologie Dietrich Bonhoeffers: Eine notwendige Klarstellung*, and Charles Marsh, *Reclaiming Dietrich Bonhoeffer: The Promise of His Theology*.

[33.] Sections of what follows have appeared previously in my book *Theology and the Dialectics of Otherness: On Reading Bonhoeffer and Adorno*, chaps. 1 and 2.

ence on Bonhoeffer's academic theology. Eberhard Bethge notes that even in secondary school, "his brother Karl-Friedrich's skepticism, against which he had to defend himself, spurred him into grappling with epistemology at an early age, and he worked hard at philosophy during his last years at [secondary] school."[34] When he went to Tübingen to study theology, in addition to hearing Karl Heim's lectures in dogmatic theology on Friedrich Schleiermacher and Albrecht Ritschl,[35] Bonhoeffer made numerous "excursions into epistemology."[36] He attended Karl Groos's lectures at Tübingen on logic and on the history of modern philosophy and joined Groos's seminar on Kant's *Critique of Pure Reason*, for which Bonhoeffer wrote a paper.[37] At Berlin he attended lectures by Heinrich Maier in the summer of 1924 on epistemology;[38] lectures by Privatdozent Rieffert in the winter of 1925 on the history of logic; lectures again by Maier in 1925 on freedom and necessity; and in 1927 those on the philosophy of culture by Eduard Spranger, who was "a leading figure of the German Neo-Hegelian revival of the 1920's."[39]

Bonhoeffer's philosophical training at Tübingen during 1923–24 and during his first year at Berlin was evidently sufficiently thorough so that, as Bethge recounts, "in 1925, when Reinhold Seeberg, after a first encounter with Dietrich, met his colleague Karl Bonhoeffer [Dietrich's father] at a meeting of the Senate of Berlin University, he expressed his surprise and admiration at the solidity of the young man's philosophical preparation and his wide knowledge of contemporary philosophy."[40] Thus we would not disagree when Bethge tells us that Bonhoeffer "familiarized himself with Seeberg's great models — Schleiermacher, Hegel and Albrecht Ritschl — and that he also acquired from Seeberg the difficult technical jargon of his student years, which is saturated with Seeberg's Hegelian concepts . . . [and] . . . Ritschl's aversion to metaphy-

---

[34.] Bethge, *Dietrich Bonhoeffer*, 27.

[35.] Ibid., 35.

[36.] Ibid., 43.

[37.] Ibid., 36.

[38.] Ibid., 50. In the summer of 1924, when the only philosophy course that Bonhoeffer was taking was Maier's "*Erkenntnistheorie*" (Epistemology), he was reading Husserl and Hegel.

[39.] L. E. Loemker, "Spranger, (Franz Ernst) Eduard," in *The Encyclopedia of Philosophy*, 8:1.

[40.] Bethge, *Dietrich Bonhoeffer*, 36.

sics."[41] But we should resist letting this suggest that Bonhoeffer's knowledge of, and opinions about, philosophy had come only at second hand, always and only filtered through, and shaped by, the theological concerns of his mentors.[42]

While Hans-Richard Reuter, therefore, has with admirable thoroughness and clarity emphasized the theological roots of *Act and Being* in his "Editor's Afterword to the German Edition" below,[43] it needs to be stressed here that Bonhoeffer's distinctive contribution to his theological problematic was to think it through in dialogue with the basic trends of modern philosophy, particularly starting with Immanuel Kant. Bonhoeffer is attempting in *Act and Being* to state the shape of a "genuine transcendentalism" and its corollary "a genuine ontology"; and he does so with constant reference to Kant's distinction between thought's unifying function (the unity of transcendental apperception) and that which resists being brought completely under the sway of reason (the thing-in-itself). A genuinely dialectical form of thinking is possible only to the extent that it sustains the reality of authentic Otherness.

In Bonhoeffer's typology in *Act and Being*, therefore, both a genuine transcendental philosophy and a genuine ontology are dependent on philosophy's being able to maintain the relationship between *both* the activity of thinking *and* something transcendent, *ein Tranzendentes*, to thought — ontologically distinct from the thinking subject — neither of which "swallows up" the other. Bonhoeffer's dialectical claim that "'being between' that which is transcendent is 'Dasein'"[44] brings to mind the dialogical philosophy of Martin Buber, whose work Bonhoeffer seems not to have known, and the whole personalist school of thought, particularly the philosophy of Eberhard Grisebach, whose influence on *Act and Being* was profound.

His explorations of the Kantian definition of the limits of philosophy — and Hegelian and Fichtean idealism's constant transgression of the limits of genuine Otherness through the pretensions of reason — led Bonhoeffer to inquire into the phenomenological and ontological tradi-

---

[41.] Ibid., 48.

[42.] Thus, the importance of part two of Reuter's Afterword in this volume, concerning the conceptual roots of *Act and Being*, should not be read as superseded by part three, concerning the theological context of Bonhoeffer's work.

[43.] See below, N. B. 168–72.

[44.] See below, page 35.

tions. He was especially concerned with the problem of intersubjectivity in the philosophies of Edmund Husserl and Martin Heidegger, whose *Being and Time* was published in 1927, just after Bonhoeffer's work on *Sanctorum Communio* was complete.[45] Throughout *Act and Being*, Bonhoeffer is arguing that what is needed is a form of theological thinking that takes seriously both philosophy's own repeated attempts to surmount its intrinsic tendency toward system, toward totality, and the reasons they must be judged a failure. He wished to clarify the extent to which theology can or cannot affirm transcendental epistemology's subject-object paradigm as appropriate for theological thinking that remembers the sociality of the Other, the ethics of difference — between humanity and God, as between one human being and another.

Description and Organization of the Text

Couched in the jargon of a doctoral thesis, *Act and Being* is a vigorous transcendental argument. That is to say, its concern is with the conditions of the possibility of theology's responsible thinking about Otherness. Bonhoeffer in *Act and Being* engages in a protracted meditation on the consequences of theology's reluctance to state clearly its justifiable reasons for its long and deep involvement in continental philosophy's epistemological subject-object paradigm, which theology has employed precisely as a means by which to explicate its categories of *transcendence* and *revelation*.

Despite his clear sense of the inadequacies for theology of many of philosophy's ways of thinking, Bonhoeffer was aware — as were few of his contemporaries — "that the passage beyond philosophy," as Jacques Derrida more recently has observed, "does not consist in turning the page of philosophy (which usually amounts to philosophizing badly), but in continuing to read philosophers *in a certain way*."[46] *Act and Being* is a theologian's proposal of that *certain way* in which to read theology's investments in the continental philosophical tradition, rather than merely turning its back when the relationship had become problematic, as seemed to Bonhoeffer to be the case with the rise of dialectical theol-

---

[45.] These need to be compared with the personalist philosophies of Bonhoeffer's contemporaries Eberhard Grisebach, Franz Rosenzweig, Eugen Rosenstock-Huessey, and Martin Buber.

[46.] Jacques Derrida, *Writing and Difference*, 288.

ogy. *Act and Being* wished to discover how to honor both theology's category of revelation and the legacy of philosophy's struggle to articulate
an authentically dialectical conceptuality — "the question that Kant and
idealism have posed for theology."[47]

To be sure, Bonhoeffer's willingness to think along with philosophy,
indeed to see a congruity between the philosophical and theological
tasks, is striking. Yet so is his trenchant critique of philosophical idealism, the epitome of which for Bonhoeffer was not Fichte, but the
attempt to "raise substance to the subject," which Hegel had worked out
most completely in his logic — namely the understanding of the object as
an a priori synthesis in transcendental apperception.[48]

Bonhoeffer is inquiring here about the totalizing urge of reason, *Vernunft*, to overcome 'the being between' that is human existence. Thinking, according to Bonhoeffer, either will be *genuinely* transcendental and
ontological, or it will be *systematic* and totalizing. The latter option recognizes *neither* the true act of thinking-within-limits (the goal of genuine
transcendental philosophy) *nor* the nature of the being of what-is-
thought, yet remains beyond-thought — something transcendent (the
goal of genuine ontology).

Act and Being is central to understanding the nature of Bonhoeffer's
movement toward a new paradigm for theological method. It clarifies
not only his thinking about the possibility of a genuinely transcendental
reading of the Kantian tradition vis-à-vis the dominant idealist reading
that he encountered in his teachers. It also more fully develops many of
the social-ontological concerns that had occupied his attention only a
short time earlier in *Sanctorum Communio*. And it points us toward the
enduring ethical problematic of the Other, the stranger, the neighbor,
to which he was to return, for example, in his fragmentary *Ethics*.[49]

Bonhoeffer, the English-speaking audience needs to be reminded
anew, was from the beginning of his career a systematic — perhaps better
stated, a philosophical — theologian. *Act and Being* beyond any doubt
presents us with a scholar more philosophically sophisticated than many
among his theological supporters heretofore have been willing to admit.
Bonhoeffer drew deeply from conceptual wells that, at least in many of
the earlier commentaries on him, were seen as merely the target of his

---

[47.] See below, page 27.
[48.] See Wilhelm Windelband, *A History of Philosophy*, 611, trans. altered.
[49.] Cf. *E*, N.B. 224ff., 248ff.

criticisms, rather than a clue to the context within which his enduring significance must be gauged.

Bonhoeffer refused in *Act and Being* to move from the perceived potential inadequacies of theoretical epistemology directly toward an apparently "more concrete" social or ethical approach. Rather, he searched in *Act and Being* for an enriched conception of human rationality that yet takes significant clues from epistemology — a form of human reason that would be adequate to the emerging social and ethical demands on theology that confronted him.

Following an introductory sketch of the contemporary theological terrain, entitled "The Problem," the argument of *Act and Being* is organized into three main sections. The first deals with the general methodological quest on which Bonhoeffer has embarked, guided by the epistemological paradigm of the subject-object relation and its ontological implications. The second places what Bonhoeffer calls "the act-being problem" in dialogue with the theological category of revelation, developing further his concern with a theology of the church, begun in his first dissertation, *Sanctorum Communio*. The third attempts to state the framework of a theological anthropology — humanity "in Adam" or "in Christ" — using the act-being framework as his guide to addressing the need for a more temporally-oriented typology.

Act and Being and Bonhoeffer's Subsequent Theology

A clearer understanding of *Act and Being* requires that we place it in the context of three other pieces in particular: (a) Bonhoeffer's inaugural lecture at the University of Berlin on July 31, 1930, "Humanity in Contemporary Philosophy and Theology"; (b) a lecture prepared in English and delivered to his peers while studying at Union Theological Seminary in New York in 1931, "The Theology of Crisis and its Attitude toward Philosophy and Science"; and (c) an article written in English in 1931 and published in *The Journal of Religion* in 1932, "Concerning the Christian Idea of God." *Act and Being* also cannot be understood without reference to Bonhoeffer's Berlin lectures from the winter of 1932–33, published as *Creation and Fall* in 1933, and his lectures on Christology from the summer of 1933, posthumously published as *Christ the Center*.

An initial difficulty in understanding *Act and Being* arises from a disparity between the text of the *Habilitationsschrift* and the explication of its themes by its author in his inaugural lecture at Berlin. For example, the subtitle to *Act and Being*[50] is "Transcendental Philosophy and Ontology in Systematic Theology." The inaugural lecture's synopsis of *Act and Being*, however, hardly mentions ontology, and certainly not as a major category in his typology. A recognition of this discrepancy should lead us to notice a further puzzling characteristic of Bonhoeffer's argument.

His own introduction to *Act and Being*, "The Problem," does indeed speak of "the decision one comes to between a transcendental-philosophical and an ontological interpretation of theological concepts," as if this simply entailed deciding between alternatives.[51] Thus Ernst Wolf's introduction to the text of *Act and Being*, which began the 1956 German edition as well as the 1961/1962 English translation, states the usual reading of this work, according to which the *Habilitationsschrift* is to be understood as a study of what Wolf calls the "confrontation between cardinal, mutually exclusive philosophical positions: Transcendentalism (Kant) and Ontology (Heidegger)."[52]

Yet already here we can see some equivocation about the study's true purpose. For example, he does speak at one moment of "how faith as act, and revelation as being, are related to one another."[53] This is as if, parallel to the concerns stated in the subtitle, the former were simply a 'transcendental' issue and the latter an 'ontological' issue. But at the next moment he speaks of revelation itself as needing to be interpreted alternatively "in terms of act [aktmäßig], and . . . in terms of being [seinsmäßig]."[54]

One begins to suspect that there is something else going on here, that the fundamental problem is more subtle than theology's categorical choice between a transcendental emphasis on 'act' and an ontological-systematizing emphasis upon 'being' — or theology's attempt somehow simply to put the two together again.[55] In addition one suspects that considerable care may need to be taken to distinguish what Bonhoeffer

---

[50.] The subtitle of *Act and Being* was omitted from the previous English translation.

[51.] See below, page 27.

[52.] "Introduction" by Ernst Wolf, *AB* 5.

[53.] See below, page 28.

[54.] Ibid.

[55.] The tendency to the latter sort of oversimplification of the task proposed in *Act and Being* seems to be one to which Ernst Feil's *The Theology of Dietrich Bonhoeffer* is prone (N.B. 10).

said he was going to do — perhaps even intended to do — in *Act and Being* itself, and what a careful reading of the text reveals.

Thus, the inaugural lecture leads one to interpret the two divisions of Section A of *Act and Being* not as the polar extremes of the argument: the transcendental endeavor versus the ontological endeavor. Rather, for Bonhoeffer *"der transzendentale Versuch,"* whose inspiration was Immanuel Kant, refers to the general rubric within which Bonhoeffer's own argument in *Act and Being* is to be understood. And *"der ontologische Versuch,"* as seen most clearly in post-Hegelian idealism, represents the dominant way in which philosophy and theology up until Bonhoeffer's time had attempted to respond to the act-being problematic inherited from Kantian transcendentalism. Stated in the most direct terms, Bonhoeffer's constructive argument is that the transcendental endeavor has been to set conditions under which both its own project and that of ontology are to be undertaken if both are not to share complicity in the system's collapse of the dialectic of 'act' and 'being'.

Bonhoeffer stated the sharpest possible formulation of the problem in his essays "Concerning the Christian Idea of God" and "The Theology of Crisis and its Attitude toward Philosophy and Science,"[56] both of which were written in 1931 when Bonhoeffer was a student at Union Theological Seminary in New York. They both carry the tone of an apology for the position of Barth, at that time largely unknown in the United States, in a climate that Bonhoeffer found to be overwhelmingly and uncritically shaped by theological liberalism. Yet they also reflect the cardinal concerns of Bonhoeffer during the time of the writing of *Act and Being*. Thus they remain instructive for our reading of the present text.

First, Bonhoeffer charges in these essays, the legacy of the system-building of idealism to theological liberalism is a conception of thought as "in itself a closed circle," which "does violence to reality, pulling it into the circle of the ego," since "thinking always means system and system excludes reality."[57] In idealism, Bonhoeffer argues,

> there are no limits for the ego; its power and its claim are boundless; it is its own standard. Here all transcendence is pulled into the circle of the

---

[56.] Bonhoeffer, "Concerning the Christian Idea of God," *GS* 3:100–109; "The Theology of Crisis and its Attitude Toward Philosophy and Science," *NRS* 361–72 (*GS* 3:110–26).

[57.] "Concerning the Christian Idea of God," 101.

creative ego. . . . One knows oneself immediately by the act of the coming of the ego to itself.[58]

Second, according to Bonhoeffer, idealism's premises exhibit the sinfulness of the human being after the fall, as understood by Protestant theology. Fallen humanity "refers everything to itself, puts itself in the center of the world, does violence to reality, makes itself God, and God and the other person its creatures."[59] In the "essential boundlessness of thinking, in its claim to be a closed system, in its egocentricity," Bonhoeffer sees "a philosophical affirmation of the theological insight of the Reformers, which they expressed in terms of the *cor curvum in se, corruptio mentis*. Human beings *in statu corruptionis* are indeed alone, they are their own creator and lord, they are indeed the center of their world of sin."[60]

Third, such thinking is therefore incapable of conceiving that "the Christian messages comes . . . entirely from outside of the world of sin. It was precisely God who came in Jesus Christ."[61] The idealist tradition, Bonhoeffer argues in Kierkegaardian fashion, cannot conceive of "God as the absolutely free personality [who] is therefore absolutely transcendent,"[62] and yet who "revealed God's self in 'onceness' . . . in a historical fact, in a historical personality"[63] — in "God's real acting for human beings in history" in Jesus of Nazareth.[64] Since humanity cannot "get outside of the circle of sin" on its own, "revelation in Christ, justification, means breaking . . . the circle of sin. . . . Since only the revelation in Christ claims to constitute the real outside of human beings, it implies that it is the only criterion of any revelation."[65]

[58.] "The Theology of Crisis," 120, trans. altered. There he also writes: "At the basis of all thinking lies the necessity of a system. Thinking is essentially systematic thinking, because it rests upon itself, it is the last ground and criterion of itself. System means the interpretation of the whole through the one which is its ground and its center, the thinking ego. Idealism saw and affirmed this as the proof of the autonomy and the freedom of human beings."

[59.] "Concerning the Christian Idea of God," 101, trans. altered.

[60.] "The Theology of Crisis," 122, trans. altered.

[61.] Ibid., 123, trans. altered.

[62.] "Concerning the Christian Idea of God," 103.

[63.] Ibid., 105, trans. altered.

[64.] "The Theology of Crisis," 112, trans. altered.

[65.] Ibid., 115–16.

Fourth what is needed is "a genuine theological epistemology" that, "as thinking per se, . . . is not excepted from the pretension and boundlessness of all thinking," but which "knows its own insufficiency and its limitations" and thereby can "leave room for the reality of God," even in theological thought.[66] What is needed is a form of theological thinking that can affirm the finitude of God's "revelation in history,"[67] — "the foolishness of the Christian idea of God, which has been witnessed to by all genuine Christian thinking from Paul, Augustine, Luther, to Kierkegaard and Barth" that "God himself dies and reveals [the divine self] in the death of a man, who is condemned as a sinner."[68] And yet such thinking must be able to distinguish between God's finite, historical "revelation in hiddenness," and humanity's sinful desire for "revelation in openness"[69] — the ironic 'openness' of "the captivity of human thinking within itself"[70] that is the truest sign of human brokenness.[71]

Thus the point of *Act and Being* for Bonhoeffer is not merely negative. Rather, if the idealist resolution of genuine transcendentalism's epistemological tension between subject and object does not know "its own insufficiency and limitations,"[72] then "the concept of revelation must . . . yield an epistemology of its own."[73] Revelation needs a form of thinking that both attends to the 'immediacy' of that historical particularity of revelation — which can "take seriously the ontological category in history"[74] — and yet continues to distinguish itself, as thought, from the reality whose presence it mediates.

[66.] "Concerning the Christian Idea of God," 102.

[67.] Ibid., 105.

[68.] Ibid., 108, trans. altered.

[69.] Ibid., 105. For a thoughtful inquiry into the theme of 'hiddenness,' see Andreas Pangritz on arcane discipline in Bonhoeffer's theology in his *Dietrich Bonhoeffers Forderung einer Arkandisziplin – eine unerledigte Anfrage an Kirche und Theologie.*

[70.] "Concerning the Christian Idea of God," 101.

[71.] See "The Theology of Crisis," 113–14: "It is revelation because it is *not* compatible with our own deepest essence, but entirely beyond our whole existence, for would it otherwise have had to be revealed, if it had been potentially in us before? . . . All that means that God's revelation in Christ is revelation in concealment, secrecy. All other so-called revelation is revelation in openness."

[72.] "Concerning the Christian Idea of God," 102.

[73.] See below, page 31.

[74.] "Concerning the Christian Idea of God," 106.

Bonhoeffer has inherited from Søren Kierkegaard the suspicion that all immediacy per se is paganism. And yet he suspects that in the theology of revelation of his mentor, Barth, mediation itself has been carried to such an extreme that God is only tangential to history, never ontologically *in* history, with graspable, "haveable particularity." What sort of thinking, then, can theology be if it would (1) avoid the pitfalls of idealism, (2) take account of sin, (3) affirm the particularity of revelation in history, and (4) still be *thought*, affirming that "in every theological statement we cannot help but use certain general forms of thinking," which "theology has . . . in common with philosophy"?[75]

Bonhoeffer takes one clue, clearly, from the 'Kantianism' of the early theology of Karl Barth. For

> although Barth knows that even [Kant's] philosophy remains in boundlessness, he sees here the attempt of philosophy to criticize itself basically and takes from here the terminology in order to express the eternal crisis of the human being, which is brought on by God in Christ and which is beyond all philosophical grasp.[76]

Bonhoeffer concludes, however, that the 'beyond' for Barth requires the theological judgment that "there is no Christian philosophy nor philosophical terminology at all."[77] Then, "what according to Barth and his friends," Bonhoeffer asks, "ought to be the task of philosophy?"[78]

Bonhoeffer's response to his own rhetorical question, intentionally or not, is significant because, coming after his dissertation *Act and Being*, it provides a revealing clue to his divergence already from orthodox Barthianism. Bonhoeffer wrote:

> Barth himself has not answered this question sufficiently, *but his friends have thought a great deal about the problem.* Philosophy remains profane science; there *is* no Christian philosophy. But philosophy has to be *critical* philosophy, not *systematic*. And yet since even critical philosophy is bound to be systematic (as we have seen before), philosophy must work in view of this fate. It must try to think truth with regard to the real existence of humanity, and must see that it is itself an expression of the real existence of human beings and that by its own power it not only cannot save human beings, but it can-

---

[75.] "The Theology of Crisis," 118.
[76.] Ibid., 123–24, trans. altered.
[77.] Ibid., 124.
[78.] Ibid., 124.

not even be the crisis of them. *By doing so it gives room, as far as it can, for God's revelation, which indeed makes room for itself by itself.*[79]

Any sympathetic reading of *Act and Being*, however critical it need be, must be willing to follow along with Bonhoeffer's brash attempt to push the transcendental tradition to give room, as far as it can, for God's revelation. He never wavered in his confidence that revelation indeed makes room for itself by itself. But neither did he waver in his sense of the urgency for theology to find for itself a form of conceptuality that is an adequate receptor for these twin demands. What was needed, Bonhoeffer argues, is a form of thinking that takes seriously philosophy's own attempt to surmount its intrinsic tendencies toward system, toward totality. Theology requires a form of thinking capable of realizing transcendental philosophy's own attempts to think critically rather than systematically, its attempts to articulate a genuine active-receptivity of revelation, a dialectics of Otherness.

The social and ethical implications of Bonhoeffer's methodological deliberations in *Act and Being* resonate throughout his other theological writings. Already in *Sanctorum Communio* Bonhoeffer had drawn the ethical inference from idealist epistemology that "the limit set by the individual person is in principle overcome."[80] It would become the guiding metaphor in *Creation and Fall*, where Bonhoeffer speaks of humanity's being created free, but only within the limits of creatureliness.[81] Indeed 'the fall' *is* for Bonhoeffer the Promethean attempt to be God, humanity's attempt to exist *sicut deus*, in the place of God, to become limitless, all-powerful, one whose very existence comes to be defined by the violent transgression of the limit of the Other (thus the Cain and Abel story which concludes the creation-fall narrative in *Genesis*).[82] Indeed the lectures on Christology would propose that Jesus *is* the Other-par-excellence, the sought-for limit to human pretensions, the center of human existence, history, and nature precisely *because* the concreteness of revelation in Christ — the new Adam — provides the creative limit that allows humanity to be authentically human, rather than a demonic usurper of divine power. Bonhoeffer returned to this theme of the limits of creatureliness and their role in human responsible action in

---

[79.] Ibid., 124; trans. altered, emphases added [WF].
[80.] *SC* 27.
[81.] *CF/T* 52ff.
[82.] *CF/T* 72–76.

The Cost of Discipleship and his *Ethics*, calling the life of the Other "a boundary which [the disciple] dare not pass."[83] This enduring theme of the transgression of the Other, the refusal to know any limits, is what *Act and Being* had warned theology against — "the I . . . [become] the *point of departure* instead of the limit-point,"[84] not just of philosophy but of reality itself. To be limitless is to be incapable of being encountered by the revelation of Christ and one's responsibilities to one's neighbor as well.

Act and Being in Bonheoffer Scholarship in English

Until recently, serious treatments of *Act and Being* in the English literature on Bonhoeffer have been few. Franklin Sherman wrote the first major explication of *Act and Being* in *The Place of Bonhoeffer* in 1962. Walter Lowe wrote an enduringly provocative essay, "The Critique of Philosophy in Bonhoeffer's *Act and Being*," in 1966, but it remains unpublished.[85] The translation of André Dumas's *Dietrich Bonhoeffer: Theologian of Reality* in 1971 offered a tantalizing but finally incomplete glimpse into the philosophical background of *Act and Being*. Heinrich Ott's *Reality and Faith: The Theological Legacy of Dietrich Bonhoeffer* appeared in English in 1972, pointing toward, but not developing, the theme of the sociality of revelation in *Sanctorum Communio* and *Act and Being*. And Thomas Day provided a brief, but less than enthusiastic, overview of *Act and Being* in his *Dietrich Bonhoeffer on Christian Community and Common Sense*, originally written as a Ph.D. dissertation at Union Theological Seminary in 1975.

The first extended treatment of *Act and Being* in English, and the beginning of a new phase of appreciation of this work especially in the United States, began two decades ago with Clifford J. Green's *Bonhoeffer: The Sociality of Christ and Humanity*, published in 1975, which for the first time took seriously the social ontology Bonhoeffer was attempting to articulate. But a decade was to pass between Green's book and the excellent English translation of Ernst Feil's *The Theology of Dietrich Bonhoeffer*, which placed *Act and Being* within the context of Bonhoeffer's entire

---

[83.] *CD* 143; cf. *E*, N.B. 233–35.

[84.] See below, page 39.

[85.] Cf. his "Bonhoeffer and Deconstruction: Toward a Theology of the Crucified Logos," *Theology and the Practice of Responsibility: Essays on Dietrich Bonhoeffer*, 207–21.

theological development and pointed out the centrality of the conceptual pair: *actus directus* and *actus reflexus*. My own *Theology and the Dialectics of Otherness: On Reading Bonhoeffer and Adorno*, published in 1988, sought to uncover the extent of the philosophical innovation and insight in *Act and Being*, and to place Bonhoeffer's developing theology of Otherness into dialogue with one other such interpretation of the Kantian-Hegelian-Heideggerian legacy, the 'negative dialectical' project of Theodor Adorno.[86] That same year, the late Jörg Rades wrote his stimulating and promising essay, "Bonhoeffer and Hegel: From *Sanctorum Communio* to the Hegel Seminar with Some Perspectives for the Later Works," sketching a longer work that will now never be written. More recently Robert P. Scharlemann's essay, "Authenticity and Encounter: Bonhoeffer's Appropriation of Ontology," published in 1994, has refocused attention on the Bonhoeffer-Heidegger connection in *Act and Being*. And Charles Marsh's *Reclaiming Dietrich Bonhoeffer: The Promise of his Theology*, published that same year, has reopened the Bonhoeffer-Barth relationship to critical inquiry, using it as a springboard to inquire into Bonhoeffer's notion of selfhood — including a sophisticated reference to the philosophical theology of *Act and Being* — and its relationship to Bonhoeffer's theology of community.

The Critical Edition, Notes, and Apparatus

The basis of the present translation of *Act and Being* is the German critical edition of *Akt und Sein*, edited by Hans-Richard Reuter, which is volume 2 of the *Dietrich Bonhoeffer Werke*, published in 1988. Since both the original manuscript of Bonhoeffer's *Habilitationsschrift* and any typescript copies are missing,[87] the two published editions of the book formed the basis for Reuter's work: (1) *Akt und Sein: Transzendental-philosophie und Ontologie in der systematischen Theologie*, by Dietrich Bon-

---

[86.] This work in particular was profoundly influenced by the work of Walter Lowe, N.B. his essay, "The Critique of Philosophy in Bonhoeffer's *Act and Being*," mentioned above.

[87.] There is no manuscript or typescript of the work in the *Habilitation* files in the archives of the Humboldt-Universität in (formerly East) Berlin. According to its director, Dr. Kossak, it was not common custom at the time to hand in the work. The archives and library of the publishing house C. Bertelsmann were burned in the war, according to its legal successor, the Gütersloh Verlagshaus Gerd Mohn.

hoeffer. *Beiträge zur Förderung christlicher Theologie*, vol. 34. Edited by A. Schlatter and W. Lütgert. Gütersloh: C. Bertelsmann, 1931. (2) *Akt und Sein: Transzendentalphilosophie und Ontologie in der systematischen Theologie. Theologische Bücherei: Neudrucke und Berichte aus dem 20. Jahrhundert*, vol. 5. Edited by E. Wolf. Munich: Christian Kaiser Verlag, 1956.

The 1931 edition was used as the textual basis of Reuter's work, although the internal pagination of the 1956 edition was retained, since it was the one most familiar to German readers. In the present English edition of *Act and Being*, the pagination of the German text of *DBW* 2 is indicated in the margins of the text in order to facilitate cross-references with that critical edition. No attempt has been made to provide the pagination of either of the former two German editions or the pagination of the previous English translation by Bernard Noble.

Bonhoeffer's footnotes have been retained in a form as close to the original as possible. They are numbered consecutively, using plain Arabic numbers superscripted, beginning anew in each of the four major sections of the book. At times, information missing in Bonhoeffer's footnotes is supplied by the editor, enclosed in brackets, where such information will help the reader not to be misled in attributing a source. Editorial notes may provide further clarification of Bonhoeffer's own notes where necessary, as is the case when missing information is crucial to identify the source being consulted.

Editorial notes provided by the editors of either the German or the English editions are printed at the bottom of the page beneath Bonhoeffer's notes. They also are numbered consecutively, using superscripted Arabic numbers in square brackets, beginning anew in each major section of the book. Translations of Latin and Greek citations, expressions, and vocabulary are placed in double quotation marks in the editorial notes. Cross references to sections of the present work have been placed in editorial notes, if they have been added by an editor or translator rather than by Bonhoeffer. Editorial notes tend to clarify or expand knowledge of persons, issues, and works during Bonhoeffer's own time, rather than providing material placing Bonhoeffer's position in dialogue with subsequent scholarship on him.

A brief chronology follows the afterword by the editor of the German edition. This is not intended to be an exhaustive timetable of Bonhoeffer's life and the events in which it was imbedded; rather it signals the most pertinent dates related directly to the influences upon *Act and Being*, its composition, and publication.

The bibliography at the end of the text provides a list of the "Literature Used by Bonhoeffer" in the writing of *Act and Being*. It provides the complete bibliographical information to supplement Bonhoeffer's own often scanty and fragmentary documentation. It gives provisional English translations of the titles of books and articles for which there are no published English editions; and it includes the full information about the published English editions of works that Bonhoeffer cites — as well as the German edition originally used by Bonhoeffer himself — where such are available. The "Literature Consulted by the Editors" is listed next in the bibliography, providing titles of the works cited by the editors in their notes throughout the book. Finally, "Other Literature Related to *Act and Being*" is listed, suggesting additional material which may be of special interest to scholars, particularly those in the English-speaking world, that are studying *Act and Being*.

The use of abbreviations in the footnotes, editorial notes, and bibliographies has been held to a minimum. The abbreviations for works written by Bonhoeffer are provided as part of the front matter just before this introduction. All other abbreviations follow the conventions of the *Chicago Manual of Style*, 13th edition.

The indexes for *Act and Being* are based on those in the *DBW* 2 German critical edition. They have been revised and expanded significantly, however, to reflect the common usage of theological terms in English-speaking contexts, in addition to material provided in the English edition that did not appear in the German volume.

Because of their technical usage by Bonhoeffer or their significance within the writings of a person to whom Bonhoeffer frequently refers, a small number of German terms have been left untranslated in the present English edition. These include *Dasein*, which Bonhoeffer virtually always uses here in a technical, Heideggerian manner to refer to human existence, and, at times, the terms *existential* and *existentiell*, which also are being borrowed by Bonhoeffer from Heidegger. Other terms proved especially difficult to translate, and editorial notes have been provided to explain the choices that have been made. Such words include *Aufhebung* (usually used by Bonhoeffer in a Hegelian sense), which has been variously translated as "subversion" or "suspension"; *Gegenstand*, the German word for "object," which Bonhoeffer wishes to be understood as that which "stands over against" the thinking subject; *Mensch*, the usual generic term for "human beings" employed by Bonhoeffer, although at times he uses the more abstract *Menschheit*, which we have translated as "humanity"; and *Gemeinde*, which can mean "congregation," "community of faith," or sometimes simply "community."

Acknowledgments

A special note of gratitude is due to several of those who contributed to the production of this entirely new, fresh, and engaging English edition of *Act and Being*. First of all, Martin Rumscheidt has produced a translation that many times reads with even more lucidity than the original and has done so with more charity and collegiality than any editor could deserve. Hans-Richard Reuter read the entire manuscript and graciously allowed much of the research for his own foreword to the German edition to be incorporated into this editor's introduction to the present volume. Jean Bethke Elshtain and Susan Ford Wiltshire served as official consultants for the volume; their careful readings of the manuscript insured greater felicity in rendering Bonhoeffer's meaning in this 'foreign' tongue. Clifford Green helped with the bibliographical apparatus for this text. Beth Orling Farrera read several provisional drafts of the text, providing always-helpful suggestions with some of the thorniest translation problems. Marshall Johnson and Lois Torvik at Fortress Press have proved invaluable mentors in the editorial process. And Mara Donaldson provided sustenance and cheer throughout a process that seemed to conform to no law save that of Zeno (whose riddles had appeared to demonstrate the impossibility of motion!), and then had the fortitude and compassion to proofread the final manuscript — gifting me in innumerable ways with that presence without whom none of this would have much meaning for her editor-husband.

THE PROBLEM

The most recent developments in theology appear to me to be an attempt to come to an agreement about the problem of act and being. On the one hand, by means of his 'critical reservation' Karl Barth seeks to hold on to the freedom of God's grace and thereby to provide a foundation for human existence.[1] Friedrich Gogarten[2] and Rudolf Bultmann[3] wish to free the human being, in its 'concrete situation' or 'historicity' ['Geschichtlichkeit'][4] from the delusion of being at its own

---

[1.] The term *critical reservation* was coined by Eberhard Grisebach's student Hans Michael Müller in his critique of Karl Barth to characterize the systematic basic process of Barth's dialectical theology. Müller's position is spelled out in full in "Credo, ut intelligam," 173. For the controversy that ensued, see Hermann Diem, "Credo ut intelligam" and Gerhardt Kuhlmann, "Zum theologischen Problem der Existenz," 37, note 2. Karl Barth comments on Müller's point of view in his "Bemerkungen zu Hans Michael Müllers Lutherbuch," 568–70. Bonhoeffer refers to this below, 86, footnote 11.

[2.] Cf. Friedrich Gogarten, particularly his *Ich glaube an den dreieinigen Gott, Theologische Tradition und theologische Arbeit*; and "Das Problem einer theologischen Anthropologie."

[3.] Cf. Rudolf Bultmann, "The Question of a Dialectic Theology," "On the Question of Christology," "The Significance of 'Dialectical Theology' for the Scientific Study of the New Testament," and "The Historicity of Man and Faith."

[4.] Standard English translations of Bultmann's works render this term as "historicity," while standard English translations of Martin Heidegger's works

disposal. Hans Michael Müller maintains that, in the contingency of temptation, people reach their decision *propter Christum*.[5] Friedrich Karl Schumann holds the epistemology of idealism culpable for the decline in theology up to and including that of Barth and tries to develop an objective concept of God.[6] On the other hand, Paul Althaus wants to salvage a theology of faith from the collapse of the theology of consciousness.[7] In line with the studies of Luther by Reinhold Seeberg[8] and Karl Holl,[9] Emanuel Hirsch seeks to establish the basis of the 'being' of Christians in consciousness as conscience, as new intention.[10] Friedrich Brunstäd brings God and human beings into a unity in the 'unconditional personality'.[11] Erich Peterson means to find in pure phenomenology the tools to counter dialectical theology; for him theological concepts portray pure concepts of essence and being.[12] Yet others consider the ontological-phenomenological analysis of Dasein[13]

---

render it as "historicality." For the sake of consistency, "historicity" has been used throughout the present work. [WF]

[5.] "On account of, or in light of, Christ" [trans. MR]. Cf. Hans Michael Müller, N.B. *Erfahrung und Glaube bei Luther.*

[6.] Cf. Friedrich Karl Schumann, *Der Gottesgedanke und der Zerfall der Moderne.*

[7.] Cf. Paul Althaus, "Theologie des Glaubens." Bonhoeffer makes no further explicit reference to Althaus in this study. *Act and Being* was published, however, on the recommendation—no longer extant—of this theologian from Erlangen.

[8.] Cf. Reinhold Seeberg, *Luther und Luthertum in der neuesten katholischen Beleuchtung; Textbook of the History of Doctrine,* 3/1; and "Zur Religionsphilosophie Luthers."

[9.] Cf. Karl Holl, *Luther.*

[10.] Cf. Emanuel Hirsch, *Die idealistische Philosophie und das Christentum,* and *Jesus Christus der Herr.*

[11.] Cf. Friedrich Brunstäd, *Die Idee der Religion.*

[12.] Cf. Erik Peterson, "Zur Theorie der Mystik"; "Der Lobgesang der Engel und der mystische Lobpreis"; and "Über die Forderung einer Theologie des Glaubens," N.B. 282, 300ff. There is no further explicit discussion of Peterson in Bonhoeffer's text. Peterson had converted to the Roman Catholic Church at Christmas in 1930. His contact with the circle of Catholic phenomenologists is documented in the obituary he wrote, "Zum Gedächtnis von Max Scheler."

[13.] In common German usage Dasein means "existence." But particularly under the influence of Martin Heidegger, whose *Being and Time* had just appeared in the spring of 1927, Bonhoeffer throughout *Act and Being* uses

by Martin Heidegger in terms of *existentia*[14] and, radically opposite to it, Grisebach's 'critical philosophy' of the contingency of the present.[15] Finally, there is Erich Przywara, a Roman Catholic and Thomist, who assesses the current theological situation of both camps with astonishing clarity. He sets an ontology of the *analogia entis*[16] against the disintegration of theology brought about by the concepts of act in dialectical theology. At the heart of the problem is the struggle with the formulation of the question that Kant and idealism have posed for theology. It is a matter of the formation of genuine theological concepts, the decision one comes to between a transcendental-philosophical and an ontological interpretation of theological concepts. It is a question of the 'objectivity' of the concept of God and an adequate concept of cognition, the issue of determining the relationship between 'the being of God' and the mental act which grasps that being. In other words, the meaning of

---

Dasein in a technical sense denoting the qualitatively distinctive mode of the being-there [Da-Sein] of human beings, in contrast to the being of all else that is. The 'there' of Dasein calls attention to human finitude, the fact that we find ourselves always already situated in time. But the finitude of Dasein is also disclosed to human beings; for only Dasein 'ex-ists', stands out, from all that is around it, aware of itself, aware that its being is for itself an issue, a responsibility. The word has been left untranslated, intending to signal, through its foreignness, a whole arena of discourse in *Act and Being* to which we might otherwise be oblivious. The present work uses the translation of *Sein und Zeit* made by John Macquarrie and Edward Robinson, unless otherwise noted, except that the word "being" [Sein] is not capitalized in English [WF].

[14.] Cf. Martin Heidegger, *Being and Time*, 67. However, in this passage Heidegger goes on to stress that with regard to the entity Dasein, "here our ontological task is to show that when we choose to designate the Being of this entity as existence [Existenz], this term does not and cannot have the ontological signification of the traditional term '*existentia*'; ontologically, *existentia* is tantamount to *Being-present-at-hand*, a kind of Being which is essentially inappropriate to entities of Dasein's character. To avoid getting bewildered, we shall always use the interpretative expression '*presence-at-hand*' for the term '*existentia*', while the term 'existence', as a designation of Being, will be allotted solely to Dasein."

[15.] Cf. Eberhard Grisebach, *Die Grenzen des Erziehers und seine Verantwortung;* "Philosophie und Theologie"; and "Brunners Verteidigung der Theologie."

[16.] "the analogy of being" [MR]. Cf. particularly Erich Przywara, *Religionsphilosophie katholischer Theologie* and *Ringen der Gegenwart.*

23   'the being of God in revelation' must be interpreted theologically, including how it is known, how faith as act, and revelation as being, are related to one another and, correspondingly, *how human beings stand in light of revelation.* Is revelation 'given' to them only in each completed act; is there for human beings such a thing as 'being' in revelation? What form does the concept of revelation have when it is interpreted in terms of act and when it is interpreted in terms of being?

It is not our intention to apply the paired concepts of act and being as a critical principle to the history of theology, not even the most recent. Nonetheless, our inquiry must of necessity engage questions that are currently debated, seeking to provide a systematic sketch of the significance of the problem of act and being for the whole of theological study [Dogmatik].

The juxtaposition of act and being is not identical with that of consciousness and being, as the latter two concepts are not mutually exclusive. Even to conscious-ness [Bewußt-Sein], predicates of being apply, precisely as the mode of being of that which is conscious. Act should be thought of as pure intentionality, alien to being. Given that the act takes place in consciousness, we must distinguish between direct consciousness (*actus directus*) and the consciousness of reflection (*actus reflexus*).[17] In the former, consciousness is purely 'outwardly directed', whereas in the latter, consciousness has the power to become its own object of attention, conscious of its own self in reflection. It is not as if the act offers no material to reflection, only that reflection cannot 'find' the act, because the intentionality that is characteristic of the act is displaced by reflection. This distinction will prove to be of crucial importance in

---

[17.] One even might say that the distinction between *actus directus* and *actus reflexus* is the central idea with which Bonhoeffer is occupied in the following. Bonhoeffer took over this terminology from Franz Delitzsch, *A System of Biblical Psychology,* 407–17, but related it back to the distinction made by early Protestantism between *fides directa* (direct faith) and *fides reflexa* (reflexive faith), which is itself more exact because it is understood not psychologically but theologically. See below, Section C, pages 158–59, notes 29 and 30. Cf. also "Man in Contemporary Philosophy and Theology," *NRS* 65ff. (*GS* 3 [1930]:80f.); "The Theology of Crisis," *NRS* 372 (*GS* 3 [1931]:124); "Concerning the Christian Idea of God," *GS* 3:102; and "Probleme einer theologischen Anthropologie," *GS* 5 (1932/33):343, 349 and 353f.

theology. Even as conscious*ness* [Bewußt-*sein*], being is not in principle contained within *conscious*-ness [*Bewußt*-sein]. As something taking place in consciousness [Bewußt-Seiendes], the act is a temporal, psychic event. But just as one fails to understand the act by 'explaining' it as an occurrence in time, so 'being' is misunderstood when it is defined as something 'existing' (even as something existing in conscious-ness [Bewußt-Seiendes]). Act can never be 'explained' but only 'understood' (Dilthey), just as being can never be 'proved' but only 'pointed out'.[18] It follows that here we are concerned with the transcending of 'what exists'. Wherever this is not understood, every transcendental beginning and every genuine ontology will founder.

At this point only general and preliminary definitions should be given about the nature of act and being in light of which we can raise further questions. On the one hand, act is comprised of relationality, the infinitely-extensive, that which is bound to *conscious*ness, discontinuity, and existentiality. (The term 'existentiality' here should be taken to designate not the sphere of the 'there is' ['es gibt'],[19] but rather the central, potential engagement of a person.) On the other hand, being is comprised of confinement-to-the-self, the infinitely-intensive, that which transcends consciousness, continuity. How the understanding of both manifests itself concretely in philosophy and theology remains to be seen. But it should already be apparent that all of theology, in its teaching concern-

24

[18.] Wilhelm Dilthey, "Ideen über eine beschreibende und zergliedernde Psychologie," juxtaposed *understanding* as the method of the human sciences, or humanities [Geisteswissenschaften], with *explanation* as the procedure of the natural sciences [Naturwissenschaften]: "We explain nature, but we understand psychic life" (144). The juxtaposition of proving [erweisen], and pointing out [aufweisen], can be traced back to a common linguistic usage in phenomenology. *Aufweisen* refers to a method of phenomenological demonstration that requires evidence but not logic. For example, cf. Heidegger, *Being and Time*, 79, 250. Further evidence of such usage can be found in Jakob Lanz, "Aufweis(ung)/Ausweis(ung)," 647–49.

[19.] Bonhoeffer here distinguishes the use of the word existentiality, when speaking of the act, from the more technical Heideggerian meaning of existence, the distinctive mode of being of Dasein. For Heidegger, it is Dasein's openness to being that distinguishes it; thus "only as long as Dasein *is*, 'is there' Being ['gibt es' Sein]" (*Being and Time*, 255). For another influence on Bonhoeffer's use of '*es gibt*', see below, Section B, page 115, editorial note 47). [WF]

ing knowledge of God, of human beings, and of sin and grace, crucially depends on whether it begins with the concept of act or of being.

Arranged systematically, the problem will be examined in the following successive stages:

The encounter with the problem of knowledge provides the first clarification of the problem of act and being. The question of whether this knowledge should be interpreted in terms of act or of being becomes acute with the concept of the object. If that concept is entirely act-oriented, this will have intolerable consequences for a scholarly pursuit that insists on the need for concepts of being, and vice versa, for the question of knowledge is the question of the I about the I, about itself. Here, the question of knowledge is the understanding of Dasein trying its wings, seeking in reflection to adapt to a world, that is, to find itself in it. It is, in other words, the question of human beings. Though the latter does not follow from the former, it is their connection that is essential: the meaning of epistemology [Erkenntnistheorie] is anthropology. Wherever the capacity of human beings to know is attacked, nothing less than being human itself is at stake, which is the reason why, ever since Descartes, the passion of philosophy has burnt so strongly here. But because the concept of knowledge comprises in itself the necessity of transcending the known through the process of knowing, and vice versa, the understanding of Dasein in reference to [in bezug auf] transcendence is, in one form or another, part of the question of knowledge. This suggests that the question of God is a part of it, too. This is true (as we shall show) even where the attempt is made to exclude the question of God altogether, or where, as perhaps in Heidegger's ontology, epistemology is allotted an entirely different place in the whole of philosophy than is the case in transcendental philosophy. This is also true because the question concerning being human is hidden in epistemology, whether or not we are dealing with transcendental attempts to interpret act or ontological attempts to interpret 'being' purely in its own terms. These two attempts represent the most sharply antithetical formulations of the two positions under discussion.

Consequently, the critical idea that governs the discussion of Section A below (AB 33) must be the possibility of applying the suggested solutions of the act-being-problem to Christian conceptions of God and revelation, from which everything else proceeds. That critical idea is tested against the underlying self-understanding of human beings at any moment. The purely transcendental or the purely ontological starting points may be useful to theology as compared to other starting points. But even if this is the case, the possibility of constructing theology on only one of these concepts of knowledge still founders on the attendant understanding of the self—which proves to be that of the autonomous I understanding itself only in terms of itself and subject only to itself. The concept of a contingent revelation of God in Christ denies in principle the possibility of the self-understanding of the I apart from the reference to revelation (Christian transcendentalism). The concept of revelation must, therefore, yield an epistemology of its own. But inasmuch as an interpretation of revelation in terms of act or in terms of being yields concepts of understanding that are incapable of bearing the whole weight of revelation, the concept of revelation has to be thought about within the concreteness of the conception of the church, that is to say, in terms of a sociological category in which the interpretation of act and of being meet and are drawn together into one. The dialectic of act and being is understood theologically as the dialectic of faith and the congregation of Christ. Neither is to be thought without the other; each is 'taken up' or 'suspended' ['aufgehoben'][20] in the other. The theological concepts of object and knowledge are shown to be determined by the sociological concept of the person and must be recast accordingly. The sphere of what exists, of what 'is given' ['es gibt'],[21] of reified concepts

26

[20.] The terms *Aufheben* and *Aufhebung* are not usually used in *Act and Being* in the straightforward sense of the 'abolition' or 'abrogation' of one thing by another, but with a Hegelian, dialectical meaning: bringing into being the unity of negating (overcoming) and preserving (sustaining). Cf. for example G. W. F. Hegel, *Encyclopedia of the Philosophical Sciences in Outline*. par. 96, Addendum. Throughout the present work, Bonhoeffer employs the crucial Hegelian term *aufheben* (verb) or *Aufhebung* (noun), which in the idealist tradition denotes the dual occurrence of something being surpassed and sustained, at one and the same time, in a dialectical process moving toward an ultimate synthesis of apparent opposites. But Bonhoeffer's own use of the term, rather than seeing this as a temporal process toward synthesis, however, invokes a tension—a 'suspension' or 'between'. Despite the frequent use in Hegel scholarship of the word "sublate" to translate *aufheben*, here words such as "subvert" or "subversion" have been used when the more 'negative' connotation is emphasized, while "suspend" and "suspension" have been used to connote the tensile, unresolved dialectical state of human existence as Bonhoeffer portrays it philosophically. [WF]

[21.] Here, Bonhoeffer uses the phrase *'es gibt'* in the more mundane sense of 'what is'. [WF]

of being, is brought into motion through the sociological category. Concepts of being, insofar as they are acquired from revelation, are always determined by the concepts of sin and grace, 'Adam' and Christ. There are in theology no ontological categories that are primarily based in creation and divorced from those latter concepts.[22] The idea of this 'being'— of sin and of human beings in sin, of grace and of human beings in grace—is developed within the wider concreteness of the thought of the church in our final chapter. The study concludes with an interpretation of 'being in Christ' as determined by past and future, reflection and intentionality. The past is 'taken up' or suspended in the future, reflection in intentionality. Out of the human being of conscience grows the child.

This entire study is an attempt to unify the concern of true transcendentalism and the concern of true ontology in an 'ecclesiological form of thinking'.

[22.] In his subsequent writings, Bonhoeffer will clarify the dual reason for the inability of theology to be based in creation alone: (1) the fundamental difference between creator and creature, and (2) the creature's sinful refusal to live within the limits of creatureliness. See *CF* 35–40, 69–72, on the creator-creature distinction, as well as *C*, 102–6, 106–13, where this is related to the difference between the incarnation and humiliation of Christ. Contrary to broad trends within his own time (and ours) Bonhoeffer refused to dispense with the theological concept of 'sin' altogether, despite his strong confidence in the human capacities of knowledge and will. Thus, there is no 'innocent' vision of creation to which Bonhoeffer can appeal, 'before' or 'apart from' human brokenness. Rather, he must speak of creation, and all created human capacities, only in terms of a fallen Adam and a redemptive Christ—as 'being in Adam' or 'being in Christ'. This was at the root of the conflict later over the efficacy in theology of any appeal to 'orders of creation' in formulating a theological ethics. See *NRS* 162: "Creation and sin are so bound up together [that] each human order is an order of the fallen world and not an order of creation. . . . [Thus] there is no longer any possibility of regarding any features per se as orders of creation and of perceiving the will of God directly in them." [WF]

A. The Problem of Act and Being, Portrayed in a Preparatory Manner as the Epistemological Problem of an Autonomous Understanding of Dasein in Philosophy

1. The Transcendental Attempt

Epistemology is the attempt of the I to understand itself. I reflect on myself; I and myself move apart and come together again. This is the basic posture of transcendental philosophers. And in this attitude of reflection the self-understanding of the I is, in one way or another, closed within itself. The I intends to understand itself by regarding itself. Here the common basis of transcendental philosophy and idealism is clear.

Two things are to be kept in mind in what follows. Genuine transcendental philosophy, such as that which Kant[1] tried to develop by rejoining a long conceptual development from the time of scholastic theology,[2]

---

1. The entire interpretation of Kant, as well as of idealism, presented here is stylized. For that reason, quotations are dispensed with. Kant is depicted as a pure transcendental philosopher, which he never was entirely, even though in our view he intended to be. The substance of the discussion concerns systematic and not historical questions.[1]

2. Cf. H. Knittermeyer, "Die Transzendentalphilosophie und die Theologie." *Christl. Welt* 1924, N.B. col. 222.[2]

[1.] In *SC* Bonhoeffer did not distinguish between Kant's transcendental philosophy and idealism as sharply as he does in this study. See *SC* 211, note 5.

[2.] Hinrich Knittermeyer's article was written for the two hundredth anniversary of Kant's birth. As a countermeasure against neo-Kantianism and its predominance in the understanding of Kant in contemporary theology, Knittermeyer proposed what he called "the trinitarian root of transcendental philosophy" (col. 222) of which Kant himself had remained ever mindful, albeit for reasons of critique. Bonhoeffer's own stylized presenta-

must be distinguished from the concept of transcendentalist philosophy as understood by post-Kantian idealism.[3] Further, we must consider the question whether Kant's transcendental critique of reason is at all identical with the crisis into which reason is placed in Luther and Protestant orthodoxy. We need to ask whether Kant did not proceed to place reason within its rights precisely by defining its limits[3] and whether, for that reason, he is not to be given from the outset the title of the epistemologist *par excellence*[4] of Protestantism.[5]

28

It is integral to the concept of genuine transcendentalism that thinking refers to something transcendent which, however, is not at its disposal. All thinking always refers to something transcendent in two ways: retrospectively and prospectively. It is *retrospective* in that thinking, *qua* thinking, lays claim to a meaning which it cannot give to itself—in that such meaning is in reference to the logos of transcendence. The reference is *prospective* in that thinking, *qua* relation, is in reference to objects, coming up against something transcendent, provided that they are truly *ob*jects—standing over against thought. (It makes no difference which

---

3. Cf. W. Lütgert's interpretation in *Religion des Idealismus*, 1, 3ff.

tion of 'genuine transcendentalism' actually follows Knittermeyer's attempt to mediate Heidegger through Kant in such a manner as to prevent the establishment of the relation of philosophy to Dasein at the expense of the primary qualification of Dasein by means of the categories of cognition. Cf. Knittermeyer, "Philosophie der praktischen Vernunft": "The ontological approach does not seem to be in error when it links philosophy to Dasein as human Dasein. Difficulties arise only when Dasein itself lays claim to an ontic dignity, instead of being seen primarily as Dasein being tempted by cognition" (352f.). Cf. Bonhoeffer, "The Theology of Crisis," *NRS* 369f.

[3.] While genuine transcendental philosophy, in Bonhoeffer's schema, may indeed still prove of service to theology, transcendentalist philosophy—by which he means a specific development of the transcendental tradition in the direction of systematic philosophies of totality—is seen by Bonhoeffer as the greatest danger to all forms of critical rationality, including theology. [WF]

[4.] Bonhoeffer draws on the assertion of Wilhelm Lütgert that, as Kant had noted, "the mind is unable to know God, not because knowledge of the mind is restricted to matters of the world, but because it restricts itself to consciousness. . . . For Kant reason is without power outside the house it has built for itself, while it is all powerful inside it. It is all powerful because it rests always at home, that is to say, it remains within itself" (*Die Religion des deutschen Idealismus*, 11f.).

[5.] The previous English edition of the text mistranslated this sentence in such a way that Bonhoeffer was left saying that it is 'impermissible' to understand Kant in precisely the way that Bonhoeffer indeed wishes us to understand him: as potentially the "espistemologist *par excellence* of Protestantism." See *AB* 20.[WF]

concept of object, from Kant to [Heinrich] Rickert, is applied here.) One may speak of genuine transcendentalism so long as the resistance of transcendence to thinking is upheld, that is to say, so long as the thing-in-itself and transcendental apperception are understood as pure limiting concepts, neither of which is entangled with the other. In knowing, human Dasein knows itself to be suspended between [eingespannt zwi- 29 schen][6] two poles that transcend it. This 'being between' that which is transcendent is 'Dasein'.4 But this acquires another, special meaning through thinking. All existing things, in the midst of which human Dasein may find itself, are by virtue of thinking 'in reference to' human Dasein. They are so by virtue of that same thinking (that understands itself in just this way) which enables Dasein to understand itself as being between that which is transcendent [zwischen Transzendentem seiend].[8] This is how human Dasein acquires a mode of being which distinguishes it from all else that exists. For in that mode the world of all else that exists is being transcended; indeed, that world has existence only in reference to thought. Whether it exists only *by virtue* of thinking is another question. For genuine transcendentalism the mode of being of human Dasein that has this remarkable characteristic is the pure *act*. This is a surprising, albeit necessary, conclusion. 'Being' is being amidst transcendence [Sein zwischen Transzendenz]. But this is so only by virtue of that will to self-understanding which is itself oriented towards transcendence. To know oneself to be oriented towards transcendence and, consequently, to be the world's reference point is what, in transcendentalism, constitutes human Dasein. From this delimitation of the self-understanding-human-being—that is, of reason—now breaks forth the radical critique of reason. Here, reason is given back its original or primordial legitimacy, because it is reason itself that causes the crisis of rea-

---

4. The concept of Dasein as the mode of being of human beings as distinct from other existing things is taken over from the terminology of Heidegger: *Being and Time*, 1962 [1927].[7]

[6.] Bonhoeffer repeatedly employs a quasi-spatial metaphor to describe human-existence as a 'between'—a 'space' or opening—within which can occur the encounter with that which is other than ourselves. [WF]

[7.] Cf. Martin Heidegger, *Being and Time*, 32: "As ways in which man behaves, sciences have the manner of Being which this entity [Seiendes]—man himself—possesses. This entity [Seiende] we denote terminologically as '*Dasein*'."

[8.] Again, one sees the tensile imagery with which Bonhoeffer conveys his dialectical approach. [WF]

son. In other words, human beings understand themselves, in the last
resort, not from the transcendent but from themselves, from reason—or,
to be precise, from the limits that reason has set for itself, whether the
limits are rational or ethical in kind. Every transcendental epistemology
or corresponding understanding of Dasein must end up in this internal
contradiction. This failure or breech, which resides in the heart of the
matter itself, has to be taken more seriously than the immediately ensu-
30   ing attempts to restore inner unity. Such attempts are always at the
expense of the transcendental point of departure.

First of all, what has to be kept in mind and explained is this: the
human being is Dasein as pure act—Dasein that understands itself from
within its self-imposed limits, that is, from itself. Transcendentalism is
not phenomenalism.[9] The issue that distinguishes Kant from phenomenalism makes clear that even though one encounters in Kant ideas that
are strongly reminiscent of phenomenalism, they are, nonetheless, contrary to his project. This is made clear by the question that distinguishes
Kant from phenomenalism. Phenomenalism asked how the I comes
upon the object, then rendered the question moot by means of the pure
phenomenality of objects in the consciousness. Kant, on the other hand,
accepted the customary reference of the I towards the object and now
asked how knowledge was possible at all, or what the meaning of that
customarily accepted reference was. His question differs from that of
phenomenalism in the same way that a question about the commonly
accepted reference differs from a question about being. Genuine transcendentalism knows no question of being pure and simple. It cannot

---

[9.] Phenomenalism is a term that was introduced by nineteenth-century Kantians. It
designated positions within the theory of knowledge that, on one hand, explained the
knowledge of entities in terms of the relation of individual subjects of cognition to the
conceptions presented to them and, on the other, left undecided the reality of entities outside of the activity of conceptualization. Bonhoeffer clearly does not wish to limit himself
to interpretations of Kant at this point such as that of Wilhelm Windelband, to whose history of philosophy he refers later in the present work. According to Windelband, the theoretical philosophy of Kant's transcendental aesthetics and logic is to be understood as a
"completely consistent phenomenalism," as a "transcendental phenomenalism," yes, even
as an "absolute phenomenalism" (*Geschichte der neueren Philosophie* 2:63–94, esp. 67, 82,
91). Rather, Bonhoeffer identifies his own position with relation to Friedrich Brunstäd's
description of phenomenalism, "which declares that we can know appearances only and
not things in themselves [Dinge an sich]" (*Idee der Religion*, 72). Bonhoeffer follows Brunstäd in stressing the sharp difference between Kant and phenomenalism (cf. Brunstäd, *Idee
der Religion*, 90f.).

know such a question precisely because its very meaning is to go beyond the 'dogmatism'[10] of the question of being. Knowing is not possible as a duplication of reality, a process in which there are no criteria for the question of truth. Instead, knowing is made possible only by a synthesis that is originally founded, and then brought to fulfillment, in the knowing subject in the unity of transcendental apperception. This synthesis must be understood as having logical precedence over the empirical, over experience. It must, in other words, be thought a priori. But this must be a synthesis with its own inner necessity and legitimacy, wherein it demonstrates its truth and validity. Knowledge is not validated through the congruence of knowledge with the object of knowledge, however their correspondence is construed, but through the necessity of the a priori synthesis.[11] Truth is only in the pure act. Thus, the concept of being is resolved into the concept of act. Being 'is' only in reference to knowing. This 'in reference to' of the original form of transcendentalism opens the space for the orientation of thinking towards transcendence, whereas the substitution of 'through' for 'in reference to' would express the full power of reason over transcendence. Consequently, the understanding of Dasein is characterized as it is for Kant as self-knowing 'in reference to'. It has the sense of *being deeply called into question* by

31

[10.] It was Kant who defined his 'critical philosophy' vis-à-vis both 'dogmatism', "the presumption that it is possible to make progress with pure knowledge, according to principles, from concepts alone," and 'scepticism', "which makes short work with all metaphysics." Kant's proposed 'criticism', to the contrary, "is the necessary preparation for a thoroughly grounded metaphysics" (*Critique of Pure Reason*, B xxxv–xxxvi, 32). Hegel, then, defined 'dogmatism' as "the opinion that the True consists in a proposition which is a fixed result, or which is immediately known" (*Phenomenology of Spirit*, par. 40, 23). Kant's search for the transcendental conditions of the possibility of knowledge thus turns into the idealistic proposal that knowing is a process, not fixed, in which the knower mediates all that is known. Finally, according to Johann Gottlieb Fichte, a full-blown idealism does away with any enduring 'otherness' to the knowing-I whatsoever, for any philosophy "which equates the I in itself with something else and sets something else in opposition to it" is 'dogmatic' (J. G. Fichte, "Grundlage der gesamten Wissenschaftslehre" [1794/1802], in *Sämmtliche Werke*, 1:119.). [WF]

[11.] With this epistemological critique, Bonhoeffer shows himself to be part of the twentieth century's enduring philosophical struggle over the nature of Kant's epistemological turn to the subject. Here Bonhoeffer shows himself to be reacting against two philosophical reactions to Kant from the nineteenth and early twentieth centuries, idealism and positivism, the former of which is clearly for Bonhoeffer at this time the greater enemy. [WF]

knowledge,[5] of never being able to rest in itself without surrendering itself. It has the sense of pure act. But as such, the understanding of Dasein must always transcend itself.[6] Constantly oriented in reference to itself, such understanding *can never attain itself.* Were it able to do so, it would no longer be 'in reference to' and no longer pure act. The attempt to understand oneself purely from oneself must come to nothing because Dasein, by nature, is not in itself self-subsistent but precisely 'in reference to'. The consummation of this attempt cannot be attained. For when I come to know myself, the 'myself' is already something completed, but no longer the 'I', for the attainment of the self, too, is completed. There is no longer 'in reference to'. The 'I', thought of as something in process, must, instead, become something completed. 'I' cannot be thought, because it is the precondition for thinking itself—that is to say, the I 'is' always there, never as an object, but always as a priori synthesis; it precedes the object.

A profound contradiction comes into view now: the I is being-already-there. It is both the very process of attainment and its precondition, and as such the I logically *precedes* thinking. But inasmuch as everything about the I is constituted by thought, *thinking precedes the I.* This means that thinking lies on the brink of the 'nonobjective', without which, just because it is the condition of the conditional, there is nothing objective. Thinking is the boundary of existence out of which human beings live; it is a boundary in that the unconditional, that is human existence, is always out in front of human beings, but already behind them every time Dasein sets out to understand its own existence as Dasein. The impossibility of Dasein is proven by its understanding itself as an accomplishment, even while it is really the performance of an act.

Now two postures are possible in the face of the scandal of the limits in the concept of the I and in thinking. By attempting to comprehend the I, thinking suspends itself [hebt es sich selbst auf]. By limiting itself through a self-subversion [Selbstaufhebung] of its power, however—con-

----

5. Knittermeyer: *Zwischen den Zeiten*, 1929, no. 4, 352f.[12]

6. It is necessary, in relation to what follows, to state specifically that this is only one side of the historical Kant. But from the days of Fichte until now, ever-new attempts have had to be made to understand Kant better than he understood himself.

[12.] Bonhoeffer cites this as *Zwischen den Zeiten* 1929, no. 4, but the correct volume no. is 7. [WF]

trasting what is objective with the I as the condition of objectivity—thinking sets itself into power once again as that which makes the separation possible at all. One possibility is that thinking can submit to this self-limitation, in the manner of genuine transcendental thinking. This response, it seems to me, is in accord with Kant's original proposal even though, admittedly, it is linked with phenomenalistic and idealistic elements in the historical Kant that are open to dangerous misinterpretation.

The other possibility, the great temptation for all genuine philosophy, is for thinking to raise itself to the position of lord over what is nonobjective by taking the process of attainment, the I, into itself in the act of thinking. Here, the I, now thinking itself, simply becomes the *point of departure* instead of the limit-point of philosophy.[13] But thinking cannot do this without losing two very different things, reality and transcendence, that is, *the one through the other*. Philosophy, thinking, the I, all come under the power of themselves, rather than transcendence. The boundlessness of the claim of thinking turns into its exact opposite. Thinking languishes in itself; precisely where it is free from the transcendent, from reality, there it is imprisoned in itself.[14] From the originally transcendental project develops a system of pure self-transcendence on the part of thinking or, which comes to the same thing, a monism unaffected by reality. It matters little whether it now is called a system of pure transcendence or one of pure immanence, as the end product is materially the same. Kierkegaard said, not without justification, that such philosophizing obviously forgets that we ourselves exist.[15] This second possibility was taken up and elaborated as much in the transition from Socrates to Plato as it was in the turn from Kant to

33

[13.] Here Bonhoeffer challenges all readings of the Kantian turn to the subject that interpret it as necessarily a turn toward the sovereign self, toward a self that wills and chooses, and sees itself as the point of departure for all understanding. Rather, Bonhoeffer emphasizes precisely the 'critical' turn of the Kantian revolution, which sustained an ontological reserve, or agnosticism, in its judgments about the power of the subject—a reserve that Hegel and Fichte then, in Bonhoeffer's view, exploited. [WF]

[14.] Thus, for the proto-deconstructionist Bonhoeffer, an irony lies at the heart of all late-modern and postmodern attempts to free the subject from any encumbrances of transcendence; for in attempting to free the subject from heteronomy, they actually leave the subject imprisoned with only itself, unable to allow the approach of that which is genuinely other. [WF]

[15.] This is, in essence, the basic point of Kierkegaard's critique of idealism. Cf. especially Søren Kierkegaard, *Concluding Unscientific Postscript*, 118–25, 189–208, 301–18.

idealism—though, of course, in an entirely different sense. Only the second of these two general possibilities conceals within itself the claim of the system, and that is its secret power.

Whether thinking is modest about itself—that is to say remains genuine transcendental thinking—or whether it lays violent hands on the unconditional and becomes idealistic thinking, is no longer a question of theoretical philosophy, which, as we saw, holds up both possibilities for the choosing. It is a decision of practical reason. Nothing can oblige thinking, precisely as free thinking, not to draw the unconditional into itself and to take control of its I. But it is no less an act of free thinking when, precisely to remain free, it contents itself with its orientation towards transcendence and does not take control of its I, simply because it is always 'in reference to'. Here at the apogee of thinking—though not to avoid the need for thinking—there comes clearly to light the decision-character[7] of thinking that is no longer held within the strictures of internal logic, the character of which Fichte spoke when he said that the kind of philosophy one has depends on what kind of human being one is.[8]

Idealism deprives self-understanding Dasein of its transcendental orientation, for it understands itself without it. That is to say, in freeing Dasein from 'being amidst transcendents', from being entwined by the transcendent, idealism seems to have resolved the concept of being—which in pure transcendental philosophy still perhaps appeared to be encumbered by the transcendent—entirely into the concept of act. Idealism has radicalized Kant's discovery. To be is to be comprehended by the I in the a priori synthesis.[9] Without the I, there is no being. The I is

---

7. The third possibility is genuine ontology. Cf. further below.

8. Cf. [Fichte]. *Werke*, 1, 434.[16]

9. Cf. Brunstäd: *Idee der Religion*, 1922. In this work Kant and idealism are brought into immediate relation; the presentation of idealism there treats with exemplary clarity the basic theme, the a priori synthesis, in the idealist interpretation.[17]

[16.] "One's choice of philosophy depends on what kind of human being one is, for a philosophical system is not an inert household effect to be taken up or abandoned as desired; the system, rather, is animated by the soul of the human being who has embraced it" (J. G. Fichte, "Erste Einleitung in die Wissenschaftslehre" [1797], in *Sämmtliche Werke*, 1:434).

[17.] Friedrich Brunstäd, *Idee der Religion*, 90–107. Brunstäd does away with "the phenomenalistic obscuring of Kant" and the "objective-idealistic one of Hegel," thereby establishing the unity of the "critical-idealistic concept of knowledge" (91). On the "clarity

creative; it alone is efficacious, going out of and returning to itself. If being were not the object of understanding, but were thought absolutely, it would lead immediately to materialism. Idealism is neighbor to materialism (Hegel–Marx). Dasein is the contemplation by the eternal I of itself; it is its coming home. Understood as eternal act, Dasein is self-understanding out of itself. Yet if the I is the creator of its world, what is there outside itself from which it might derive knowledge of itself? Spirit understands spirit [Geist].[18] Therefore, I can understand myself from myself—one may even say 'from God', to the extent to which God is in me, and to the extent that God is the unconditional personality, which I am.[10] It would appear that thereby all concepts of being have fallen by the wayside, and that a purified concept of act governs epistemology and anthropology. And yet, something surprising has come to pass in this apparent radicalization of the transcendental position. If in original transcendentalism the human spirit was suspended between transcendence [eingespannt zwischen Transzendenz] and, consequently, irrevocably in reference to them, now the movement of the spirit is turned in upon itself. In Luther's words this is *ratio in se ipsam incurva* [*reason turned in upon itself*].[11] Spirit has, in principle, come to rest. Only in the   35

---

10. Cf. Brunstäd's idea of the unconditional personality in which God and I are one.[19]

11. [Luther,] *Lectures on Romans*, 291 [trans. altered, MR].[20]

of presentation" with which Brunstäd has presented the essence of idealism, see further Emanuel Hirsch, *Die idealistische Philosophie und das Christentum*, 40, note 1.

[18.] Bonhoeffer uses 'Geist' to mean "spirit" in a broad range of ways—including mind; the ethos or 'spirit' of a time; as well as the religious sense of the term. The present work translates 'Geist' as "spirit," 'geistlich' as "spiritual" (religious), and 'geistig' as "intellectual." When the context does not make clear the sense in which a term is used, a brief note may be employed to remind the reader. [WF]

[19.] Cf. Brunstäd, *Idee der Religion*, 99f. A distinction is made here, however, between a general I (I, awareness [Bewußtheit], personality) and a particular I (self, consciousness [Bewußtsein], person); cf. below, 51, note 22.

[20.] "Ratio est quia natura nostra vitio primi peccati tam profunda est in se ipsam incurva, ut non solum optima dona Dei sibi inflectat ipsisque fruatur (ut patet in iustitiariis et hypocritis), immo et ipso Deo utatur ad illa consequenda, verum etiam hoc ipsum ignoret, quod tam inique, curve et prave omnia, etiam Deum, propter se ipsam querat. Sicut propheta Hiere. 17: 'Pravum est cor hominis et inscrutabile, quis cognoscet illud?' i.e. ita curvum in se, ut nullus hominum, quantum libet sanctus (seclusa tentatione), scire possit." ["The reason for this is that our nature, on account of the defilement of the first sin, is so turned in on itself beyond measure that not only does it twist God's best gifts to

power of remaining in itself is spirit enabled to step outside of itself.
Accordingly, the spirit remains fully in control of itself in this movement
and never gets into the embarrassing position of merely 'being in reference to transcendence'. But, spirit at rest in itself, even if in a dialectically unreal movement, is substance, that is, absolute being. So Hegel
could well say that essentially the one thing he felt obliged to hold
against Spinoza was that he did not define substance as subjectivity.[12]
Idealism, especially Hegel, actually appears to have reached or attained
a synopsis of act and being that would be capable of satisfying the
demands of the problem, if only those doing the philosophizing themselves did not founder on the resistance of their own reality to this philosophy. Hegel wrote a philosophy of angels, but not of human beings as
Dasein [menschliches Dasein].[22] Even the philosopher simply is not in
full possession of the spirit. All who countenance that they need only to
come to themselves, in order to be in God, are doomed to hideous disil-
lusion in the experience of being-, persisting-, and ending-up-turned-in-
upon-themselves utterly—the experience of utmost loneliness in its
tormenting desolation and sterility. Such people see themselves placed
in a contingent here-and-there. As people who are questioning, thinking,
and acting, they have to find their way in the midst of it, and have to
relate every given situation to themselves so that they can decide 'in

36

---

12. [G. W. F. Hegel]. *Lectures on the History of Philosophy*, 3:330–31.[21] Cited by
Hirsch: Die idealistiche Philosophie und das Christentum, 1926, 61, n. 4.

its own purposes and seek self-enjoyment—something that is obvious among both the just
and hypocrites—but it even uses God for those purposes. And then it misunderstands that
it falsely, crookedly and perversely desires everything, including God, for selfish reasons
only. In the seventeenth chapter of Jeremiah it says: 'devious is the human heart and
inscrutable, who can fathom it?' This means that it is so turned in on itself that no one,
however saintly—subject to temptation or not—can understand it."] Luther, *Lectures on
Romans*, 291.

[21.] Bonhoeffer quotes here Hegel's *Werke*, 15, 409, cited in Hirsch: *Die idealistische
Philosophie und das Christentum*, 1926, 61, note 4; although this section does mention Spinoza in contrast to the philosophy of Leibnitz, it does not directly raise the complaint
against Spinoza that Bonhoeffer claims.

[22.] Bonhoeffer generally uses Dasein in a Heideggerian sense, to speak of the existence of human beings in particular. At times he seems to lapse back to a more generic
usage of Dasein simply to mean "existence" in general, in which case he often will qualify
it, when speaking of human existence in particular, by saying "human Dasein"—a formulation that is, speaking strictly in the Heideggerian sense, redundant. [WF]

reference to it'.[23] And the violation that people thereby themselves do suffer at being 'in reference to' an other, at being in reference to a transcendent which 'is already there', is something fundamentally different from the certainty of bearing within themselves the possibility of mastering the world. In other words, in the purely transcendental understanding of Dasein even the character of the act is expressed more purely than in the conflation of act and being in idealism. Only where Dasein cannot understand itself in abiding transcendental orientation or, to put it another way, is able to understand that it does not understand itself, is the true meaning of act brought to expression: act as an 'in reference to' that never comes to rest, as intentionality pure and simple, as giving proof of itself in the psychic process but as understandable only on the far side of it, act as 'direct' consciousness (*actus directus*). Here philosophizing itself is essentially related to Dasein, because it places itself within the responsibilities of human Dasein and raises its questions only from within that context. Accordingly, the questions themselves belong to Dasein and so do not involve the answer in advance. Thus, philosophizing partakes of the act-character of Dasein and does not make its case on the basis of a trait, a having [Haben] that is grounded in a being [Sein].

To be sure, the transcendental starting point seems to have prevailed in idealism also insofar as the reality of the external world is to be understood in it only from the I. Kant's a priori synthesis and Fichte's intellectual perception appear to be identical, as far as the founding of the reality of the external world in the I is concerned. And yet, even here genuine transcendentalism must judge more circumspectly than idealism, because for the former there is no knowledge capable of going beyond the proposition that phenomena, the external world, are 'in reference to' the I and are, consequently, knowable only via the I. It does not lie within the competence of a purely transcendental thinking to draw from this a subsequent judgment about being, negative or positive. If idealism sees a need to complete transcendentalism by replacing the transcendental reference with the ontological judgment concerning the creative power of the I, it distorts the meaning of transcendentalism by radicalizing it. It is no coincidence that idealism, beginning as it does   37

[23.] Bonhoeffer's indictment of late modernity's solipsism and narcissism is nowhere more strongly stated than here. [WF]

with an ontological judgment, ends up, as shown, close to having a new concept of substance. Thus the pure concept of act belongs, after all, to transcendentalism. It is a transcendental judgment to say that the objects of my knowledge, the world, are 'in reference to me', whereas in idealism the world comes about 'through me'. We should not let this distinction be disregarded in systematic theology simply because it remains blurred in the history of philosophy. On the contrary, it is not hard to see its importance for theology as well as for the philosophical understanding of God at a given time. The reason why Kant could not take Fichte's side in the dispute over atheism[24] was that, at bottom, Kant understood himself even better than Fichte thought he had understood Kant. If the world comes to be through the I, then the I and God the creator exchange roles. God no longer can be the object of knowledge, but—since God is inconceivable as the creature of the I—somehow is brought into unity with the I itself. Thus, for idealism God 'is' only to the extent to which I think, only insofar as in thinking, I end up with myself.

Transcendentalism distinguishes itself from this position in that it does not make the I into a creator but thinks of the I only as something to which the world must be thought of as related. In this way, to be sure, the decisive boundary of the Creator's integrity is honored in principle, that is, to the extent to which this is at all possible in philosophy. Certainly, here, too, God cannot be the object of knowledge. Were that possible, God would be oriented with the phenomena of the world as God is towards the I and, consequently, would be thought of as essentially for the I. Given the transcendental point of departure, the objectivity of God is an impossibility, since all being is understood as something existing [Seiende], as what 'there is' in the a priori synthesis. The objectivity of God is translated into act, and absolute being becomes an unfulfillable thought, because it is not objective. Thus, the concept of God, as the basis of possibility for Dasein and thinking, remains nonobjective. Transcendental thinking can never say 'God is', for that would be objectifying, finitizing, 'dogmatizing'. Truth 'is' only in the act itself, the act in reference to transcendence. Only in the execution of the act, in Dasein seeking to understand itself, 'is' God in existence as condition, possibil-

38

[24.] A controversy about atheism followed the publication of Johann Gottlieb Fichte's article "Über den Grund unseres Glaubens an eine göttliche Weltregierung" (*Sämmtliche Werke*, 5:177ff.). In the article Fichte had maintained that there was no reason to postulate a 'particular being' beyond the divinity of the moral order of the world as the 'cause' of this order (186). This led to his dismissal from the University of Jena in 1799.

ity, always in process and never completed. Thus, God always remains at the back of human beings, no matter which way human beings may turn.

We should not conceal how close God and the I come together here. Still, both remain limit-concepts 'in reference to' which thinking, or Dasein, permanently 'is'. But while this presentation of transcendentalism is noticeably uncertain here, we can scarcely refrain from directing to it a broader question: What is this transcendent, towards which everything is said to be in orientation? If it can never be objectively knowable, how can reason fix its limits over against something unknown? Even if this is a free decision of practical reason, it remains the self-chosen limit by reason of itself, by which reason once again legitimates itself as that which put the boundaries in place. This innermost unclarity in Kant's concept of the transcendental leads to the insight that here, too, despite the strenuous attempt to go beyond itself or establish its boundaries, reason remains by itself, understands itself not 'in reference to' that which transcends it, but 'in reference to' itself. The miscarriage of the endeavor to ascertain the boundaries of reason is due to the fact that there are for reason essentially no boundaries, for even the boundaries are thought away until they are no longer genuine boundaries. Reason can only be brought into obedience: the obedience of speculation, the obedience to Christ, or however else one may name it. There is a boundary only for a concrete human being in its entirety, and this boundary is called *Christ*.

It remains to be said that in Kantian transcendentalism as in idealism, reason gets entangled in itself. 'To understand oneself' consequently can mean only 'to understand oneself from or out of oneself'. 'I am', therefore, means: I think (*cogito, sum*).[25] Similarly, 'God is' means: spirit comes to itself, it knows in the unity of consciousness. A genuine belief in God finds that the ground seems to crumble beneath its desire to be able to assert the being of God outside the I, for there is only reason alone with itself. It is clear now that, on its own, the I cannot move beyond itself. It is imprisoned in itself, it sees only itself, even when it sees another, even when it wants to see God. It understands itself out of itself, which really means, however, that it basically does not understand itself. Indeed it does not understand itself until this I has been encountered and overwhelmed in its existence by an other. The I believes itself

39

[25.] "Cogito, ergo sum" ("I think, therefore I am") is the foundational assertion of the philosophy of René Descartes's *Discourse on Method*, 4:101.

free and is captive; it has all power and has only itself as a vassal: that is what Protestant theology means by the corruption of reason. It is the ontic inversion into the self, the *cor curvum in se*.[13] [26] If Kant suspected this, as we may surmise from what he had to say about radical evil,[27] he nevertheless finally struggled in vain to overcome the difficulty by means of the transcendental point of departure, whereas idealism, in the course of its development, at this very point allowed the I to celebrate untroubled the triumph of its liberation.

Everything converges in the decisive question that must be put to transcendentalism and idealism alike: Can the I understand itself out of itself? Or must fundamental objections be raised already at this point?

'Understanding' ['Verstehen'][28] (as distinct from explanation [Erklären])[29] extends to mental states of affairs and includes the immediate consciousness of evidence. Such consciousness is only possible in the case of that potential productivity aimed at something to be understood, be it a deed, a thought, or an artistic composition. To understand means to be creative in one way or another; at this point, the technical abilities required are of no consequence. The object of understanding here should be Dasein itself—that is, Dasein in its unity—for there is no 'understanding' save on the basis of unity. If Dasein is so structured that the will-to-understand-itself belongs to its essence, the problem arises of how the unity of Dasein can be gained by means of self-understanding from, or out of, the self [Sich-aus-sich-selbst-verstehen]. The eye does not see itself.[30] If unity were to be gained in that manner, the self-under-

40

---

13. Luther, *Lectures on Romans*, 291 [trans. altered, MR].

[26.] "the heart turned in on itself." Cf. above, 41–42, editorial note 20. [WF]

[27.] Cf. Immanuel Kant, *Religion within the Limits of Reason Alone*, Book 1, "Concerning the Indwelling of the Evil Principle with the Good, or, On the Radical Evil in Human Nature" (15–49).

[28.] The hermeneutical signficance of 'understanding' would have been evident to Bonhoeffer from his reading of Heidegger's *Being and Time* (e.g., 182ff. and 385ff.). [WF]

[29.] This distinction refers to Wilhelm Dilthey's attempt to distinguish the 'natural' sciences from the 'human' sciences on the basis of the goals of their methods: explanation and understanding, respectively. See above, "The Problem," page 29, editorial note 18. [WF]

[30.] This allusion to the metaphor of the eye and the sun goes back to Plato (*Republic*, 508 a 4ff.). Also see Bonhoeffer's sermon on Matthew 5:8, where he cites the first two lines of Goethe's "Xenia": "if the eye were not like the sun, it could never see the sun; if god's own power did not lie in us, how could we delight in the divine?" (*GS* 5 [1928]:448). In the

standing Dasein therefore would have to be able to think of itself as the creator of itself in its entirety. This would have to include its self-understanding, even its own existence, in which this creator *must* live, now as one who has or does not have self-understanding. This is self-contradictory inasmuch the 'I' must already be there in order to be able to create. Aware of this situation, the I of idealist reason[14] can pass itself off as the ultimate entity—the 'I am who I am',[31] which is ontologically meaningful only with regard to the concept of God. The I, by a paradox beyond possible meaning, makes itself its own creator. Alternatively, human beings perceive this existentiality of theirs in its full mind-body configuration as a 'being between' ['Sein zwischen'], 'in reference to' something to which even Dasein is an as yet uncomprehended pointer. Of course, the understanding of the self given here signifies no real understanding of existence. Rather, it characterizes only the final possible position human thinking and self-understanding can assume. In the final analysis, a new problematic of act and being must be disclosed.

Neo-Kantianism tried to carry through the transcendental approach anew, in order to resolve the problem of thinking and being. But by doing away with the thing-in-itself, neo-Kantianism expresses an onto-   41
logical judgment in the place of a referential one and follows the path of Fichte by making thinking the foundation of being.[32] It remains problematic how, say, [Hermann] Cohen's concept of method, derived from the transcendental approach, is linked with Fichte's substantially similar concept of the creative mind.[15] Although [Paul] Natorp here initially follows Cohen, he later, while trying again to master the problem of being, worked out the idea of a 'universal logic'.[16] The logos lies beyond think-

---

14. And, in the final analysis, also Kant's transcendental I.

15. Cf. H. Cohen: *System der Philosophie*, 1. *Logik der reinen Erkenntnis*, 1902.

16. Cf. particularly P. Natorp's last work: *Praktische Philosophie*, 1925, 1–27.

original version Goethe had written "how could we see the light?" instead of "it could never see the sun." Emanuel Hirsch cites a sonnet by Johann Gottlieb Fichte that has a very similar theme (Fichte, *Sämmtliche Werke*, 8:461f.) in Hirsch's *Die idealistische Philosophie*, 58.

[31.] Bonhoeffer alludes here to the meaning of the tetragrammaton, the name of God given in Exodus 3:14.

[32.] Here Bonhoeffer turns to the contrast that is fundamental to his argument, that between genuine transcendentalism's recognition that reality is always, but only, 'in reference to' the subject, and idealism's (and neo-Kantianism's) misguided ontological judgment that 'through me' as thinking subject, reality has its being. [WF]

ing and being as that through which both are possible in the first place. Neither can be transposed into [aufgehoben], and thereby reduced to, the other. Thinking is 'thinking-in-being' and being is 'being-in-thinking'. Clearly, with this speculation we approach Hegel, as is evidenced by the interrelationship of act and being.

What, in sum, results for the problem of act and being from the transcendental and idealistic attempts? Common to both is the attempt to "raise substance to the subject,"[17] which Hegel had worked out most completely in his logic, namely the understanding of the object as an a priori synthesis in transcendental apperception. Here, being becomes the knowing consciousness. But this assertion is by no means unequivocal. Its positive or negative interpretation leads in totally opposite directions. The thesis that being is given in the knowing consciousness is certainly not identical with the converse, that where there is no knowing consciousness, there is also no being. The difference we have noted comes to the fore here. In the positive phrasing the relatedness of consciousness and being that is transcendent is expressed, while in the negative phrasing, the dissolving of the latter into the former is expressed. Unquestionably both interpretations are urgently interested in focusing on the mental act of the person. There is a person only in consciousness. In his phenomenology Hegel described step by step how the I becomes a real person, a goal which in the last resort is attainable only by philosophizing. If anything is to manifest itself to me as being, the thinking spirit must be able to apprehend it; consequently, the person is apprehended only where matters of logic are under consideration—that is to say, the existence of the person is attained through 'meaning'. An exceptional place is alloted to the 'word' here, as the only material means of communicating matters of logic clearly. The person is cradled in freedom. In freedom comes knowledge; in freedom alone can the existence of human beings apprehend itself and change. Act, meaning, and freedom belong together. Thus, the essence of the person is freedom, autonomy, coming-to-itself or being-with-itself.

If they are at one at this point, transcendentalism and idealism part company when they define the character of act. Transcendentalism succeeds in preserving the purity of the act by regarding Dasein only as

42

---

17. Windelband: *Geschichte der neueren Philosophie*,[33] 337.

[33.] Bonhoeffer refers to vol. 2.

'being in reference to' something transcendent. But since according to Kant this something transcendent cannot prove itself to be genuinely transcendent, Kant's original conception comes to naught. Hence it is that idealism draws the transcendent into itself, uniting being and act within itself, with all the consequences that arise for anthropology. This indicates that concepts of being cannot be dispensed with in the orientation towards transcendence, which marks Kantian philosophy, any more than in the profusion of transcendence that marks idealistic philosophy. This conclusion, however, is at variance with the original intention of both.[18]

Now, if theology espouses this transcendentalist-idealist epistemology, it forfeits a certain right by necessity. (Transcendentalist, as distinct from transcendental, is the term which denotes that manner of transcendental philosophy which, on the basis of the transcendental approach, develops a system of reason.) The *raison d'être* of transcendentalist-idealist epistemology is the claim that it involves an understanding of existence and, hence, of the world and God. Were this epistemology to forget this claim, it would forfeit its legitimacy. Epistemology is the turning of spirit to spirit. In the unity of the spirit beyond the subject-object dichotomy, the fulcrum for the understanding of Dasein, world, and God was discovered. If theology wished to call itself transcendentalist-idealist, it would have to accommodate this claim. This imposes very rigid limits on its own concept of knowledge. Furthermore, such a theology would have to locate all being in consciousness. The object, reality, is an *a priori* synthesis. A judgment is no longer true as a judgment about a reality transcending consciousness, but rather in the

43

---

18. In the history of philosophy one could seek a parallel between idealism's attempted dissolution of the concepts of being and the project of nominalism. There is no absolute being, not even of concepts, for they 'are' only in the act of being comprehended. To conclude from this that reality resides only in individual things, as was done most radically by Roscelin de Compiègne,[34] is to present idealistic philosophy with a proposition wholly alien to it. Individual things are for that philosophy merely objects of cognition by means of the application of general thought-forms and concepts.

[34.] Roscelin de Compiègne died in 1120. He is regarded as a typical representative of early scholastic nominalism. His characterization of universal concepts as *flatus vocis*—empty formulae—is known only from the writings of his opponents; nearly all of his writings have been lost.

"unconditional unity of experience of the personality."[19] This must hold true even for statements about God. Correspondingly, as we have already shown, such a theology may espouse no objective concept of God, since the object 'is' only in the transcendental unity of apperception; God 'is' in this unity, never conceivable, but only acting in the process of the conscious spirit. The identity of my not objective I with God is stated here in what is called the 'unconditional personality'.[20] This puts theology in the dilemma either of making the objective God the content of consciousness, that is to say, an object of the I-subject, or

44   of letting the I discover God in its non-objective selfhood [Ichheit] , in its coming to itself.

God 'is' not outside the spirit coming to itself. "The ultimate, true reality is that which is attested in our self-activity, in our selfhood."[21] But if we take nonobjectivity seriously, then God is indeed only in the act of the self-knowing spirit. In philosophical reflection God is not an objective existent but is only in the execution of that philosophizing. While genuine transcendental philosophizing is in reference to transcendence—that is, basically not self-contained—idealistic philosophical reflection implies the system in which God's own self resides. The philosophical reflection of idealism manifests itself in this as a phantom movement within self-contained repose. I discover God in my coming to myself; I become aware of myself. I find myself—that is, I find God. The perspective is introspective. In the genuinely transcendental act God remains nonobjective in the process; even though inaccessible to the reflection of consciousness on itself, the existential act of thinking God takes its course in consciousness. The idealistic act, on the other hand, is

---

19. Brunstäd, 154.

20. Brunstäd, 217: *"revelatio specialis [special revelation]*[35] is the disclosure of the unconditionally synthetic personality as such. It is being grasped by God as this unconditional personality—the founding, effected by God, of the oneness of the consciousness of God and of the self."

21. Hirsch, *Philosophie des Idealismus*, 54.[36]

[35.] 'Special revelation' refers to the revelation that comes about by means of the history of redemption and God's Word.

[36.] The actual title of Hirsch's book is *Die idealistische Philosophie und das Christentum.*

quite capable of finding God in the reflection of conscious-ness [Bewußt-sein].[22]

The language of idealism about the spirit that finds itself in God, and God in itself, was so enchanting that theology could not resist it; unhesitatingly, it concluded that if being is essentially consciousness, then God must be in religious experiences, and the reborn I has to find God in the reflection on itself. Where else was God to be found but in my consciousness? Even though I can never go beyond it, consciousness is nonetheless constitutive for being in general. God is the God of my consciousness. Only in my religious consciousness 'is' God. Philosophically speaking, however, this was jumping to conclusions. For if the philosophical system of idealism is the explicit form of the pure spirit coming to itself, then an analogous theology would have to be the explicit form of the self-consciousness of the reborn [Wiedergeborene]. As a complex measure, the latter is essentially different from pure self-consciousness (which brings together in the I the absolutely individual and the absolutely general); it is bound up with experiences of particular content, and if God is indeed to be found in this reborn consciousness, God must be extracted from these experiences. But this means that God once again becomes 'objectified' in consciousness and is thereby taken into the unity of transcendental apperception, becoming the prisoner of the consciousness. Unintentionally, God, who was to be thought of solely as the functional correlate of the mental act, has become a reified object.[38]

45

---

22. Brunstäd's distinction between individual consciousness and general awareness—of which the former is the symbol—both of which, however, come together in the I, does not change anything (*Idee der Religion*, 89ff., 92). Brunstäd's attempt to reduce the interrelation of being-conscious [Bewußtsein] and aware-ness [Bewußtheit] to that of the part to the whole, in order to ensure for conscious-ness a being independent of individual consciousness (cf. 112f.), is arbitrary and leads directly back to realistic concepts.[37]

[37.] The references indicated are not precise. The passage on 'awareness' and 'consciousness', as well as that on the symbolic interpretation of the relation of the part to the whole, is found in Brunstäd, *Idee der Religion*, 101–4.

[38.] Here Bonhoeffer shows a keen sense of the dynamics of much popular religiosity, as well as academic theology, particularly its emphasis on the endless self-referentiality of intention, motive, and experience. [WF]

There are two ways of recovering from this setback. (1) The first is to radicalize the long-established initial position on the basis of idealism in such a way that the experience of God becomes the very experience of the self on the part of the transcendental I that is the foundation for all other experiences. This course, as far as I know, has been decisively and expansively adopted and developed in theology only once, namely in Friedrich Brunstäd's *Die Idee der Religion*. Here the point of identity of God and humankind is the concept of the unconditional personality. The experience of God must be the experience of this unconditional personality in myself.[23] Consequently, the certainty of the experience of God lies nowhere but in my experience of the unity of the I. And just as the transcendental unity of the I is the foundation of all truth, religion demonstrates its truth only by the fact that—precisely in its character as experience of the unconditional personality—it itself becomes the ground of the possibility of all truth.[24] How the I now can enter into communion [Verkehr][39] with God is unfathomable; obviously, here again God is posited behind the I as the ground of its possibility, for if God could stand over against the I, God would be an object. The I can never say 'God is' without at the same time saying 'God is not'—that is to say, not like anything else is as an object, but rather never objectifiable, always wholly subjective. It is just the same with the I itself, so that wherever I really say 'I', I also could say 'God'. But just as I can have no communion with my transcendental I, I can have none with God. The I remains fixed in itself; its looking into itself, its innermost depths, is religion, but also the revelation of the divine spirit. Revelation is no more than that. What reason can perceive from itself (as Hegel puts it)[40] is

46

---

23. Brunstäd, 151f: "Religion as experience, as being grasped by the unconditional personality, by the unconditional value-reality of personal life, is the condition of the possibility of all truth and validity."

24. [Brunstäd,] 154f.: "The truth of religion does not lie in the fact that science arrives at conclusions which are in accord with affirmations of faith but that religious insight [Erfahrung], religious experience [Erlebnis], are a necessary precondition of all truth. Religious insight has its certainty wholly through itself. . . . Religion has truth, is truth, because it comprises the basis of all possible truth in the experience of the unconditional synthetic unity of the I."

[39.] This is an allusion to Wilhelm Herrmann's *The Communion* [Verkehr] *of the Christian with God*.

[40.] Cf. Georg Wilhelm Friedrich Hegel, *The Philosophy of History*: "Philosophy seeks to know the substance of the reality of the idea of God and to justify disdained reality. For reason [Vernunft] is the perception of the divine work," 36, trans. altered.

revelation, and so God is completely locked into consciousness.[25] In the living reflection on itself, the I understands itself from itself. It relates itself to itself, and consequently to God, in unmediated reflection. That is why religion = revelation; there is no room for faith and word, if they are seen as entities contrary to reason. Yet *Deus non potest apprehendi nisi per verbum*, A.C. 2, 67.[41]   47

Here, as in the whole of idealism, the inmost identity of I and God, which underlies everything, is merely an expression of the proposition that like is known only through like.[42] If God is to come to human beings, they essentially must already be like God. If theology is to grasp the relationship of God and humankind, it can do so only by presupposing a profound likeness of one to the other and finding precisely here the unity between God and human beings. One is like the very God one comprehends.[43]

---

25. Brunstäd would contest this (cf. 214). But: "It (the unity of experience) *is* revelation, is the effect of revelation; revelation is through this subjectivity, by entering into and by going through this inwardness" (216). "We know God insofar as we are 'I', insofar as we experience. The limits of our knowledge of God lie in the limited nature of the content of our consciousness" (218). (!)

[41.] "God does not let the divine self be known or grasped save in and through the Word alone" ("Apology of the Augsburg Confession," *The Book of Concord*, 116, trans altered MR).

[42.] This is a principle of the psychology of knowledge, dating back to pre-Socratic philosophers such as Empedocles. See Hermann Diels and Walter Kranz, eds., *Ancilla to the Pre-Socratic Philosophers*, chap. 31, no. 109:63, passim. Aristotle formulated it in the concept of ἡ γνῶσις τοῦ ὁμοίου τῷ ὁμοίῳ, "the knowledge of the like through the like." Erich Seeberg believes that the Thomistic doctrine of the knowledge of God was shaped by this Greek philosophical dictum, as was the system of mysticism (cf. *Luthers Theologie*, 1:3). Karl Barth made this formula the basic principle of his theological doctrine of knowledge; see "Das Schriftprinzip der reformierten Kirche," where Barth expressed this understanding for the first time (220). Bonhoeffer takes this up in "Lässt sich eine historische und pneumatische Auslegung der Schrift unterscheiden" (Is it permissible to distinguish between a historical and a spiritual interpretation of Scripture?), from the summer semester of 1925, and "Luthers Anschauungen vom Heiligen Geist" (Luther's views on the Holy Spirit), from the winter semester of 1925/26 (*DBW* 9:312f., 370, 393, and 396). Bonhoeffer in *SC* already has spoken of the basic social relation in Stoicism as always "thought of as that of like to like," as in the basic social relation of idealism (24), in which like is bound only to like, excluding the possibility of encounter by any genuine 'Other' (31). [WF]

[43.] Cf. Johann Wolfgang von Goethe, *Faust*, 1, lines 512ff.:16. Also, God must be conceived only as fundamentally like the one who does the conceiving. Idealism, and all its heirs, according to Bonhoeffer are unable to appreciate any genuine Otherness, especially God's. Everything is to be conceived according to its inner push toward identity. [WF]

That such assertions are theologically intolerable becomes apparent when they are stated with such sharpness. It is not because human beings are like God that God comes to them—on the contrary, God then would not need to come—but precisely because human beings are utterly unlike God and never know God from themselves. That is why God comes to them, that they may know God. Then, but only then, do they indeed know God. This idea has to find a place in Christian epistemology. But that subverts the presuppositions of all that has gone before. It seems that everything depends on the transformation of the concepts of being into those of act. In the first instance, there is no other place for God in this operation than the I that is in the process of completion of the spiritual act, or in what makes the process possible. In that case, the

48 I becomes the creator of the world. This causes the understanding of human beings, who in their concreteness of spirit and flesh are the very ones with whom Christian theology is crucially concerned and who invariably find themselves already present in their given worlds, to be entirely lost. This resolution of ontological concepts had become possible in idealism only on the basis of an unexpressed ontological judgment and is, for that reason, without legitimacy. The negative judgment—that this 'is' not, or that this is only through me—remains in every instance an ontological judgment that does not lie within the confines of the transcendental approach but represents, rather, a violation of limits with most grave consequences.

(2) The second way of recovering from this setback is to pull back to the purely transcendental approach. God is not objective. In this context, that means that God is no longer accessible even to the reflection of consciousness on itself. God 'is' in the pure process of completion of the act of consciousness but evades every attempt on the part of reflection to grasp God. God 'is' as *actus directus*. Act is always 'in reference to' transcendence. Therefore, 'being' that is independent of the I is rendered possible by the transcendental approach, even if it is not a given fact, whereas in idealism being and I were merged into one. If the transcendental approach is not to end once again in the system of reason, it clearly requires a new formulation of the 'limits' of reason—that is, of the concept of being and that of the act which is 'in reference to' this being. It was here where the first attempt had failed.

It is not the problem of a 'real external world', let alone its proof, that

is the issue for us in relation to being.[26] It is, rather, the sort of being of 49
God's revelation. The meaning of conceptions of transcendence, of the
'external', of being, is expressed far more clearly in this context than in
connection with the problem of the external world, particularly since
idealism merges both into one. The implications of the Christian idea of
God for, let us say, the reality of the external world, are to be discussed,
in outline, in the positive section of our study.

The conceptual world of Karl Barth has affinity with the transcendental approach.[27] Still, the encroachment of idealism on negative judgments of being (see above) and their incompatibility with the idea of
God have almost always somehow been felt and often have come clearly
to expression.

Likewise, the epistemology of Reinhold Seeberg[28]—in unmistakable
contrast to that of Brunstäd—may be far more correctly denoted as Kant-

---

26. If, to give an example, A. Riehl[44] seeks in his work *Der philosophische Kritizismus* (2,1ff. and 172)[45] to provide proof for the reality of the external world by
means of the dependence of consciousness on sensations, the logical-epistemo-
logical problematic of idealism remains quite unaffected. Even idealism does
not doubt the existence of an empirical external world; the argument is insuffi-
cient for the epistemological way of thinking because it confuses supporting evidence from psychology and epistemology. The same is to be said about the
inference from 'social feelings' to the external world. W. Dilthey's inquiry into
the reality of the external world, which at first sight seems very traditional in
form, is based in the experience of the will and the resistance it offers and
attempts fundamentally to overcome the whole of the idealistic theory of knowledge in favor of a philosophy of life shaped by history. Thus interpreted,
Dilthey's work is of decisive significance for current philosophy of history, especially as it has recently acquired influence on theology. Cf. W. Dilthey, "Beiträge
zur Lösung der Frage vom Ursprung unseres Glaubens an die Realität der
Aussenwelt und seinem Recht" 1890, in *Ges. Schrift.*, 5, 1st half, 90ff., N.B. 134.

27. On this point see the chapter [below] on "The Interpretation of Revelation in Terms of the Concept of Act."

28. [R. Seeberg,] *Dogmatik*, 1, N.B. 70–110, 257–84.

[44.] Alois Riehl (1844–1924) was a precursor of Marburg Neo-Kantianism and a representative of a theory of science of 'Critical Realism'. For Bonhoeffer's counterargument
see below, pages 127–28.

[45.] The actual reference is Alois Riehl, *Kritizismus*, 2/2:172.

ian-transcendental than as idealist; the same may be said of Seeberg's concept of religious transcendentalism. The struggle of theology with transcendental epistemology becomes apparent in the entire nexus of his thought. Underlying it is an idea of God conceived of as *actus purus*.[46] There is no potentiality in God, only actuality, a notion that leads Seeberg to pure voluntarism. As primal will, God operates as act on human beings, encountering them as beings whose nature is conscious spirit in their will. Epistemology now tries to comprehend transcendentally this encounter of God and human beings . Even though human beings are both potentiality and act, while God is pure act, their encounter is possible only in the act of consciousness; therefore, the essence of human beings resides in the spiritual act [geistiger Akt]. It is noteworthy, however, that the notion of potentiality is clearly intended to depict human beings in their concreteness, something that Seeberg believed himself unable to grasp in the pure notion of act. Now if the encounter of human beings with God can take place only in consciousness—that is, in full spiritual clarity about the meaning of the procedure and in complete freedom[29]—then for Seeberg here is given the point of departure for his transcendentalism.[30] As the consciousness 'has' God, so God 'is'; if it has not God, God 'is' not. What counts as real is what the subject thinks of necessity.[31] Being appears to be merging into act (perhaps in Brunstäd's sense). Precisely at this point, however, Seeberg refuses to take the step into idealism. Instead, a number of statements

50

---

29. [R. Seeberg, *Dogmatik*, 1]: "If this is to be a spiritual encounter, then it cannot persist for one moment without entering consciousness or becoming thought" (103). (The encounter of God with human beings takes place in such a manner that the latter), "conscious of their freedom, consciously and willingly perform the movement which the Spirit of God has accomplished in them" (91).

30. [R. Seeberg, *Dogmatik*, 1]: "Inasmuch as this spiritual entity [dies Geistige] shows itself to be real in a particular disposition of people, and can be known by us to be real only in the form given by this disposition, we have to term the sensation and knowledge under consideration here transcendental" (87).

31. [R. Seeberg, *Dogmatik*, 1]: "For transcendentalism the necessity of subjective knowledge is the demonstration of the objective reality of what is known" (279).

[46.] "pure act" Cf. Reinhold Seeberg, *Dogmatik*, 1:342. "By *actus purus* we mean an activity that occurs uninterrupted, yet without alternating between this and a state of potentiality. Accordingly, God knows no rhythm of rest and activity, has no need for relaxation and makes no distinction in will and thought between beginning and completion."

abruptly follow one upon the other that locate the existence of the supramundane, as well as that of concepts, in the human spirit alone, as well as those that acknowledge without reservation an 'objective being'—that is, a being of the supramundane that clearly transcends consciousness.[32]

In this manner the danger of identifying God and the I is averted.[33] God is the supramundane reality transcending consciousness, the creator and lord. This sentence is an unconditional requirement of Christian theology and is elaborated by Seeberg throughout his dogmatics. But, on the other hand, it can also be said that God is existent only in, or for, the consciousness of human beings. This is where Seeberg's theory of the religious a priori comes into play; there is in human beings a 'compelling ability' to "come to an unmediated awareness of pure spirit."[34] [47] By means of this ability, human beings can receive God into themselves, that is, experience God's immediate contiguity in feeling and intuition. On these premises it is now a thoroughly justified inference of transcendental thinking to attribute being to God only insofar as a conceptualization of God corresponds to it. At the same time, it is genuinely transcendental to refrain from making an absolute negative judgment about being, such as occurs here. But then we read about an unmediated perception of, or contact with, God on the part of human beings. The religious a priori is supposed to be fundamentally open to the divine will; there is, it is said, a mold in human beings into which the divine content of revelation, too, may pour.[35] In other words, revelation

51

32. [R. Seeberg, _Dogmatik_, 1]: "And so, just as concepts as such are not in the objective world but exist only in the mind of people, the supramundane [Überweltliche] has no other existence but that which it has in the religious movement of the will and intuition of the human mind. In this sense, here, too, it is a matter of transcendental perception and vision. But just as transcendentalism does not cast doubt on the objective being of the world, so the objective being of the supramundane is not made doubtful by the ideas expressed here. Only it should be said that the supramundane is perceptible to the human mind—which is to say, existent—in no other form than that of a specific, spiritual perception" (105).

33. [R. Seeberg, _Dogmatik_, 1,] 93.

34. Cf. Seeberg's distancing himself from idealism (81).

35. [R. Seeberg, _Dogmatik_, 1]: "As a formal spiritual disposition, the religious a priori has no content of its own. [. . .] The positive content of faith is given by

[47.] Seeberg, _Dogmatik_, 1:105.

must become religion; that is its essence. Revelation is religion. But that is a turning away from pure transcendentalism toward idealism in that the absolute, to use Seeberg's terminology, enters again into 'immediate' contact, into union, with the I; my will is subjected to the primal will and God's will is active in me. The difficulty lies in the concept of the religious a priori, in spite of the latitude Seeberg accords it. If we are to assume that the compelling ability to receive revelation and, by implication, to believe, is given with this a priori, we have already said too much. The natural human being has a *cor curvum in se*.[49] Natural religion, too, remains flesh and seeks after flesh. If revelation is to come to human beings, they need to be changed entirely. Faith itself must be created in them. In this matter, there is no ability to hear before the hearing. These are thoughts that Seeberg has expressed himself and supported with reference to Luther.[36] Having been wrought by God, faith runs counter to natural religiosity, for which the religious a priori noted by Seeberg certainly holds good. According to Luther, revelation and faith are bound to the concrete, preached word, and the word is the mediator of the contact between God and human beings, allowing no other 'immediateness'. But then the concept of the religious a priori can be understood only to imply that certain mental or spiritual forms are presupposed for the formal understanding of the word, in which case a specifically religious a priori makes no more sense. All that pertains to personal appropriation of the fact of Christ is not a priori, but God's contingent action on human beings. This holds true also for what Seeberg calls feeling and intuition, for the purely formal understanding of the word needs no other forms of thought than are supplied by the pure a priori of thought itself.

In Seeberg's outline of epistemology the two great concerns of theology clearly come together: first, to affirm being transcendent of consciousness and to make possible the formation of concepts of being; second, to show that the reference of revelation to human consciousness

---

revelation; the a priori is merely the inner capacity, in this context, by which we are able to become aware of the being and activity of the supramundane God and, accordingly, to receive the content of divine revelation, as divine, into the soul" (104).[48]

36. [R. Seeberg,] *Dogmatik* 2, 506ff.

[48.] In Seeberg's text the given citation reads "formal disposition of the spirit" at the beginning and ". . . and, accordingly, to receive the content of revelation, as divine, into the soul" at the end.

[49.] "heart turned in upon itself" [MR]

is, in character, an act. It is a corollary of these concerns that the necessary philosophical concepts for their solution are provided not by the
transcendentalist-idealist position but only by that of the genuinely tran-   53
scendental approach. It will become apparent later that even transcendentalism is in need of radical completion and inner transformation.

2. The Ontological Attempt

Act pointed to being. Hegel again honored the ontology Kant had
dethroned.[37] Kant's thing-in-itself had been transformed into the concept of substance that Hegel found indispensable in defining spirit.

It is the concern of *true* ontology to demonstrate the primacy of being
over against consciousness and to uncover this being. Ontology initially
wishes to say no more than that there is "a real being outside consciousness, outside the sphere of logic and the limits of ratio"—that "the
knowledge of objects is in relation to this something that exists
[Seiende] . . . but is not coincident with it."[38] [52]The real problematic of

---

37. Cf. [G. W. F. Hegel,] *Encyclopedia*, par. 33.[50]

38. N. Hartmann, *Grundlagen*[51] *einer Metaphysik der Erkenntnis*, 1925, 180ff.
"Something that exists" [Seiendes] means the same thing here that Sein does in
our terminology.

[50.] On first reading, one might be inclined to see par. 33 of Hegel's *Encyclopedia*, to
which Bonhoeffer refers here, as unsuitable to support the claim he wishes to make.
Indeed, in pars. 26ff., Hegel discusses ontology as the "teaching of the abstract determination of Being" and depicts it as the first part of an earlier metaphysics "as it existed among
us before Kantian philosophy" and as a "mere perspective of understanding [Verstand] on
the objects of reason [Vernunft]" that is always extant. A careful reading, however, makes
clear that the 'ontology' Hegel describes in this passage was merely the first part of the
older project of metaphysics that Hegel is claiming has been superseded by logic (par. 18).
Thus, when Bonhoeffer speaks of Hegel's 'ontology', he is not claiming that Hegel has
reverted to this older metaphysics, but that despite his 'Logic', Hegel is still making ontological claims. Such a closer reading of the context of par. 33 shows Hegel to be claiming
with respect to Kant's critical philosophy just the sort of *Aufhebung* that Bonhoeffer says.
For in par. 31 Hegel argues against Kant's having reduced reason [Vernunft] to a regulative
role alone; in par. 32 Hegel argues that Kant has had to use reason itself in order to critique it; and in par. 34 Hegel criticizes Kant's reduction of the *Ding an sich* (thing-in-itself)
to a limit-role, arguing instead for a more comprehensive, dialectical form of ontology
(which in par. 36 Hegel reminds his reader he has described in full in the *Phenomenology of
Spirit*). [WF]

[51.] The correct term in the title is *Grundzüge*, not *Grundlage*.

[52.] The second part of the citation from Nicolai Hartmann, reads: ". . . the knowledge
of objects is in relation to this being [Seiendes] and reflects a piece of it, however incomprehensible the possibility of this reflection may be; but the concept formed from cogni-

ontology lies in its concept. Two equally major claims meet in its com-
bining of logos and ὄν.[53] The ὄν, which is in itself free, resists the claim
of the logos as presented in the previous chapter. How then is a scholarly
activity called ontology possible? Clearly it is possible only if one of the
two—in this instance it must be logos—surrenders its claim, or if one
adapts itself to the other. But this can take place only in the movement of
thought, in such a way that the movement of thought itself, in one way
or another, essentially belongs to being. Here the step from Husserl–
Scheler to Heidegger is foreshadowed.

If the logos really surrenders its claim, it abandons its system of immanence. The question is whether the logos *per se* can possibly carry this
out. There is also a cunning of logos, by which it can give itself up only to
recover in greater strength. As long as being is a matter of thought, it
remains an 'existing' object. The attempt to think of thought itself as
being is the critical juncture at which transcendental philosophy, idealism, and ontology diverge on account of decisions made by each that are
no longer generally applicable to one another. Transcendental philosophy regards thinking to be 'in reference to' transcendence; idealism
takes transcendent being into thinking; and, finally, ontology leaves
being fully independent of thinking and accords being priority over
thinking. Genuine ontology, therefore, must always remain a *critical*
scholarly pursuit that does not cause being itself to be seen as a given,
but rather thinks of itself as always already something existing only within the logos, in self-understanding. For being, of course—which also
includes Dasein and being there in thought [Denksein]—transcends the
given, what exists. Ontology must be the pursuit that ponders this fact of
'always already existing'[54] and is itself mindful of this correlation; thinking must again and again be 'suspended' ['aufgehoben'] in being.

Here, the logos must refrain from usurping the power of the creator;
whether it does so in genuine *kenosis*[55] or *krypsis*[56] remains to be seen.

---

tion *is not congruent with* what is (das Seiende), for the image is neither complete (adequate) nor similar to what is.

[53.] Here ὄν is the Greek word for "being"; logos means "speech," "word," "account,"
or "reason." The word logos will not be italicized in the present text unless Bonhoeffer
himself did so.

[54.] See Heidegger, *Being and Time*: "Dasein's totality of being as care means: ahead-of-
itself-already-being-in (a world), as being-alongside (entitites encountered within-the-
world)" (375). [WF]

[55.] "the giving up of something" [MR]

[56.] "secrecy, hiddenness" [MR]

For the sake of the freedom of being, spontaneity must become receptivity—that is, creative thinking must become a viewing, pure intuition (*intueri* = to look upon, to take into consideration). It is but one step from here to *systematic* ontology that opens being itself to viewing. But this clearly represents an endeavor to go behind the way transcendentalism and idealism put their questions. Wherever thinking or viewing stands over against an object without mediation, there is no genuine ontology, for in such ontology thinking is again and again 'suspended' ['aufgehoben'] in being and, therefore, criticallly involved in the process of knowledge.

Systematic ontology seeks to present pure being as transcending consciousness. If, however, being is obscured by something that exists, it becomes the task of thinking to uncover or 'clear the way'[57] to this being. There are different ways of regarding this task of clearing the way to 'the essence'. But in principle people have eyes to see; they bear within themselves the potential to arrive at the eternal essentials. In Platonic terms, people have beheld the ideas, and now they eternally bear the *anamnesis*[58] within themselves until they attain pure vision once again. Human beings understand their nature from what they have beheld— that is, they see themselves disclosed in their eternal core. That is naive, systematic ontology and is maintained in such unbroken form among more recent philosophers only by [Nicole] Malebranche, in his theory of the participation of all knowledge in the idea of God, and, later, by Vincenzo Gioberti in his ontologism.[59]

As in the preceding chapter, the following presentation is structured systematically-typologically, using several outstanding examples of recent ontologies.[60]

[57.] Although Bonhoeffer has encountered the notion of ontology's task as 'clearing' in his reading of *Being and Time* (171), Heidegger's word there is *lichten*, which is used in German normally to mean the thinning of trees, the creation of a "clearing." Bonhoeffer's term is *freilegen*, meaning "to uncover," to "clear off." [WF]

[58.] "recollection"; cf. Plato, *Meno*, 81d 4f, 36b 1.

[59.] Vincenzo Gioberti (1801–1852) referred to 'ontologism', the philosophical position that he championed, as "anti-psychologistic." According to him, true knowledge is grounded in the a priori, nonconceptual, and intuitive knowledge of the presence of the absolute being in the finite intellect. Gioberti's ontologism derives from the doctrine of illumination of the Augustinian-Franciscan tradition, which Nicole Malebranche (1638–1715) had elaborated into a systematic epistemology. In 1861 a decree of the Holy Office condemned the major ontological teachings (see cf. Heinrich Denzinger and Adolfus Schönmetzer, *The Sources of Catholic Dogma*, nos. 2841–47.

[60.] The following typology of the ontological approach, as manifested by Edmund

The ontology of the Husserlian school, though it has an intense pre-
occupation with ontology, is in a way still under the spell of idealism.
The consequences will be briefly elaborated. For Husserl, phenomenol-
56   ogy[39] is the science of the phenomena of pure consciousness. Phenomenology is concerned only with such phenomena given to consciousness.
The question of existence is 'bracketed out' from the outset. Creatures
of fantasy and reality are ranked in the same order, next to each other.
As a result, a rift appears between essence and reality (*essentia* and *existentia*). Every act, indeed, intends an object; consciousness is always
'consciousness of' some entity. But whether this 'intentional object'
envisaged by consciousness is also a real object is quite irrelevant to the
question of pure essentiality. *Noesis* refers to *noema*, but the 'noetic-
noematic parallel structure'[61] remains immanent in consciousness.
This follows necessarily from the concept of what is given to transcendental consciousness. For example, an empirical tree is not yet 'given' in
'simple perception'. For it, or anything else, to become a given, a method
of 'bracketing'—that is, of 'phenomenological and eidetic reduction'—
must be brought into operation. This is a preliminary step, namely, the
way through theory to the pre-theoretic givenness. All interpretation
spoils simple givenness, and everything real is already an interpretation,
since reality is constituted by consciousness,[40] and so everything real
must be utterly 'ruled out of bounds'.[41] The task of phenomenological-
eidetic reduction, therefore, is to eliminate what is empirical-factual
from the *eidos*, from the essence, so that pure transcendental consciousness, no longer engaged in interpretation, and essence face each other
in simple givenness. In these two reductions the specifically phenomenological method of knowledge, the perception of essence [Wesens-

---

39. E. Husserl, *Logical Investigations*, 1922; vols. 1 and 2 are particularly relevant. *Ideas: General Introduction to Pure Phenomenology*, 1922.

40. *Ideas: General Introduction to Pure Phenomenology*, [par. 86:] 230ff., [pars.
47–56:]133–55.

41. Ibid., [par. 31:] 96ff.

Husserl, Max Scheler, and Martin Heidegger, shows the influence on Bonhoeffer of Erich
Przywara's study, "Drei Richtungen der Phänomenologie."

[61.] See Robert Winkler, *Phänomenologie und Religion*, 41, which Bonhoeffer quotes in
support of his interpretation of Husserl. Cf. Husserl, *Ideas*, par. 97. Here *noesis* means the
act of the intellect; *noema* means the intended object of knowledge. [WF]

schau], comes into play. Just as there is a purely sensory perception, so there is a purely conceptual perception [geistige Anschauung]. "The beholding of essence, too, is perception, just as the eidetic object is object. . . . Thus, the beholding of essence *is* perception; it is beholding in the most meaningful sense and not a simple, and perhaps vague, calling to mind. It is, therefore, a perception giving data *at first hand*, grasping the essence in its 'bodily' selfhood."[42]   57

Here two trains of thought seem to intersect in Husserl.[43] The concept of the perception of essence seems to imply that over against the beholding subject there stands an independent, self-contained being, the concept of which the subject forms in the beholding,[44] that is, without interpretation or inventive production. What meaning could there be in reduction to the *eidos*, if in the end that too were to be seen as a product of consciousness? We might say that a transcendental realism corresponds to this train of thought. Against this stands the assertion that consciousness is the constituent of all that is—that is to say, the insistence on the immanence of all being in consciousness. To speak of that which transcends consciousness is only a rule that consciousness projects beyond itself so as to order reality within it.[45] No longer can the process of cognition be understood as the perception that reproduces the *eidos* in 'ideation'—even Husserl rejects the realistic epistemology of the mirroring of being by consciousness[46]—but must be represented as creative, as 'generating' the object (Cohen), as spontaneity.[47] In other words, the a priori belongs not on the side of the object but on that of consciousness. In this way Husserl moves over to the side of pure idealism which, it would seem, is contrary to his original intentions. One would quite rightly expect systematic phenomenology to develop an idea of God that

---

42. Ibid., [par. 3:] 49.

43. Attention has already been drawn to this, especially by R. Winkler, *Phänomenologie und Religion*, 1921, 63ff.; J. Geyser, *Neue und alte Wege der Philosophie; Max Schelers Phänomenologie der Religion*, 1924; and W. Ehrlich, *Kant und Husserl*, 1923.

44. [Husserl] *Ideas*, par. 22, par. 24.

45. See for example Husserl, *Ideas*, [par. 51:] 142: [Nature] "*is* only in so far as it constitutes itself within ordered organizations of consciousness."

46. Ibid., [par. 90:] 241ff.

47. Ibid., par. 23: 82.

58   resembles the Platonic idea of God;[48] Husserl, however, in his demand
that the transcendence of God be bracketed out, teaches something
else.[49] Phenomenology poses no questions of being, only of essence. Yet
Husserl finds room in the question of God at least for an aside or footnote about the possibility of a somehow unique, 'intuitive' intimation of
God, which would require not a 'mundane' concept of God but a special
kind of transcendence.[50] Even if Husserl does not achieve real clarity
here, his phenomenology rests on the belief in the possibility of grasping intellectually, out of pure consciousness, the absolute as something
given—whether by means of an originally given intuition or in some
spontaneous manner. But now the I, or consciousness, is once again
restored to the place of God—an assertion which Husserl would deny,
but which is an inescapable consequence of his philosophical starting
point. The human logos has overcome the ὄν, preventing any clear grasp
of the concepts of being and God. Being as *existentia* has been dissolved
into *essentia*, and with that the transition to idealism is sealed.

What Husserl had confined to pure logic strives, as can be seen in
Scheler,[63] to embrace the 'totality of life'. Scheler evidently noticed the
idealistic character of Husserl's phenomenology and adopted only his
genuinely phenomenological position in order, first, to rid it of every
idealistic notion and, second, to develop it consistently in the fields of
ethics and philosophy of religion. While Husserl still gave a noticeable
priority to the logos over the ὄν—despite his intention of securing the
freedom of the latter from the former—Scheler, however, reverses this
position by lucidly working out the priority of the ὄν over against consciousness. A decisive step was taken when he transferred the a priori
from the formal, from what pertains to consciousness, to the material, to

---

48. Cf. *Logical Investigations*, 1/2, par. 64: 168.[62]
49. *Ideas*, par. 58.
50. Ibid., par. 51, "Note":142–43.

[62.] Bonhoeffer's reference here to the 1922 German edition of Husserl is itself
unclear. Bonhoeffer's footnote, therefore, simply has been reproduced as given; in the
English edition of the *Logical Investigations* there is no paragraph 64 in volume one, section two.
[63.] In relation to Scheler, also see Bonhoeffer's inaugural lecture at Berlin in 1930,
"Man [*sic*] in Contemporary Philosophy and Theology," *NRS* 53f., 56 (*GS* 3:65ff.).

what belongs to the domain of value, to the given.[51] This is a proper   59
development of the phenomenological position. The object of inquiry is
no longer how anything can possibly be given, but what it is that is
given.[52] Clearly, a being transcending consciousness is presupposed
here; otherwise, there would be no philosophizing at all. The Kantian-
idealistic question is dismissed as formalistic, and thus wrongly framed,
because it was burdened with unwarranted presuppositions. To be
beheld is that which is given in values in the rich fullness of every living
thing, from the least up to the highest values of the good and holy.[53] But
those values are predicates of being—that is, such predicates as are connected with, or belong to, a being logically independent of consciousness. They lie exposed to the consciousness just as conscious*ness*, *being*
conscious [Bewußt*sein*], lies exposed to the *conscious*ness, being *conscious*
[*Bewußt*sein]. But this has profound significance, as we shall see, for the
doctrines of guilt, original sin, and grace.

In relation to the idea of God, the priority of being preserves God's
transcendence of consciousness. God and I do not finally coalesce,
become one. Still, two difficulties arise. *First*, Scheler's way of thinking
about the positing of God's reality, God's existence [Dasein Gottes],
remains as problematic in his "material ethics of value" as in "the eternal
in human beings."[66] It would appear that the object of Scheler's investigation is the essence of the idea of God, rather than the existence of
God [Dasein Gottes], and that he does not proceed to the positing of the
reality of God.[54] Scheler is not prepared to accept as a proof of God's

---

51. M. Scheler, *Formalism in Ethics*, 48–89.[64]

52. Ibid., 55.

53. Cf. Przywara: "Drei Richtungen der Phänomenologie," *Stimmen der Zeit*,
1928, and the previously cited work by J. Geyser.[65]

54. Cf. the discussion of this in J. Geyser, 35ff. and in E. Przywara, *Religionsbegründung*. Also relevant to this is [M. Scheler,] *Formalism in Ethics*, 396, esp.
note 34, and *On the Eternal in Man*, 255ff.

[64.] Presumably the reference is to Scheler, *Formalism in Ethics*, 48–81 ("The A Priori
and the Formal in General").

[65.] The reference here and in Bonhoeffer's footnote 54 is to Johannes Geyser, *Max
Schelers Phänomenologie der Religion*.

[66.] Bonhoeffer is alluding here to Max Scheler's two books, *Formalism in Ethics and
Non-Formal Ethics of Values* and *On the Eternal in Man*. [WF]

existence that belief in the reality of God is given as part of the religious
60   phenomenon. Such reticence in making assertions about existence is of
a piece with Husserl's bracketing of reality. When Scheler declares that
the demand for a proof for God outside the basic religious experience
"is tantamount to demanding that the existence of colors should be
rationally demonstrated before they are seen, or of sounds before
they[67] are heard,"[55] his readiness to posit reality is clearly manifest. But
so is the failure of the undertaking in the manner of Cartesian demonstration. Be that as it may, Scheler has difficulties with the problem of
reality. This is because he had readily made the transcendence of consciousness on the part of *essentia* the presupposition of his philosophy
without doing the same for *existentia*; the consequence is that now Scheler cannot find his way back to the latter.

The *second* difficulty stems from the question of the interrelation of
human logos—under the concept of which may be included what Scheler
calls 'the feeling of values'—and being. No doubt, a sphere transcending
the logos, yes, even a priority, is reserved for being, that is, for the
'essence'. Nevertheless, according to Scheler, in this 'feeling of values'
the beholding I is capable of taking into itself the whole world, the fullness of life, the good and the very deity; being person, the I bears within
itself that which enables it to behold the highest value, to understand
God and itself. In this way the being of God, the world, and the I have
once again been delivered into the hands of the person understanding
itself from, and remaining in, itself. It is not as if the person produced
being, only as if being were accessible to the I from itself,[56] as if human
beings had the power to to make righteous, or to 'justify', themselves and
the world. Although Husserl leaves room for a transcendence of God,
without probing further, Scheler's vision, however, particularly in his last
literary period, does violence to God, first ascending to God in love and
61   then pulling God down to its level.[68] The all is closed in by the I, and in
this all God, too, is found.

---

55. [M. Scheler,] *On the Eternal*, 263.
56. [M. Scheler,] *Formalism in Ethics*, 294, bottom.

[67.] The cited text in Scheler reads "of sounds before they — are heard."
[68.] Cf. E. Przywara, "Drei Richtungen der Phänomenologie," concerning Scheler:
"once, at the outset, an exuberant rush into God's blessedness of love but then, at the end,
a desperate and raging tearing of God down into the world's misery" (258).

This accords with the 'will to have a system'[57] [69] which, at first glance, seemed incompatible with the phenomenological approach, but which is there in Husserl no less than in Scheler. The goal of philosophy is not a 'picture-book phenomenology' but a system. A system is made possible, however, only by an immanent idea of God or, rather, by the exclusion of the idea of God from the context of philosophy altogether, assuming that this were possible in practice, which we would, of course, deny. In the system lies the mastery of being by the knowing I, hence its claim to divinity, "the path to the usurpation of divine beholding."[58]

Earlier, the mode of God's being stood in question; here it is determined, by the force of the beholding I, to be that of something which exists, over against which stands the I in freedom of vision. The being that transcends what exists, and whose mode of being thinking and beholding know themselves to be, has been lost to sight. And the result is the system of pure immanence.

Phenomenology since Husserl has itself done violence to a problem, the clarification of which would have been indispensable for its very presuppositions: the problem of being itself. Not until the arbitrarily bracketed existence, or 'reality', is put on a new ontological foundation can we expect a clarification of the problem of act and being, which neither Husserl nor Scheler offers.

Here the most recent and encompassing phenomenological investigation comes onto the scene, taking ontology itself for its object: Martin Heidegger's *Being and Time*.[70] In what appears to be the bluntest reversal of phenomenology thus far, *existentia* is made the *essentia* of *esse*.[59] [71] Precisely where Husserl 'brackets', Heidegger discloses being itself. Correspondingly, where Husserl and Scheler speak of timeless essences and

62

---

57. [Husserl,] *Logical Investigations*, 1[/1], chap. 11; [M. Scheler,] *Formalism*, xix.

58. Przywara, *Drei Richtungen der Phänomenologie*, 262.

59. [M. Heidegger,] *Being and Time*, 67.

[69.] Bonhoeffer appears to refer here to Edmund Husserl, *Logical Investigations* 1/1, chap. 11, pars. 62–64:225–31. Philosophical systems are satirized by Kierkegaard in his *Concluding Unscientific Postscript* (117–22); and Nietzsche says "the will to a system is a lack of integrity" ("Twilight of the Idols," in *The Portable Nietzsche*, 470). [WF]

[70.] Cf. on Heidegger "Man [sic] in Contemporary Philosophy and Theology," *NRS*, 55ff. (*GS* 3:68ff.) and "Karl Heim's *Glaube und Denken*," *GS* 3:140.

[71.] Existence [existentia] is made the essence [essentia] of being [esse].

values as the being of what exists (insofar as this distinction is made at
all!), Heidegger interprets being essentially in terms of temporality. This
is possible only because the place of Husserl's 'pure transcendental consciousness' is taken by those who concretely ask the question of being,
who themselves are something existing in the specificity of their manner
of being as 'Dasein'. An understanding of being can be gained in principle only on the basis of a "hermeneutic of Dasein"[60] which is an "analysis of the existentiality [of][72] existence." Being is understood from
Dasein, since Dasein[73] at all times already "*is* in such a way as to be
something which understands something like being."[61] Dasein is, in
every instance, my Dasein. "Understanding of being is itself a definite
characteristic of Dasein's being."[62] Dasein is "'being in such a way that
one has an understanding of being'. That kind of being towards which
Dasein can comport itself in one way or another, and always does comport itself somehow, we call existence [Existenz]."[63] This existence is not
mere 'being-at-hand' ['Vorhandensein'], a manner of being that is not
proper to Dasein but only to the *res*, to things. Existence is, rather, what
at that point is an already taken, real decision of Dasein's 'ability to be'.
"Dasein is not something present-at-hand [ein Vorhandenes] which possesses its competence for something by way of an extra; it is primarily
being-possible. Dasein is in every case what it can be, and in the way in
which it is its possibility."[74] We need to be aware of the fact that the concept of possibility has a dual meaning for Heidegger. His main concern
is the ontological analysis of the existentiality of existence, that is, the
"analysis of what constitutes existence."[64] Here the existential, ontologi-
63   cal possibilities of Dasein are uncovered; they are to be distinguished
from the ontic-existentiell possibilities about which philosophy is silent.
Neither kind of possibility can be called absolute possibility, since each
is precisely concerned with the existentiality of historical existence. "But
the roots of the existential analytic, on its part, are ultimately *existentiell,*

---

60. Ibid., 62.
61. Ibid., 39.
62. Ibid., 32.
63. Ibid.
64. Ibid., 33.

[72.] "Of" is missing in Bonhoeffer.
[73.] Bonhoeffer's text has 'das Sein' here, not 'Dasein' as in Heidegger.
[74.] Heidegger, *Being and Time*, 183.

that is, *ontical.*"[65] [75] "Yet [humanity's] *'substance'* is existence."[66] Dasein always finds itself already in a world. It is 'to be in the world' existential-ontologically.[67] [76] Dasein is in 'being with others',[68] in 'being fallen into captivity to the anonymous' [im Verfallensein an das Man],[69] to a day-in, day-out sameness [Alltäglichkeit]. Dasein understands its 'being in the world' as its 'having been thrown' ['Geworfenheit'] into that world. Dasein is the being in the world of Dasein; its being, as the ability to be, is epitomized in the sentence: Dasein is 'care' ['Sorge'],[70] understood also in strictly ontological-existential terms. As temporal Dasein within historicity, it must order itself upon its own end so as to attain its original wholeness. And this end is death.[71] In the most proper sense, Dasein is 'being towards death'. But instead of living in the 'resoluteness [Entschlossenheit] to death', in this its authenticity, Dasein always finds itself already 'fallen into captivity' to the 'anonymous'. But the call of conscience[72] summons Dasein out of that captivity and into "its own-most potentiality-for-being."[73] But Dasein itself is the caller, "which, in its thrownness . . . is anxious about its potentiality-for-being."[74] Dasein seeks to return to itself from the world's 'uncanniness' ['Unheim-lichkeit'], which offers no home anywhere.[77] In the call of conscience Dasein experiences itself as guilty in its fallenness to the world, in its nul-

---

65. Ibid., 34.
66. Ibid., 153.
67. Ibid., 78ff.
68. Ibid., 149ff.
69. Ibid., 163ff.
70. Ibid., 225ff.
71. Ibid., 279ff.
72. Ibid., 315ff.
73. Ibid., 322.
74. Ibid.

[75.] Philosophy's inquiry into the most primordial, underived, level of questioning is what Heidegger called the inquiry into *Sein*, being, as opposed to inquiries into an object of ordinary experience, *das Seiende*. The first sort of inquiry is what is called ontological questioning; the latter is what is called ontic. The sort of human self-awareness necessary for ontological questioning is what Heidegger called *existential* self-awareness; that for the inquiry into the ontic realm he termed *existentiell*. Since otherwise we would miss a crucial distinction being made by Heidegger, the present work renders the German *existenzial* as the English "existential" and leaves the German *existentiell* as "existentiell" in English [WF]

[76.] Heidegger's way of writing this phrase is *In-der-Welt-Sein*: being-in-the-world.

[77.]The German word *unheimlich* has both a literal sense of "not being at home" and a more common sense of "uncanniness." [WF]

64 lity, and enters into its most authentic possibility: the decision unto death. It does so not by withdrawing from this world but by accepting its fallenness in the world as its guilt. Insofar as Dasein lays hold of the possibility, the existence, most authentic to it, Dasein grasps its own wholeness.

What is important for our inquiry here is the unconditional priority given to the question of being over that of thought. It had been the basic mistake of Descartes and all his followers that, in explicating the *cogito sum*,[78] they neglected to put the question of being to the *sum*.[75] But this question cannot be raised unless there "*is* something like an understanding of being."[76] All thought is but a determination of the being of Dasein. Thought does not, therefore, produce its world for itself. Rather, it finds itself, as Dasein, in the world; in every instance, it is already in a world just as, in every instance, it is already itself. Dasein is already its possibility,[77] in authenticity or inauthenticity.[78] It is capable both of choosing itself in authenticity and of losing itself in inauthenticity. The decisive point is, however, that it already 'is' in every instance what it understands and determines itself to be. This helps make sense of a leaning toward philosophical realism.[79] It is evident that Dasein, which is in the world, is in fact in a real external world. In this, realism is right; it is wrong when it tries to supply a proof for that external world. "The 'scandal of philosophy' is not that this proof has yet to be given, but that such proofs are expected and attempted again and again. . . . If Dasein is understood correctly, it defies such proofs, because, in its being, it already *is* what subsequent proofs deem necessary to demonstrate for it."[80] The attempt to supply proof presupposes an isolated subject, on the one side, and an isolated existing thing [Seiendes] on the

65 other. But being can never be elucidated by means of what exists [Seiendes], but can only be understood within Dasein (in the reflection of idealism on the I!). Here, too, idealism receives its due. Being is essen-

---

75. Ibid., 44ff. and 254.
76. Ibid., 244.
77. Ibid., 69.
78. Ibid., 68.
79. Ibid., par. 43:244ff.
80. Ibid., 249.

[78.] "think therefore am" [MR]

tially Dasein, but Dasein is spirit[81] in its historicity. This Dasein must go beyond idealism and inquire about its ontological structure, for in this way only can light be shed on the meaning of being in general.[82] Therefore being has priority over thought, and yet being equals Dasein, equals understanding of being, equals spirit. This completes the picture of Heidegger's ontology for us. Being understands itself in Dasein, in spirit. But Dasein is the existence of human beings in their historicity, in the momentariness of the decisions that they, in every instance, have already taken.

From the perspective of the problem of act and being, it would seem that here a genuine coordination of the two has been reached. The priority of being turned out to be the priority of spirit-being in which the spirit does not annihilate being, but 'is' and understands it. This solution, though reminiscent of Hegel, is fundamentally different from Hegel's theory, in that being is Dasein, 'being in the world', existing in temporality. Thus, pure consciousness in Husserl's sense does not dominate; neither does the material a priori in Scheler's sense. Heidegger has succeeded in forcing together act and being in the concept of Dasein; both what Dasein itself decides, and the fact that it is itself determined, are brought into one here. In not deciding there is already determination. Dasein does not have an absolute ability to be. The ontological-existential structure cannot be entirely separated from the ontic one. Dasein is neither a discontinuous succession of individual acts nor the continuity of a being that transcends time. Dasein is constant decision-making and, in every instance, already being determined.   66

Two factors enabled Heidegger to reach this conclusion. The *first* is that he interprets being so much in terms of time that even God's eternity, if it could be at all philosophically conceived, would, in principle,

---

81. Cf. Przywara, 259. In relation to Heidegger he writes: "The spiritual being (of human beings) is the essence of being altogether. . . . What Heidegger calls 'being', however much he talks of the reduction from truth to being, is actually nothing other than the being of consciousness."[79]

82. Heidegger, *Being and Time*, 251: "If what the term 'idealism' says, amounts to the understanding that being can never be explained by entities but is already that which is 'transcendental' for every entity, then idealism affords the only correct possibility for a philosophical problematic."

[79.] "Drei Richtungen der Phänomenologie."

have to be thought of as having been drawn into time.[83] Thus, Dasein always already 'is' whenever it makes a decision. If it were functioning out of a time-transcendent sphere, it would always have to constitute itself anew. 'Being' just cannot be statically comprehended as something that exists [Seiendes]. It is interpreted in reference to the understanding of being, and thereby drawn into the movement of decision-making existence, that Dilthey calls the 'totality of life'.

The *second* factor is that, in making its decisions, temporal Dasein is always directed upon itself so as to be able to decide, even though this 'itself' already 'is'. It is able to seize what its existence offers to it: its own-most possibility. It can come to itself, for it is able to understand itself, but this means that Dasein is contained in the world or, better, the world is contained in Dasein.

It is the basic thesis of this ontological metaphysics that Dasein in temporality already possesses in every instance an understanding of being, that it is, so to speak, 'open' to itself and in this way that Dasein is the window on being. The genuine ontological accomplishment of the 'suspension' ['Aufhebung'][80] of thought in being is conditioned by the view that human beings, *qua* Dasein, have the understanding of being systematically at their disposal. Still, it must be highly instructive for theology to see worked out in philosophy a metaphysical definition of the interrelationship of act and being. In this definition, it is true, the concept of being remains self-contained, notwithstanding the high degree of internal consistency. Heidegger's philosophy is a consciously atheistic philosophy of finitude. Everything in it is related to the fact that finitude is enclosed in itself through Dasein. It is decisive for the existential analysis of Dasein that finitude is conceived to be closed in. *Being enclosed* is something that can no longer be separated from finitude. Like all other existential characteristics [Existentialien] of Dasein, the existential ability to be does not become disclosed as a general existential characteristic of finite Dasein but as something essentially determined by the fact that finitude is closed in. In its essence the philosophical concept of finitude is that of closed-in finitude. Here, then, no

67

---

83. *Being and Time*, 499, note xiii.

[80.] 'Suspension' is used here in the sense it might be used by a chemist to speak of one substance that is mixed with, but not dissolved in, another—but not in the sense of a temporary withholding from, or abrogation of, the one by the other. [WF]

room has been left for the concept of revelation. With the knowledge, gained in revelation, that finitude is creatureliness—that is, open for God—all concepts of being must be formed anew. It follows that Heidegger's concept of being, despite its enormous expansion through the discovery of the existential sphere, remains unsuitable for theology.[84]

Building on the anti-idealistic presupposition of the unconditional priority of being over consciousness, Catholic-Thomistic philosophy demolishes the fundamentally closed concept of being in order to open it up for the transcendence of God. *Esse* and *essentia* are rent apart within being.[85] In human beings the two are separate, whereas in God they coincide so that one might wonder whether '*that* God is' [Dasein] incorporates '*how* God is' [Sosein] into itself or vice versa,[86] seeing that God essentially is always what God should be. The *essentia* of human beings is related always to their *esse*. But it is always different from the *esse*, because human beings are in 'becoming' while God is in 'being'. God is the eternal 'is' that abides in all 'was' and 'will be',[87] yet also infinitely beyond them. It is not that the *esse* of human beings is divine and the *essentia* nondivine, or the reverse, but the ontological relationship of human beings to God lies in the entirety of the *essentia-esse* difference of human beings and the *essentia-esse* identity of God. The relation between God and human beings takes the form neither of pure exclusivity, even if only partial, nor of pure identity, again even if only partial; both wholes can be considered, rather, in a relation of 'likeness' to one another, as being is like becoming. That is the Thomist principle of the *analogia entis*, which Przywara especially has restored in our time with methodical brilliance to the center of Roman Catholic philosophy of religion and dogmatics.[81] On this ontological foundation Thomas–   68

---

84. Cf. below, footnote 89.
85. Cf. Thomas Aquinas: *On Being and Essence*.
86. Przywara: *Religionsphilosophie katholischer Theologie*, 1927, 24.
87. Przywara: *Ringen der Gegenwart*, vol. 2: 923ff.

[81.] The term *analogia entis*, or "analogy of being," which Bonhoeffer's reading of Erich Przywara introduced into the discussion (see "The Problem" above, page 27, editorial note 16), is not to be found in Thomas Aquinas. It was used first, on several occasions, by Francisco de Suarez (1548–1619) (see *Opera Omnia*, 26:14, 16, 21 and 320–22). Initially, Przywara used the term as an element of the church's traditional teaching (*Schriften*, 2:7). This aspect is examined in detail by Bernhard Gertz, *Glaubenswelt als Analogie*, 235ff.

Przywara[82] seems, indeed, to have succeded in opening the concept of being to the transcendent. God is not enclosed in Dasein nor Dasein in God, but just as God is imagined to exist in abolute originality, so human beings are thought of as existing in their relative but authentic reality before God (*causae secundae*).[83] The concept of likeness requires two substances that stand over against, yet in relative independence from, each other. According to Przywara, 'is' stands 'in-over' becoming, and the latter 'comes from the former'. Therefore, God is not divorced from the creature but is in it to the degree to which God grants it relative but authentic reality. (Here arise the inferences of all-efficacy [Allwirksamkeit] vis-à-vis sole-efficacy [Alleinwirksamkeit], the doctrines of nature-supernature and grace.) This is how Thomas succeeds in interpreting Dasein in terms of temporality without sealing it in itself. The question remains whether the transcendence of God's 'is', or the analogy of divine being, is really adequate to express God's transcendence as Christians understand it, or whether a metaphysics of immanence still lurks behind the scene. Thomistic ontology is valid in relation to the being of human beings *qua* creatures, inasmuch as the being of human beings is determined, according to Thomas, essentially by creatureliness. This includes a continuity of the mode of being in *status corruptionis* and *status gratiae*.[84] With the continuity of their own ontological condition there is also guaranteed to human beings by the *analogia entis* a continuity of the ontological condition of God. Thus their being, whether in the original state of Adam or in Christ, may always be certain of its analogy to God's being. God remains 'in-over' human beings; but if that is to make any concrete theological sense and not remain purely formalistic-metaphysical, the modes of being 'in Adam' or 'in Christ' must be understood and interpreted in their own right. We must ask, in other words, whether there is in fact a being of human beings in general that is not already determined in every instance as their 'being-in-Adam' or 'being-in-Christ', as their being-guilty or being-pardoned, and only as such could lead to an understanding of the being of human beings. But

---

[82.] This awkward construction is Bonhoeffer's; he apparently took Przywara's position to be akin to, and representative of, that of Thomas Aquinas himself, indeed Thomism in general. [WF]

[83.] 'Secondary causes', that is to say, causes which in relation to the first mover are of a second order. Scholastic thought uses the term to depict the work of the creature as distinct of that of the creator. Cf. Erich Przywara, *Religionsphilosophie*, 39.

[84.] 'The status of the human being after the fall' and 'the state of grace.'

then, a priori, the possibility of a guarantee of the divine continuity of being loses any basis. The eternal 'is' remains a speculative notion which is continuously 'in-over' becoming, and which even admits of being broadened into an a priori system of the natural insight of reason, but which is inadequate for a theological ontology. God is not primarily the sheer 'is'. Rather God 'is' the righteous one; God 'is' the holy one; God 'is' love. The ontological foundation for theological concepts of being must remain precisely the realization that this 'is' can in no way be detached from the concrete definition. A formalistic retreat to something 'more general' behind that kind of specificity fundamentally destroys the Christian idea of revelation. The contingency of God's revelation in law and gospel is twisted into a general theory of being with requisite modifications, thereby blocking the road to a genuinely theological concept of sin and grace. Only general attributes can be deduced from the concept of the analogy of being; the two like-unlike images of being are fixed in their interrelation. But from this point of view, neither human nor divine contingent activity—thus neither sin nor grace—is conceivable; everything must already be patterned, in principle, on the ontological concept of analogy. But this brings us to the concept of existence in Thomas–Przywara.[85] Human beings, existing in the tension of *esse-essentia*, must already bear within themselves, as a possibility of existence, the possibility of beholding the 'is'—that is, the *esse-essentia* identity. It follows from this, however, that in this concept of existence one regards as implicitly already 'present' ['vorhanden'] what can only be made explicit in the ways God is related to human beings (and vice versa) that are possible within the limits of the *analogia entis*. But now, human existence is, once again, comprehensible through itself and also has access to God. This is the inevitable consequence of all systematic metaphysics. And so the attempt to open the concept of being to the transcendent also ends up with an illusory transcendence. The basic features of the ontological proof of God's existence come into view; if there is in the creature a tension between *essentia* and *esse*, then there must be, underlying that tension and making it possible, an identity of the two beyond that: the divine being as *essentia* and *esse*. Just as Anselm surely arrived at a being[88] but not God, and thus remained in the closed

70

88. Cf. R. Seeberg, *Lehrbuch der Dogmengeschichte*, 150, note 3.

[85.] See above, page 74, editorial note 82.

world,[86] the Thomistic ontological concept of God cannot go beyond a metaphysics locked in the closed world. This is the case as long as it discovers in the existence of human beings possibilities to understand themselves and, therefore, God—in other words, to "project themselves on the lines of their most authentic ability to be," as Heidegger puts it.[87] This is the case as long as the world together with its idea of God are combined in the I—but this means that one cannot successfully make room for a revelation, that is, one cannot form theological concepts of being and act.

Does this prove that every ontological approach is of no use for theology? It proves this with regard to an ontological approach just as little as it does with relation to a transcendental approach. Insofar as both, the foundation of being in act and of act in being, become a system confined in the I, a system in which the I understands itself through itself and can

71 place itself into the truth, they are of no help in the understanding of the concept of revelation. This occurs, on the one side, even if the genuinely transcendental approach sets free a being transcendent of consciousness, a being 'in reference to which' Dasein is conceived—while remaining itself nonobjective. And this occurs even if, on the other side, genuine ontology really intends to conceive of being as the a priori of thought in such a way that such thought suspends itself in being. For the inevitable conclusion must be that, in the first place, reason itself determines the limits and that, in the second place, being somehow falls into the power of the thinking I, so that in both instances, the I understands itself from itself within a closed system. *Per se*, a philosophy can concede

---

[86.] This is an allusion to the proof of God's existence of Anselm of Canterbury (ca. 1034–1109), found in the work *Proslogion* (*Anselm of Canterbury*, 1:89–112). Bonhoeffer's formulation 'a being' is somewhat confusing, since Anselm's ontological proof, put forth in terms of the concept of *id quo maius cogitari nequit*, "that than which a greater cannot be thought" (94), sets God forth as absolute being, encompassing concept and reality. The part of Seeberg's work to which Bonhoeffer refers cites the key statements of Anselm's *Proslogion*, chap. 2, in order to guard against all misinterpretation of Anselm's argument as an expression of metaphysical realism. Karl Barth agrees with Reinhold Seeberg's correction of the prevailing, traditional reading of Anselm; at the same time he goes further in his interpretation when, in the context of his theological program, he places the proof within the context of the form and language of prayer. Cf. Karl Barth, *Anselm: Fides Quaerens Intellectum*.

[87.] Martin Heidegger, *Being and Time*, par. 31.

no room for revelation[89] unless it knows revelation and confesses itself

---

89. If Paul Tillich[88] believes that there is no possibility of distinguishing between philosophical and theological anthropology (*Religiöse Verwirklichung,* Berlin 1930, 300), one need only refer to the concept of revelation. If, from the viewpoint of revelation, theological anthropology sees human existence as essentially determined by guilt or by grace—and not merely as 'under threat in an unconditional sense'—then philosophical anthropology is able to adopt such concepts from theology only at the expense of bursting its own framework. For in doing so, philosophical anthropology turns its analysis of human existence, too, into an analysis of humanity's attempt to lay hold of itself; that is to say, it can do so only at the expense of becoming theological anthropology. This leaves the question of truth untouched. It is to be tested only in conjunction with the concept of contingency inherent in revelation. Cf. relevant passages below, as well as Fr. Gogarten, "Das Problem einer theologischen Anthropologie," *Zwischen den Zeiten,* no. 6, 1929.[89] In a recent article, "The Historicity of Man and Faith" [which Bonhoeffer knew from *Zeitschrift für Theologie und Kirche,* 1930, no. 5, 339–64], R. Bultmann formulated the relation of philosophy to theology in such a way that it is the task of philosophy to examine phenomenologically those structures of Dasein which represent the existential-ontological possibilities (as distinct from ontic ones, of course) for believing and unbelieving Dasein: "Philosophy sees that Dasein is in every case a concrete Dasein, characterized by a definite 'how' [Wie]; philosophy speaks of the 'actual fact' of this 'how', but not of the 'how' itself" (Bultmann, "The Historicity of Man and Faith," in *Existence and Faith,* 94, trans. altered). The theme of philosophy is existentiality [Existentialität], whereas the theme of theology is concrete (believing) existence [Existenz]. The same line is followed by the following statements on the concept of revelation: Believers can state no more accurately or completely than unbelievers what revelation is. "What 'more' do believers know? Just this, that revelation has touched them, that they are in life, that they have received grace and are forgiven" [Bultmann,] 100). The event-character of revelation and the event-character of faith can be thought within the existential-ontological possibilities of Dasein. The presupposition for all this is to be found in Bultmann's

[88.] Bonhoeffer is referring to Paul Tillich's *Religiöse Verwirklichung,* chap. 9, "Klassenkampf und Religiöser Sozialismus" (Class struggle and religious socialism), 300. Concerning Tillich, see also "Man [sic] in Contemporary Philosophy and Theology," *NRS* 58f. (*GS* 3:71f.). Bonhoeffer's footnote 89 in its entirety leaves the impression that it was an excursus that Bonhoeffer wrote after the completion of the manuscript of *Act and Being* and inserted here. The articles by Tillich, Bultmann, and Löwith indeed appeared just at the time when Bonhoeffer was completing his *Habilitationsschrift,* the deadline for which was February 1930. [WF]

[89.] Bonhoeffer mistakenly cites Gogarten's "Das Problem einer theologischen Anthropologie" as appearing in *Zwischen den Zeiten* 6 (1929); it is actually found in volume 7 (1929).

72   to be Christian philosophy in full recognition that the place it wanted to
     usurp *is* already occupied by another—namely, by Christ.

---

assertion, which he does not further substantiate: "believing Dasein is still
Dasein, in every instance" (["The Historicity of Man and Faith,"] 94, trans.
altered). But this leads to further questions, for here is the root of the un-
bounded claim of philosophy. It must be asked whether one can assert this [unity
of Dasein],[90] even only of its existential-ontological possibilities, apart from revelation without making revelation impossible. If the answer is yes, then believers
do in fact know nothing 'more' about revelation than unbelievers. From the perspective of revelation the matter appears differently: believers know everything
about revelation and unbelievers know nothing. The reason for this is that the
essence of revelation lies in its event-character. For the existential-ontological
analysis, revelation can be thought within the static possibilities of Dasein; but
then it no longer has the essential character of an event, one that comes from
God's freedom. Only where forgiveness of sins is an event do I know of revelation as a believer. And where this event does not take place, the forgiveness of
sins of which I 'know' is no longer the forgiveness of sins attested by revelation.
Were it not so, the doctrine of justification would be in jeopardy. But if revelation is essentially an event of God's free activity, then it supersedes and challenges also the existential-ontological possibilities of Dasein. Then Dasein is no
longer essentially identical with itself on account of itself, whether revelation is
event or not. Then revelation claims to be the initiator of the unity of Dasein and
have the sole right to do so; then the deepest root of philosophy, the one from
which it derives its claims, is cut. The letting go of the ontic by retreat into the
ontological [unity of Dasein] is considered futile by revelation. In the existentiell
event of revelation, the existential structure of Dasein is touched and changed.
There is no second mediator, not even the existential structure of Dasein. For
revelation, the ontic-existentiell and ontological-existential structures coincide.
From the perspective of revelation—inasmuch as they are consistently regarded
apart from the event of revelation—the phenomenological definition of Dasein
(according to its existential structure as historical, as 'care', as 'being-towards-
death') is as much an abstraction and a postulate as is the biological definition of
human beings. That is why, finally, this interpretation of Dasein is also irrelevant
for theology. Cf. especially Kurt[91] Löwith, "Phänomenologische Ontologie und
protestantische Theologie," *Zeitschrift für Theologie und Kirche*, 1930, no. 5,
365–99. I am in substantial agreement with Löwith's comments against Bultmann and the 'ideal of existence' which is at the base of existential analysis, and
which opens up the concept of existential analysis to criticism. I have learned
much from this article.

[90.] "Unity of Dasein" does not appear in the two German manuscripts consulted for
the critical edition; the phrase is conjecture.
[91.] Löwith's correct first name is Karl.

In what follows, nevertheless, genuine transcendental philosophy and genuine ontology—as distinct from idealism and phenomenology—are said to make a contribution to the understanding of the problem of act and being within the concept of revelation. That is so for two reasons. The first is that genuine transcendental philosophy and genuine ontology have thoroughly grasped and thought through the philosophical problem of act and being. The second is that questions concerning the interpretation of act and being can be put to revelation in the sharpest possible manner because of their view that not only are human beings pure act 'in reference to' but also that thought is ontologically 'suspended' in being. The concept of revelation itself will restore an entirely new form to those questions and it will become clear in the process that, on the basis of that concept, the 'in reference to' ['in bezug auf'] and the 'suspension' ['Aufgehobensein'] of the act in being are basically amenable to a theological interpretation and, therefore, of help in the understanding of the concept of revelation. We shall see that in the concept of revelation both are brought together, surmounted, and transcended [aufgehoben] in an original fashion.

The offense against Christian thinking in any autonomous self-understanding is that it believes human beings to be capable of giving truth to themselves, of transporting themselves into the truth by themselves, since the 'ground' of existence must somehow surely be in the truth, in the likeness to God. But here, truth means only that reference to God which Christian theology does not hold possible save in the *word* of God that is spoken about and to human beings in the revelation of law and gospel. It is in this sense that formal validity may be granted to the assertion, common to the transcendental-idealist position, that knowledge of the self and of God is no "possession without context"[90] but is one that places the knower in an immediate 'possessing' relation to what is known. In a terminology to be further explained later on, knowledge in

73

74

---

90. Cf. F. K. Schumann, *Gottesgedanke und Zerfall der Moderne,* 1929, final chapter.[92]

[92.] Schumann in *Der Gottesdedanke und der Zerfall der Moderne* (333f.) follows Johannes Rehmke and his study *Logik oder Philosophie als Wissenslehre* (39ff.) in defending the thesis, critical of idealism, that knowledge is a final, most simple, primordial datum that is to be seen as a *having* of what is known *without any other relationships,* rather than as an activity of one kind or another *in relation to* what is known.

truth about oneself, as well as about God, is already 'being in . . . ', whether in 'Adam' or 'Christ'.

It is never possible for a systematic metaphysics to know that "one cannot give oneself truth," for such knowledge would already signify a placing of oneself into truth. But neither is such knowledge a possibility of 'critical philosophy'.[91] A philosophy with such an expectation of itself would be uncritical in the strongest sense. Thinking is as little able as good works to deliver the *cor curvum in se* from itself. Is it merely a coincidence that the most profound German philosophy resulted in the enclosing of the all in the I? Even this realization is a matter of placing oneself into truth—seeing that the world of the I without grace is locked in the I—albeit not the truth of the divine word, because it 'is' not in that truth. If it were in the truth of the divine word it could not celebrate the triumph of the I, of the spirit, but would have to recognize in its eternal loneliness the curse of lost community with God [Gottesgemeinschaft]. Only a way of thinking that, bound in obedience to Christ, 'is' from the truth can place into the truth. We are sent onward to revelation itself, yet we cannot understand this step as one, the final one, open to us; rather, we need to see it as one that must already have been taken so that we may be able to take it at all.

This is something that recently a group of theologians and philosophers, whose reflections have a common focus on the central problem of existence, has understood and accepted. It remains to be seen whether they have succeeded in interpreting appropriately the concept of revelation from the perspective of the problem of act and being.

---

91. Cf. the passage on Grisebach in Section B below.

B. The Problem of Act and Being in the Interpretation of Revelation and the Church as the Solution to the Problem

1. The Interpretation of Revelation in Terms of the Concept of Act

a) The Contingency of Revelation

To say that human beings cannot place themselves into the truth is not the kind of self-evident proposition on the basis of which one must or can postulate a revelation capable of supplying truth. On the contrary, the untruth of human self-understanding is made clear only from within revelation and its truth, once it has taken place and has been believed. Were it not so, revelation would itself be pulled into the untruthfulness of self-understanding as the final postulate of human thought, with the result that human beings would be put in the situation, from the postulates of their own existence, of adjudging themselves right and placing themselves into the truth. But this is something that only revelation can accomplish, if it is truly understood as such. Therefore, only those who have been placed into the truth can understand themselves in truth. Having been placed into the truth, they may now come to understand themselves in that fashion—precisely as a foreshadowing of their re-creation, of their 'being known' by God,[1] (see above, pages 45ff.). That is to say, they may now recognize themselves as having been created anew from untruth for truth. But they recognize themselves as that only from within truth, within revelation—that is, in Christ, whether judged or par-

---

[1.] Cf. 1 Cor. 13:12. Also see Karl Barth, *The Epistle to the Romans*: "[grace] is the knowledge . . . by which we know . . . [that we] are known by [God]" (206). See below, pages 91f., 107–8.

doned. This is what furnishes the theological concept of existence: existence is envisaged in reference to revelation as an existence touched or not touched by revelation. There is no more potential engagement (see above, page 29): existence has or has not been truly touched as a concrete, spiritual-embodied whole at that 'boundary' that is no longer located in or can be established by human beings, but which is Christ himself. This concept of existence will have to be made explicit in the following pages and must demonstrate its validity in the context of our subsequent discussion.

The concern of every theology since Duns Scotus and Occam that has emphasized the contingency of revelation is to be understood from this perspective.[2] But the transcendence of reason is asserted along with its contingency—that is, the absolute freedom of revelation as opposed to reason and, consequently, to all possibilities that could be developed, for example, from existence understood as potentiality. Revelation, which places the I into truth, which gives understanding of God and the self, is a contingent event that is to be affirmed or denied only in its positivity—that is to say, received as reality; it cannot be extracted from speculations about human existence as such. Revelation is an event that has its basis in the freedom of God, positively as the self-giving or, negatively, as the self-withholding of God.

The claim about God's freedom in revelation admits a twofold interpretation. There is a *formal* one: God is free inasmuch as God is bound to nothing, not even the 'existing', 'historical' Word. The Word as truly God's is free. God can give or withhold the divine self according to absolute favor, remaining in either case free. Never is God at the disposal of human beings; it is God's glory that, in relation to everything given and conditional, God remains utterly free, unconditioned.[1] "The rela-

----

1. But cf. Luther, *LW* 37:72 (*WA* 23:157): "It is the honor of our God, however, that, in giving the divine self for our sake in deepest condescension, entering into flesh and bread, into our mouth, heart and bowel and suffering for our sake, God be dishonorably handled, both on the altar and the cross"[3] [trans. altered MR].

[2.] John Duns Scotus (ca. 1270–1308) and William of Occam (Ockham) (ca.1285–1347) were the main representatives of Franciscan scholasticism. They taught that the origin of revelation (and creation) is contingent, not necessary, and lies in God's free will alone.

[3.] From Martin Luther, "That These Words of Christ, 'This is my Body', etc., Still Stand Firm against the Fanatics" (1527), *LW* 37:13–150. Bonhoeffer had transposed Luther's text into modern German for his dissertation.

tion between God and human beings, in which God's revelation to me, to a human being, is truly imparted, would have to be free and not static in the sense that its constancy could never mean anything other than the constancy of an action that is not only continuous but in every instance beginning, in all seriousness, at the beginning. This relation should never be thought of as already given, already obtaining, nor from the viewpoint of a law of nature or a function of mathematics, but always as *a matter of action [aktuell]*, that is, with all the instability of a deed being done right now."[2] Revelation is interpreted purely in terms of act. It is an event that happens to someone who listens, free to suspend the relation at any moment. How could it be otherwise, since it is "the majestically free favor of God" (Barth),[4] which establishes the relation and remains its lord. God is understood as pure act. God's freedom is the possibility grasped in the concrete act—but just that: possibility.

It must seem strange at first that the relation between God and human beings should dissolve into pure acts precisely where, at the outset, the transcendence of consciousness on the part of revelation is unequivocally asserted. The consequent assumption is confirmed, namely that transcendentalism is lurking here. God is made known only in acts that God freely initiates. "Human beings are always pardoned in this way, that God's word comes to them, not otherwise, not beforehand and also not afterwards. The heavenly manna in the wilderness does not, as we know, let itself be saved up."[3] God's Word 'is' not independent of revelation itself happening to human beings and of being heard and believed by them. But this is where the transcendental approach becomes apparent. Because it is God who creates the hearing and believing, and because it is indeed God who does the hearing and believing in human beings,[4] the Word of God is only in the act of belief and never "in these abstractions from the event of grace . . . the event over which God has sole control,

77

78

---

2. [Karl] Barth, [*Die christliche*] *Dogmatik* (1927), 295.

3. Barth: "Fate and Idea in Theology," 39f.

4. Barth, [*Die christliche*] *Dogmatik*, 1, 357f. Cf. ["Das Schriftprinzip der reformierten Kirche"], *Zwischen den Zeiten*, 1925, no. 3, 239ff., and [*Die christliche*] *Dogmatik*, 284ff.

[4.] Karl Barth, *Die christliche Dogmatik*, 297. For Bonhoeffer's remarks about Barth, cf. particularly "The Theology of Crisis" (1931), in *NRS* 361–72 (*GS* 3:110ff.).

and which is strictly momentary."[5] [5] God's being is only act[6] and, therefore, is in human beings also only as act, in such a way that all reflection upon the accomplished act takes place at a distance from it, with the result that the act cannot be grasped in conceptual form or become part of systematic thought. It follows that, even though Barth readily uses temporal categories (instant, now, beforehand, afterward, etc.), his concept of act still should not be regarded as temporal. God's freedom and the act of faith are essentially supratemporal. However, if Barth nonetheless stresses the act that always "begins at the beginning" again,[6] and in each instance is free, so that one can never make inferences from one act to the next, then he endeavors to give the transcendental concept of act a historical meaning. This endeavor is bound to fail because, according to Barth, no historical moment is *capax infiniti*,[7] so that empirical human activity—be it faith, obedience—is at best reference to God's activity and in its historicity can never be faith and obedience itself.

---

5. Barth, "Fate and Idea," 40.
6. Barth, "Fate and Idea," 36.

[5.] Earlier versions of Bonhoeffer's text began the citation with the words: "the Word of God is only in the act of belief. . . ."

[6.] Cf. Barth, *Die christliche Dogmatik*, 295.

[7.] This is an allusion to a formulation that had caused controversy within Protestantism. Lutherans had spoken of the *extra calvinisticum*: "Finitum non capax infiniti" ("the finite is not capable of bearing the infinite"). Reformed theology, on the other hand, adhered to the traditional scholastic assertion that "quod finitum est, infinitum comprehendere non potest" ("what is finite cannot understand the infinite") (Wolfgang Musculus, *Loci communes sacrae theologiae*, 430). The counterposition of the Lutherans was formulated first by J. Brenz as a basic assertion of theology of revelation to be distinguished from philosophical insight: "Si autem consulamus oracula spiritus sancti, manifestum est, quod finitum possit fieri capax . . . infiniti. . . ." ("But when we consult what the Holy Spirit says, it becomes apparent that the finite can become capable of bearing the infinite.") (J. Brenz, *De maiestate Domini nostri Iesu Christi*, 30). This Reformed position was first expressed as a dogmatic formula by Timotheus Kirchner, *Apologia oder Verantwortung des christlichen Concordienbuchs*, 45b; cf. Theodor Mahlmann's article "Endlich II" in *Historisches Wörterbuch der Philosophie*, 2:487f. Karl Barth adopted the formula during the dialectical period of his theology (cf. *Die christliche Dogmatik*, 188, 268ff.), but in a form different from that expressed in the *Church Dogmatics* (1/1:466f., 407f.). Cf. the seminar paper that Bonhoeffer wrote as early as 1925, "Lässt sich eine historische und pneumatische Auslegung der Schrift unterscheiden" (Can we distinguish a historical and a spiritual interpretation of [holy] scripture), *DBW* 9:305–23; cf. *NRS* 61f. (*GS* 3:76ff.).

Thus, the problem of transcendental philosophy, discussed at the beginning, presents itself anew. God recedes into the nonobjective, into what is beyond our disposition. That is the necessary consequence of the formal conception of God's freedom, which might be demonstrated without difficulty also in the relationship between nominalism and the concept of contingency at the close of the Middle Ages.[7]

God remains always the Lord, always subject, so that whoever claims to have God as an object no longer has *God*; God is always the God who 'comes' and never the God who 'is there' (Barth).[8]   79

Such a formal understanding of God's contingent activity could not but lead Barth to develop the concept of the 'dialectical'. "God's Word is not bound, nor ever will be bound. Theological dialectic can be genuine theological dialectic only insofar as it is open to this conception—only as it serves this and only this conception, that is, as it serves the freedom of God's Word."[8] The freedom of God's Word cannot be captured in unequivocal theological statements. It breaks them apart, and that is the reason why theological statements are there only under a 'critical proviso'.[9] [9] All of Barth's theological statements are based on the necessity of saying not-God when I speak of God—because it is *I* who speak of *God*—and not-I when I speak of the believing I. This acknowledges that   80 all genuinely theological concepts do not fit into an undialectical system; were it otherwise, the act-concepts would have petrified in the sys-

---

7. Admittedly, the concept of the freedom of God of late scholasticism appears to speak only of unreal possibilities. In that way the positivity of the church's order could be preserved. In Barth, God's freedom is asserted within the positive order as the explosive disruption of all historical forms.

8. Barth, "Fate and Idea," 59.

9. Even though R. Bultmann derives the concept of dialectic chiefly from the historicity of *Dasein*, I do not think that there is a fundamental difference between him and Barth, even though they hold different concepts of existence. In their historical situation human beings pose, or 'are', the question to which God gives the answer in freedom; the only way to talk about this answer in historicity is dialectically. 'Dialectical' does not mean so much 'determined by the opposite' as determined by historical reality, by the concrete question of the context and by God's answer. Cf. [Bultmann,] "The Significance of 'Dialectical Theology' for the Scientific Study of the New Testament," 163–64.

[8.] Cf. Barth, "Fate and Idea," 39ff.
[9.] Ibid., 29. See above, page 25, editorial note 1, and below, page 86, footnote 11.

tem into being-concepts, eliminating the concept of contingency in the process and turning the 'coming' God into one who 'is there'. Revelation would have become static in the theological system. This is what the critical proviso opposes. Yet it is not as if a dialectical theology had, after all, discovered a 'systematic' formula for a theology of revelation; no, "even for theology there is justification only by faith."[10] The proviso made by dialectical theology is not a logical one that might be canceled by the opposite but, in view of predestination, a real one in each case.[11][12]No

81   theological idea can as such ever comprehend God, it remains "strictly

---

10. Barth, "Fate and Idea," 60.

11. Their untenable philosophical and theological presuppositions aside (to be discussed later in the text), the reproach of Barth made by Grisebach and his friends—that Barth basically is no different from Catholicism since his theology of the proviso is, after all, also a system with a proviso—seems to me to do Barth no justice. The theology of the Word is not something one can take or leave; a "real theology of the Word[10] is the sort of thing by which one can only *be* taken or left. . . . Not because my dialectics are so great, but because God condescends to make use of me and this doubtful tool[11]—therefore, not because I have unearthed the tablets of wisdom, or squared the circle, or discovered the magic point at which reality and truth intersect, . . . but rather because it has pleased God . . . to confess himself to me" (Barth, "Fate and Idea," 59). My interpretation of Barth differs at this point from that of H. M. Müller, ("*Credo, ut intelligam.* Kritische Bemerkungen zu Karl Barths Dogmatik," *Theologische Blätter*, 1928, no. 7) and of that of Gerhardt Kuhlmann, ("Zum theologischen Problem der Existenz," *Zeitschrift für Theologie und Kirche*, 1929, no. 1, p. 33, note 1), both of whom argue that Barth's critical proviso constitutes his systematic method. Theological cognition can "never capture God" (Barth, "Fate and Idea," 60). God can only confess himself to it in freedom. Both parts of the sentence are meant in an existential [existentiell] sense, so that such a negation does not purport to contain the secret approach to the general truth about God, to the system but, rather, the witness of obedient thought to be uttered anew in every instance. There is, of course, another inference with which we will deal later, namely that there must be obedient theological thought without the critical proviso.

[10.] In Bonhoeffer's citation of Barth, he misquotes the phrase "theology of the Word of God" as "theology of the Word."

[11.] In Bonhoeffer's citation of Barth, he misquotes the phrase "this my doubtful tool," omitting the word "my."

[12.] Here Bonhoeffer rescinds the ninth thesis of his doctoral defense, which stated that "the dialectic of the so-called dialectical theology has logical not real character, and thus runs the risk of neglecting the historicity of Jesus," NRS 33.

speaking [. . .] a witness to the devil." [12] God remains free, nonobjective, pure act. But God can, from sheer pleasure, make use of a theology in order to witness to the divine self in it. That, however, is not something within the power of theology but within God's freedom. Thought is a cohesive whole, incapable of radical self-disruption. Of this Barth himself is conscious: even dialectical thinking is no way to capture God. How could it be otherwise, we might ask, since before all thought there stands unfathomable predestination.

There is a new development in philosophy, itself very interested in what is happening in recent theology, which parallels this attempt of unsystematic thought conforming to a formal understanding of God's freedom. E. Grisebach[13] has set out in several works to clarify, or more precisely, to point the way to, the concept of reality.[13] One way or another, every system blends reality-truth-I into one; it arrogates to itself the power to understand and to have disposition over reality. People are tempted, as with a 'satanic propensity' ['Satanie'], to draw reality, the absolute, their fellow beings into themselves. But they remain, instead, alone with themselves in their system, unable to arrive at reality. Theory can never form a concept of reality. Reality is 'experienced' in the contingent fact of the claim of the 'others'. Only what comes from 'outside' can direct people to their reality, their existence. In 'taking on' the 'claim of the other', I exist in reality, I act ethically.[14] That is the meaning of an ethic, not of timeless truths, but of the 'present'.[14] People can never have   82 disposition over the absolute, that is, bear it within themselves, and for that reason they never arrive at the system.

Friedrich Gogarten and H. Knittermeyer have developed this position

---

12. [Barth,] "Fate and Idea," 59.

13. Cf. particularly *Die Grenzen des Erziehers und seine Verantwortung*, 1924, and *Gegenwart. Eine kritische Ethik*, 1928.

14. On Grisebach's concept of time, see *Gegenwart*, chap. 12, "Vom Gestern, Heute und Morgen."

[13.] For Bonhoeffer's remarks about Grisebach, see "Man [sic] in Contemporary Philosophy and Theology," *NRS* 59, 63 (*GS* 3:72f.), and "The Theology of Crisis," *NRS* 370f. (*GS* 3:121 f.).

[14.] Bonhoeffer works out this position in detail in the notion of *Stellvertretung*—responsible action on behalf of, and in the place of, another person—in *Ethics*: "*Stellvertretung* and thus responsibility exist only in the complete surrender of one's own life for that of another" (*DBW* 8:258). But the roots of *Stellvertretung* lie here in the early, 'academic' theology, particularly the engagement with the personalism of Eberhard Grisebach. [WF]

for theology in such a way that in place of the encounter of human
beings with the absolute, with God, stands the encounter with the You
[Du] of the neighbor, the limitation[15] by the other as something that
takes place in, and really constitutes, history. Faced with this You, all
'humanistic-systematic' thought, all thought in search of ontological concepts, fails. For it is a matter of history, i.e., the encounter of I and You.
The meaning of the gospel is that the claim of the neighbor has been ful-
filled once and for all in Christ.[16]

The inevitable objection against this position is that in the attempt to
avoid all absolutizing, it is the You which is absolutized. But if the claim
of the I to absoluteness is merely transferred to the You, and not the one
who is above both and the absolute, then not only do we appear to be
heading toward a purely ethicized conception of the gospel, but also the
concept of history as well as of theology is obscured. And that means
that revelation is lost from sight.

If now, as was stated, the I is called into reality by the You, is directed
83   into its existence, then clearly the I and the You are given the possibility
of being in reality, of understanding themselves in it, of 'placing' one

---

15. [Paul] Tillich's thought also strives for humanity's 'de-securing' [Ent-
sicherung]. But he does not escape speculation in the attempt to define the
nature of Protestant proclamation as, firstly, the insistence on "living through
the boundary-situation" and, secondly, the declaration of "the yes, which befalls
people in the boundary-situation that is taken with utter seriousness" (*Religiöse
Verwirklichung*, 40; the third definition is of no relevance in this context). The
same holds in relation to the rejection of all "religious contents, even God and
Christ" (38). What else is the boundary-situation of human beings, speaking in
entirely concrete terms, but sin? What else is Protestant proclamation to proclaim but the 'religious content' of the forgiveness of sin and grace? But the
boundary-situation must be proclaimed to people through the word of judgment
and grace. Were I able to place myself into the boundary-situation without that
preaching, I could place myself also into truth and the *lumen naturae*[15] would
come into force after all.

16. This is the orientation of Gogartens 'dogmatics', *Ich glaube an den dreieini-
gen Gott*, 1926, and Knittermeyer's *Die Philosophie und das Christentum*, 1927. Cf.
Gogarten, ["Das Problem einer theologischen Anthropologie"], *Zwischen den
Zeiten*, 1929, vol. 6.[16]

[15.] "the natural light of reason" or "the natural ability to comprehend" [MR]

[16.] Bonhoeffer mistakenly cites Gogarten's "Das Problem einer theologischen
Anthropologie" as appearing in *Zwischen den Zeiten* 6 (1929); it is actually found in vol. 7
(1929). [WF]

another mutually 'into the truth' without God, and without revelation. If this is so, then it is on account of the postulation of the You as absolute. Therefore, such 'critical' philosophy cannot serve as a basis for theological thinking that rests on revelation as the sole possibility for human beings "being placed into the truth."[17] Therefore, Grisebach's critical philosophy, as 'thought', remains a system. Were it to be genuinely 'unsystematic', it would have captured reality once again; it would have entered into reality on its own. Thought is bent on wholeness if it is genuine thought, for it is capable of taking the claim of the other into itself. Grisebach is right, and he comes a long way to meet Christian thought, when he insists that human beings are directed into their reality only from outside. But natural human beings do not perceive this 'from outside' in the claim of the neighbors, whose only function is, finally, to act ethically themselves by bearing that claim. No, the 'from outside' is perceived alone in what in the first place enables human beings to understand the 'from outside' adequately, namely in revelation through faith.

The will to refrain from a system, as a deliberate act of ethical modesty toward the other, is no more a basis for the understanding of revelation than are good works. Godless thought—even when it is ethical—remains self-enclosed. Even a critical philosophy cannot place one into the truth, because its crisis emerges from within itself, and its apparent reality is still subservient to the claims of the *cor curvum in se* that have lost the power to claim anyone. Revelation gives itself without precondition and is alone able to place one into reality. Theological thought goes from God to reality, not from reality to God. Accordingly,   84 the will to refrain from a system must come to naught; thought remains within itself, in sin as in grace. The genuine system remains an eschatological possibility. That thought tends toward system, unable to disrupt itself, containing itself within itself—this is its designation by virtue of creation and *eschata* [consummation], in which thought no longer needs to disrupt itself because it is in reality, placed by God eternally into the truth, because it sees. But that is why any system of human beings, who *are* not eternally in the truth, is an untrue system and must be shattered so that the true system may become possible. This breaking-apart

---

17. Human beings can be 'in reality' and 'in truth' only through God. True reality is reality interpreted by the truth of the Word of God, so that whoever is in reality also is in the truth, and vice versa.

happens in faith through preaching. Here we meet the problem of theology, preaching, and faith for the first time; it is treated explicitly below.

In sum, all thought remains within itself as long as existence remains within itself. But existence is led out of itself into the crisis of self and placed into the truth by revelation, by the Word. Even when existence is placed into the truth, its thinking about itself and about God remains within itself; but it is disrupted ever anew by the reality of revelation, so that it may distance itself from profane thought, in a manner to be explained later. This means that human beings must *be* placed by God into reality, if there is to be room for reality in their thought.

If the knowledge of self and of God that God has implanted in human beings is considered purely as act, it is for the purpose of utterly excluding any kind of being. The act stays inaccessible to reflection; it runs its course each time in 'direct consciousness' (see above). That follows from the formal understanding of God's freedom. Theological thought seems, therefore, destined to remain essentially profane; it can only, in each event, stand "under God's blessing" (thus Barth). But one must object: what can it mean to speak of a justification by faith, as required by theology (see above, page 86), when it can always be a question only of the justification of thinking theologians themselves? What remains in question is precisely whether their existence, having been placed into truth, constrasts their systematic thinking with profane thinking—whether such a possibility exists at all and upon what it is grounded. Pure actualism in thinking about revelation must, on the basis of its formalistic understanding of God's freedom, deny the possibility of a distinction between profane and theological or—in anticipation of what needs development later—[17] ecclesial thought.

The entire situation raises the question whether the formalistic-actualistic understanding of the freedom and contingency of God in revelation is to be made the foundation of theological thought. In revelation it is not so much a question of the freedom of God—eternally remaining within the divine self, aseity—on the other side of revelation, as it is of God's coming out of God's own self in revelation. It is a matter of God's *given* Word, the covenant in which God is bound by God's own action. It is a question of the freedom of God, which finds its strongest evidence precisely in that God freely chose to be bound to historical human beings and to be placed at the disposal of human beings. God is

85

[17.] See below, pages 125ff.

free not from human beings but for them. Christ is the word of God's freedom. God *is* present, that is, not in eternal nonobjectivity but—to put it quite provisionally for now—'haveable', graspable in the Word within the church. Here the formal understanding of God's freedom is countered by a substantial one. If the latter can be shown to be a true understanding of God's freedom, then we are guided toward concepts of being by the understanding of revelation as pure act. From such a position, however, with a new understanding of revelation, the problem of the theological system, too, could be raised and solved in quite a different way. It would subsequently have to be shown what justification remains for the interpretation of revelation in terms of act.

In what follows, we will examine first the epistemological problems resulting from the interpretation of revelation in terms of act. The concept of existence is to be looked at from the same perspective, in light of which the need to look for concepts of being will become apparent.

b) Knowledge of Revelation   86

The interpretation of revelation in terms of act has its philosophical counterpart in the genuinely transcendental approach. Epistemologically this signifies that one can speak about the object of knowledge only in reference to the knowing subject. Nothing essentially is being said thereby about the being of what exists beyond its being known. The transcendent can never be an object of knowledge, inasmuch as it, being the basis of the very possibility of all knowledge, always evades the act of knowing. Anything objective is drawn into cognition, that is, is formed by it. Only the basis of what is known and of the knower remains free from the I—that is to say, being, unlike the entity, is not taken into the I, but remains transcendent to it. The faulty conclusion of idealism, the identification of the I and being, is impossible the moment the I knows itself as existing in time, bound to its existence in history.

If one now tries to place revelation into this frame, the only option is to consider revelation as objective or nonobjective. Epistemologically speaking, only the nonobjective position leaves room for revelation, since the objective position is drawn by the I into itself, which still leaves free the being of what is, although it cannot become objective. But if revelation is nonobjective, it follows theologically that God always remains subject and always evades humanity's cognitive clutches. If, on the other hand, we are truly to speak of *revelation*, it must somehow be manifest to human beings and knowable by them. And, as a matter of fact, God's revelation has somehow become knowable in Christ. How is that to be understood? God can never become the object of consciousness. Revelation can be understood only in such a way that God is kept in view as subject. But this is possible only because God is also the subject of the cognition of revelation since, if human beings did gain knowledge, it would not be God whom they knew. But this cognition of revelation is called 'believing', what is revealed is called Christ, and the subject of understanding is God as Holy Spirit. God is in revelation only in the act of understanding oneself. The reflection on this act will never meet God in my consciousness. The representation of God in my consciousness is, in essence, not God as such. God is only in the act of believing. In 'my' believing the Holy Spirit attests itself. That this is so is not a matter of demonstrable fact. It is so only in the act of believing, which, otherwise, remains a psychic act like the others. It is true 'existentially' ['existentiell'], that is to say, in the situation of being encountered. Accordingly, my knowledge of God depends in each instance on whether God has known me in Christ (1 Cor. 13:12; Gal. 4:9), on whether God is effecting faith in Christ in me. There is, therefore, no method for the knowledge of God; human beings cannot place themselves into the existential [existentiell] situation from which they could speak of God, for they are not able to place themselves into the truth. They can try to think in reference to this situation, but as long as they speak 'about' God, their thinking will remain self-enclosed outside the truth.

This consistent development of the transcendental position opposes every manner of objectification of God, whether in the Catholic canonization of history—that is, in the concept of the church—or whether in the Protestant idea of verbal inspiration, or in nineteenth-century theology of consciousness. God is not the God of our consciousness (Barth contra Schaeder).[18] It is certain that when we speak of God, this idea of God comes naturally to mind; but it is equally certain that God as such is not reached through it—inasmuch as we cannot speak of God as of something there for the finding. On the contrary, God alone can speak of God. To make God the content of my consciousness means to understand God as an entity. This has two consequences.

[18.] Cf. Barth, *Christliche Dogmatik*, N.B. 1:92–7; and Erich Schaeder, *Das Geistproblem der Theologie*, N.B. 2–5.

1. God 'is' not in the sense that an objective entity is. God is in God-understanding-God's-self[19] in human beings in the act of faith. God is in the self-understanding of human existence, in revelation. Only faith itself can say whether God 'is' also outside the act of faith. The transcendental approach leaves room for such an I-transcendent being without, however, placing it into the reach of the I. For that reason, faith ought not to be thought of as essentially a psychic event, though it is that too, of course, but as the pure deed of God and of God alone.

2. If God is thereby perceived as the subject of cognition, it is an equally pressing matter, on one hand, to reach an understanding of the human I as the subject of the knowledge of God, without which the act of faith would have no contact with the existence of human beings, and, on the other hand, to avoid the identification of the divine and the human I. That is, the question has been put concerning the mediation between the divine and the human act of faith—in other words, the question about the relation between grace and religion, revelation and history, with reference to the problem of cognition.

This is where the profound difference between genuine transcendentalism and idealism comes to light. If, as was shown in the latter, revelation was in essence religion as a consequence of the identification of I and being, the two are in sharp contrast in the course of the transcendental project. True, God 'is' only in faith, but it is God as such who is the subject of believing. That is why faith is something essentially different from religion. But it remains unclear (even in Barth) how the religious act of human beings and God's action in faith are to be thought, without dividing them into two—by nature different—spheres, or without suspending either the subjectivity of God or the fact that human beings were encountered in their existence. People can inspire religious acts of every kind, but God alone can give faith as utter readiness to hear; only God indeed can hear. The act of faith upon which we reflect cannot be distinguished from the religious act, whereas faith, being effected by God, is only in the act and never something one just comes across. But from that it follows that the I of faith, which is to be God's as well as mine, also can never be something one just comes across but is something that acts only in each act of faith. Whether I do or do not believe is something that no reflection on my religious acts can determine; it is

88

[19.] Hyphenation added for clarity. [WF]

89   equally impossible for me, in the process of believing, to focus on my
      faith [Glaube], so that I would have to believe in my faith.[18] Faith is never
      directed towards itself but always towards Christ, toward that which
      comes from outside. Thus, only in faith in Christ do I know that I believe
      (which is to say that here I do not know it), and in reflection on faith in
      Christ I know nothing. From the nonobjectivity of God follows neces-
      sarily the nonobjectivity of the I which knows God—and this implies that
      revelation should be the nonobjectivity of faith.

      When the interpretation of the concept of revelation is changed, a
      wholly different situation arises. Such an interpretation is possible, how-
      ever, only in connection with a critique of the transcendental concept of
      knowledge that the purely actualistic view of revelation and God's free-
      dom had employed. Only here could the nonobjectivity of God be given
      clear philosophical expression and could objectivity be repudiated. But
      if one can raise objections at this point, it may be that the concepts of the
      objectivity and the nonobjectivity of God, understood in a nontranscen-
      dental sense, show themselves to be inappropriate in relation to what
      they are meant to express.

      Knowing and Having: Through the act of knowing, the known is put at
      the disposition of the I; it can be classified within the system of knowl-
      edge. As something known, it 'is' only in this system. The aim of cogni-
      tion is to close this system. If this happens, the I has become lord of the
      world. For that reason, revelation stands against the system, for God is
      lord of the world, and the true system is but an eschatological possibil-
90   ity.[21] From that it seems to follow necessarily that God can be known
      only in the act, that is, existentially. Otherwise, God would be delivered

---

18. Even Luther could speak this way: *WA* 5:164. Cf. O. Piper, *Theologie und
reine Lehre*, 1926, 5.[20]

[20.] Martin Luther, *Operationes in Psalmos* (Writings on Psalms), 1519–1521 (*WA* 5:165):
"Oportet enim non modo credere, sperare, diligere, sed etiam scire et certum esse, se
credere, sperare, diligere." ("One must not only believe, hope, and love, one must also
know and be sure that one believes, hopes, and loves.") Within the tradition of
Lutheranism, Otto Piper approaches the problem of the certainty of faith by distinguishing between what faith is in essense and what it is psychically (*Theologie und reine Lehre*, 5).
In his criticism of self-reflective faith, Bonhoeffer corrects his own comments in *SC* 124.

[21.] Here Bonhoeffer challenges both the nominalist God as absolute, arbitrary willing
and the philosophical systems that would, mimetically, make human beings willing-sover-
eigns of (their own) creation. [WF]

into the system. For to know is to have. Thus, a chasm opens up between systematic and existential knowledge. True, the latter necessarily enters into the former but, in becoming something known, it gives up its existentiality. It seems that God's claim to sole lordship can be protected only in this manner.

The world of my systematic knowledge remains in force even when I know about God and my neighbor. Bultmann concluded from this that talk of God is possible "only as talk of ourselves,"[19] since "to apprehend our existence" would mean "to apprehend God."[20] One finds oneself, at least through such a formulation, ominously close to ignoring the fact that faith can be directed solely and exclusively to God. It is talking of God that first enables us to talk of ourselves. In a reflective theological form of thinking I have no more intimate reference to my existence than to God. On the contrary, one might say paradoxically that God is closer to me than is my existence,[21] inasmuch as it is God who first discloses my existence to me. One cannot come to a 'knowledge' of God from here either. It would be possible to talk of God, or to know about God, and to have theology as a scholarly discipline only if revelation were not understood as pure act, if there were somehow a being of revelation outside my existential knowledge of it, outside my faith, on which my faith, my thought, my knowledge could 'rest'. Like transcendental thought, the theology originating in the transcendental approach is integral to the reference of existence to transcendence. Its knowledge is part of the question of existence. But a discipline, the essence of which is not to ask but to know, must be passionately interested in concepts of being. The mode of being in which they are to be conceived remains open for the time being.

91

---

19. R. Bultmann, "What Does It Mean to Speak of God?" 61.
20. Bultmann,"What Does It Mean to Speak of God?" 63.
21. Cf. Luther, *LW* 37:58 (*WA* 23:135).[22]

[22.] Luther, "That These Words of Christ, 'This is my Body', etc., Still Stand Firm against the Fanatics" (1527): "Therefore, indeed, he himself must be present in every single creature in its innermost and outermost being, on all sides, through and through, below and above, before and behind, so that nothing can be more truly present and within all creatures than God himself with his power" (58), which is said with reference to Genesis 1, Psalms 118:15f. and 139:7, Isa. 66:1f., Jer. 23:23, Acts 5:31 and 17:27f., and Rom. 11:36.

c) The Person of Decision

If existence is in the truth only in the act of being encountered by God, then it faces falling into untruth at every turn. Since it is unable to place itself into the truth, it 'is' only in the instance of God's decision for it, which must also be understood, of course, in some way as its decision for God. In other words, existence 'is' in its 'being in reference to God', which is founded in God's 'being in reference to the I'. Only that existence which stands in the truth—that is, which stands in the decision—understands itself and does so in such a way that it knows itself placed into the truth by Christ in judgment and in grace. Only here is it true to say: I am a sinner, or I am pardoned. Outside the decision, it is 'known truth' but not truth for me. Falling into untruth, occurring at every turn, must be understood as a decision against God and, therefore, as God's decision, God's wrath, against us. Thus, holding-oneself-back-from-decision is already decision.

This is the consequence for the concept of existence that comes out of the interpretation of revelation purely in terms of act, which stands at the center of dialectical theology. "Whether we know it or not,"[22] the human being is the question to God to which only God can provide the answer. However, this question which we are is not our fate but our deed. "We ourselves are [. . .] the authors of our life."[23] Human beings's "being is not thought of as a phenomenon of nature, nor as a substance; it runs its course in its response to God's claim on it and therefore in its action. But this action is understood not as a process going on in time (like the action of a machine) but as a deliberate and responsible act."[24]

92

---

22. Bultmann, "The Question of a Dialectic Theology: A Discussion with Peterson," 259.

23. Barth, [*Die christliche*] *Dogmatik*, 72.

24. R. Bultmann, "The Significance of 'Dialectical Theology'," 163. Bultmann continues: "Just for that reason, man does not have his being at his own disposal, for at every moment it is being risked. That is, for Paul, man's being stands under the possibility of being determined by God or by sin" (163). The concept of possibility, as used here, is clearly suggested to Bultmann by Heidegger's existential-ontological analysis of Dasein as the possibility of ontic existence. Consequently, it includes the possibility of an ontological understanding of Dasein unaffected by revelation. But, seen from the position of revelation, 'to be possible' in relation to sin or grace (whether *existential* or *existentiell*) always means to be already really in one or the other. Bultmann differs widely from Barth here. G. Kuhlmann has pointed this out very clearly in *Zeitsch. f. Theol. u. Kirche*, 1929,

For human beings, to exist means to stand, act, and decide under God's claim. Existence is in pure actuality. Consequently, self-understanding is given only in the act itself. There are no concepts of existence prior to existence. The existence of human beings is either in sin or in grace. Through revelation there is only sinful or pardoned existence, without potentiality.[23]

The danger of a concept of existence derived apart from revelation lurks in Bultmann's attempt to interpret the insecurity of Dasein in the sense of 'always-being-already-guilty', on the basis of its historicity.[24] The historicity of being can be interpreted only from the position of sin, but not vice versa.

The original transcendental approach comes into its own in the indissoluble and exclusive reference of existence to revelation. The I is 'in reference to' transcendence. It decides ever anew but, on account of revelation, in such a way that decision about itself always has already been determined by the transcendent [das Transzendente], given that the 'in reference to transcendence' has as its basis the orientation of being toward Dasein. It remains problematic how Dasein as decision can be perceived also as something that has continuity. It would appear to be simple if Dasein could be understood as deciding ever anew for its "own unique possibility,"[25] that is, for sin, in which case this possibility is already reality. Deciding and not deciding are understood as already deciding for sin. But even here one must still indicate the position on the basis of which the being of sin is understood as a whole. The new

93

---

no. 1. It hardly needs pointing out that Bultmann here has moved equally far away from a pure understanding of act.

[23.] Other criticisms of the category *potentiality* or *possibility* in theology are found in *SC* 89ff.; "Man in Contemporary Philosophy and Theology," *NRS* 52, 64 (*GS* 3:64, 78); and *Creation and Fall*, 52.

[24.] Cf. Rudolf Bultmann, "The Historicity of Man and Faith," 97: "And just as I can clarify *conceptually* what Christian eschatology is when I know what *in general* 'future' can mean for man [Dasein], so also I can only clarify the concept of '*sin*', for example, by referring to the concept of guilt as an original ontological determination of existence."

[25.] Cf. Bultmann, "The Historicity of Man and Faith": *Dasein* which "is involved in care for [itself] chooses [its] own unique possibility. This choice is a genuine resolve only when it is a carrying out of the *resolution* that grows out of man's seeing in death his properest possibility and letting himself be thrown back by death into the now—of understanding the now from the standpoint of death and thus resolving in the situation" (102). In relation to this, cf. Martin Heidegger, *Being and Time*, section 74, "The basic constitution of historicality."

existence of faith appears to resist even more an understanding in continuity as 'being'. How is 'being in faith' to be conceived, given that faith is
a decision wrought ever anew by God? The continuity that is called for
applies as much to the new existence, as such, as it does to the unity of
the whole I, to the empirical, total I in general. The question is, how and
with what right is existence, especially new existence, to be thought of as
a unity?

The question of continuity makes it clear that Heidegger's concept of
existence is of no use for the elucidation of being in faith. Heidegger's
Dasein is something that has continuity, since it is already in the state of
having fallen subject to the world, for which it makes its decision. Dasein
is always already guilty.[25] In conscience it can summon itself out of the
world back to itself, but then it always finds itself already in guilt. But it
is impossible to understand this always-being-already-in-guilt as ontolog-
94   ically analogous to being in faith. For being, in the sense of the ability to
be, is confined to its limits, whereas faith is not a human ability as such[26]
and, consequently, also no being in which existence, in the process of
coming to itself, finds itself. If the understanding of being is regarded as
an ontological characteristic of Dasein, it becomes questionable whether
and how, on the basis of revelation, this being of self-understanding existence is conceivable. It is unthinkable in terms of Heidegger's sense of
existence, since that existence remains confined within its existential-
ontological possibilities. But only a being could provide the foundation
for the continuity of the new existence in unity with the I.

Two further possible solutions are proposed in the attempts (1) to pre-
serve the continuity of the new existence at the expense of the continuity of the total I (Barth) and (2) on the contrary, to assert the continuity
of the total I at the expense of the continuity of the new existence (Bultmann.)

1. In Barth the new I is presented formally as the 'non-being' of the
old I. The new I is initially clearly 'not I'.[27] It is not open to view; it is the

---

25. The term, 'guilty', is used by Heidegger in an existential-ontological and
not in a concrete-Christian sense; for that reason, 'being' in sin cannot be interpreted on the basis of his concepts.

26. Neither in the existential-ontological nor in the ontic sense: faith is not
even an impossibility but a contingent happening of revelation in reality. Sin also
is no human possibility, not even of fallen humanity, nor is it an absolute possibility; it is an occurring reality.

27. Cf. [Barth,] *The Epistle to the Romans*, N.B. 149ff., 271ff.

cancellation [Aufhebung] of the old I. It is "the nonbeing[26] of the first world which forms the being of the second world, just as the second world has its ontological ground in the nonbeing[27] of the first world."[28] "Those [human beings] to whom God is revealed are the very ones to whom God cannot become revealed. . . . They would have to conceive of themselves as not existing in order to conceive the Word of God coming to them. Make no mistake. They[28] to whom God is truly revealed must recognize this as their own impossibility for revelation."[29]

But the reason for Barth's view is that he can think of revelation only   95 as 'nonrevelation'. Thus the new human being can, indeed, be understood through the continuity of the I, as the negation of the old human being. And yet, two considerations are in order.

a) Is the new I to be thought of in unity with the empirical total-I, or does it remain its 'heavenly double'?[29] This is where Barth's concept of act becomes an issue. If the act of the new I has its continuity in the supratemporal, then the danger of a theology of experience is indeed wholly averted; but this occurs at the expense of the historicity of human beings and, hence, of the existential character of act. As utterly supratemporal, the act of the new I (being the act of the Holy Spirit) has to be thought on the horizontal plane as well as from the infinity of the vertical perspective; this makes more intelligible Barth's peculiar wavering between the rejection of the temporal characteristics of the act of faith[30] and their employment in practice (see above, pages 83f. and the preceding citations). The eternal act comes, by nature, 'before' 'every' historical act; it does so, objectively, because it is free and, logically, because for that very reason it was conceived in pure negation. Barth is quite aware that he has to define the total I as historical, and yet his concepts are already overdefined before he even takes up the concept of the historical. Barth does say everything that has to be said here, but he says

---

28. *The Epistle to the Romans*, 165 [trans. altered, MR].

29. [Barth, *Die christliche] Dogmatik*, 1:287.

30. Cf. Barth's "Bemerkungen zu H. M. Müllers Lutherbuch," in *Zw. d. Z.*, 1929, no. 6 [7].

[26.] Barth's text reads "non-being."
[27.] Barth's text reads "only in the non-being."
[28.] Barth's text reads "precisely the person."
[29.] Cf. Bonhoeffer's seminar study, "Luthers Anschauungen vom Heiligen Geist" (Luther's views of the holy spirit), *DBW* 9 (Feb. 22, 1926):377, and *TF* 449–50 (*GS* 3:29).

too much else beforehand. That is why it is not possible any more to make the I comprehensible as a historical, total I. In face of this we maintain that the essence of the *actus directus* does not lie in its timelessness, but in its intentionality towards Christ, which is not repeatable because it is freely given by God. Its essence, that is to say, lies in the way Christ touches upon existence, in its historical, temporal totality. For this reason alone the *actus directus* is not accessible to the demonstrative 'here and there', even though it occurs in concrete, conscious, psychic [psychisch] events that are substantially open to reproduction and reflection. Here the statement made earlier (see above, pages 28–29) comes into its own: it is not that the *actus directus* offers no material to reflection; it is only that in its intentionality—here directed to and founded in Christ—it does not enter into reflection.

b) If I and not-I are held to be in a relation of mutual negation, then the faith of the I must direct itself towards its identity with the not-I. But this pushes the act of faith in an erroneous direction. Faith knows only an outward-going direction towards cross and resurrection, and knows itself, as an act of the empirical total I, to be affected together with it by those events. It is in this sense that dogmatics must take up the problem of continuity. For Barth there would remain the further question as to how the believing I, which as such is in every instant already the not-I, could still believe in this not-I. Or are there are two separate acts of faith, one of the I and another of the not-I? But that also leads us back to the problem of the *actus directus*.[31]

2. Bultmann's concept of historicity enables him to conceive the continuity of the new I with the total I.[32] The whole I stands under God's claim—in the decision for God it is the new I as a whole, while in fallenness to sin it is the old. Always it is wholly itself. "We [. . .] are always being tested about the way in which we will grasp the possibilities of our historical existence. Since the historical fact of Jesus Christ, we are

---

31. It cannot be denied that Barth is determined to have faith be faith in God alone; it is on this very point that dialectical talk of God is based. But there is a significant difference whether I in faith still enquire about my identity with myself, or about the grace of God in which my identity in each instance has its basis. By its very nature, faith can no longer call itself into question, since it is based in unity, whereas unfaith can doubt Christ and thereby bring reflection into the act of faith. This distinction, however, has decisive consequences for the concept of existence.

32. Cf. [Bultmann,] "The Significance of Dialectical Theology," 163f.

asked: will we listen to God or to the devil?"[33] The word of forgiveness directs us into historicity.[34] That is certainly true as such. But how can   97
the new I be conceived in continuity? Is being in Christ constituted only by every conscious act of decision for Christ? And what does decision mean anyway? What does *"wanting* to belong to God or the devil" really mean? Clearly a decision by God is presupposed, for this decision is neither an *existential* nor an *existentiell*[30] possibility of my existence. As I find myself ever anew already in guilt, so I would have to find myself ever anew as a believer already in Christ. But it is not clear how 'I', being already in guilt, can be thought of as now being in Christ. Unless a discontinuous new I were to be assumed, everything would depend on somehow bringing the being of the new I into conjunction with the concept of existence.[35] That, however, appears possible to us by means of the idea of the church.

It is R. Seeberg who provided a cohesive picture of this matter in connection with his Luther studies. On the basis of his consistent voluntarism he introduced the concept of the new direction of the will; he does so by veering from the genuinely transcendental approach toward idealism.[31] The new I is the new will which has been turned by God into the direction that points to God, and which now in virtue of that direction can do good of its own accord. The historicity of the I, and the continuity of the total I with the new I as well as that of the new I itself, are preserved thereby. The problem of *everydayness*[32] seems to be satis-   98

---

33. [Bultmann,] "On the Question of Christology," 142.

34. Cf. [Bultmann,] "The Significance of Dialectical Theology."

35. Even supposing the possibility of an existential-ontological unity of Dasein, an explanation would still be required of what 'being in Christ' might mean.

[30.] See above, Section A, 69, editorial note 75.

[31.] Cf. Reinhold Seeberg, *Dogmatik*, 1:209ff.; 2:2ff. and 506ff.

[32.] In *Being and Time*, Heidegger defines *everydayness*, within the context of the analysis of Dasein, as the 'averageness' [Durchschnittlichkeit] of Dasein, which is insensitive to every differentiation of existence (69). His interpretation of it should help "work out the idea of a 'natural conception of the world'" (76). Heidegger recognizes that "One's own Dasein . . . is encountered proximally and for the most part in terms of the with-world with which we are environmentally concerned," and that "when Dasein is absorbed in the world of its concern . . . it is not itself," leaving us to ask, "who is it, then, who has taken over being as everyday being-with-another?" (163f.) Who is responsible? Finally, the 'everydayness of Dasein' manifests itself in the "falling and fleeing *in the face of* death," which 'attests' "that the very 'they' itself has the definite character of *Being-towards-death*" (298). Cf. below, 147.

factorily solved by the concept of direction. 'Being in Christ' means to have the new direction of will. The interpretations of revelation in terms of act and being are truly combined. One must have grasped the manifest simplicity of the conception first before one raises further questions. They arise in the first place from the concept of sin. The justified one remains sinner. What can that mean according to Seeberg save that a false direction still marks the justified one? If accordingly the new direction may not be regarded as continuous but as being infringed upon again and again by the old, how is the continuity of the total I to be conceived?

Furthermore, is there a will not directed consciously to God that could be called the will of someone justified? Is the everyday direction of the will truly direction to God? For if it is not, we would be left with a new I that again and again perishes and revives. Continuous being would have to be sought elsewhere. Given that the new direction has to be sought or given again in every act, it would appear that we cannot find an answer here to our question.

The concept of direction does not guarantee the unity of the concept of person. As a psychologically demonstrable fact, direction is still subject to disintegration into individual acts and arbitrary interpretation. Here Seeberg gave new life to Luther's valuable discovery in opposition to nominalism, namely, that if human beings are to be seen in light of the unity of God, they themselves must be seen in unity. But a psychological concept is unable by nature to convey this unity; even according to Luther human beings in their psychology elude self-comprehension. People do not know their motives; they do not know fully their sin; they are unable to understand themselves on the basis of their own psychic experiences, for they are amenable to any arbitrary interpretation. But since there is to be a self-understanding of human beings only in terms of unity—as was suggested above—and since, in addition, the understanding of human beings presupposes a potential re-creation, that unity must be sought where human beings have been created, or are created anew, and where this creation both happens to them and is something in which they participate. That oneness must be sought, furthermore, where human beings must know themselves, without interpretation, in clarity and reality. This means they must know that their unity and that of their existence is founded alone in God's Word. It is this word that lets them understand themselves as 'being in Adam' or 'being in Christ', as

99

'being in the community of faith of Christ', in such a way that the foundation of unity in the Word becomes identical with the foundation of that unity in the being in Adam or in Christ. This, too, is not a datum of experience but is given to faith as revelation. Only in faith does the unity, the 'being', of the person disclose itself.

2. The Interpretation of Revelation in Terms of Being

a) The 'Being' of Revelation

Agere sequitur esse:[33] this ontological, fundamental thesis of Catholic and orthodox Protestant dogmatics expresses quite unmistakably the antithesis to the transcendental approach. It is a matter of the interpretation of the *esse*; the issue of the interpretation of being emerges out of the understanding of the continuity between revelation and human beings. It must be true of revelation that God 'is' in it, and of human beings that they 'are' and act only out of that being. The ontological interpretation of the being of revelation defines it, in principle, as transcending consciousness and 'objective'. This being must somehow be made visible as a fact—it is there, at hand, accessible, existing; it is not dependent on act and does not fall under its power. This view is open to quite diverse interpretations within ontology.

In sharp contrast to the transcendental attempt, three possibilities present themselves for the interpretation of revelation in terms of being. 100 Revelation can be understood (1) as doctrine, (2) as a psychic experience, and (3) as an institution.

1. Revelation is interpreted in terms of concepts of being wherever its essence is taken to be doctrine, for doctrine is basically continuous and accessible; it can be freely accepted or rejected. When God is bound within a doctrine of the divine nature, then God is to be found in that doctrine, understandable and subject to classification within the human 'system'. But this makes for no encounter with the existence of human beings. Even a doctrine of a gracious God, one which declares that

---

[33.] "doing follows upon being." This proposition derives from Thomas Aquinas's statement "agere sequitur ad esse in actu" ("doing follows upon being in actuality") (*Summa Contra Gentiles* 3:69, 230, trans. altered) and "esse est prius natura, quam agere" ("the being of a thing is by nature prior to its doing") (*Summa Theologica*, 3:34, 2 ad 1).

wherever God and human beings come together there must stand the cross, is, certainly to our modern way of thinking, no offense at all but, rather, an entirely welcome addition to our 'system'. The offense arises for the first time when our existence is actually encountered, when we, wherever we hear about cross and judgment, must ourselves submit to them so that grace may abound. To declare that doctrine can be appropriated only through a divinely created faith is to make clear that there is something to revelation as a doctrine which somehow goes beyond human ontological possibilities. From this it follows that wherever revelation is understood only as doctrine one comes short of the Christian idea of revelation, because God is tied down by an ontological conception of that kind.

2. The attempt to understand revelation as an experience of consciousness, which was discussed earlier, is before us again here. This is because the fusing of the concepts of being and act, that we had shown earlier to be present in idealism, comes to view here, now seen from a different perspective. Revelation, when it is understood as a religious experience, is elevated to the 'objective status' of being. Here God is found in my experience, understandable and subject to classification within the human system of experiences. Thus, here too, existence remains without encounter. In understanding revelation, it is not a question of bringing forward this or that experience—basically, every experience, including the religious, is reproducible—but of knowing that, as I hear revelation, my existence is being encountered, disclosed, and transposed into a new manner of existing. Therefore, we are again speaking of something else that lies beyond revelation as experience. It follows that this understanding of revelation as experience falls far short of being decisive. On this basis the being of the new human being cannot be understood because existence itself is not encountered.

3. If these attempts in the final analysis submit revelation to the power of the human subject, the last possibility of defining revelation transsubjectively seems to consist in conceiving it as an institution of God. The Catholic church and the notion of Protestant orthodoxy that the Bible is verbally inspired are representative of this approach. In the institution, God 'is' bound immediately and is at the disposal of human beings. For Catholicism this means that whoever is in this institution is in God. Yet the being of the human being lies entirely in the transsubjective. Correspondingly, the grace the church infuses into human

beings is represented initially as a being [seinshaft], in the form of a habitus (*habitus entitativus!*).[34] The entire stress is laid on the being of the human being. That the substance remains untouched by the accidental quality of grace is a problem we cannot deal with here.[36] It shows nonetheless that, here too, human existence is obviously not being encountered. The being of human beings is seen to have its foundation in the transsubjective, for human existence can be encountered only from 'outside'. Therefore, the new being must be founded and sustained from outside—for which the sacrament of ordination, which is the foundational sacrament of the Catholic concept of the church, is warrant. To this condition of 'from outside' is joined, however, another equally indispensable one, namely, that it is really the whole existence of human beings which is transposed into a new manner of existing. Otherwise even the outside is no genuine outside, which is defined precisely by the fact that it originates beyond every possibility of existence while yet impinging on and creating it anew. But this is what the Catholic interpretation of the being of revelation cannot warrant. Being, conceived as an institution, as in an institution, is not capable of encountering the existence of human beings *qua* sinful existence—being in the truest sense ob-jective for it. That can happen only in the real encounter with another person. It follows that, on the one hand, the orientation of the interpretation of the being of revelation toward the concept of the church is justified, but that, on the other hand, this concept of the church is to be developed not in terms of institutions but in terms of persons. But this points us again in the already indicated direction.

102

The reason the three possible interpretations of the being of revelation that we have discussed fail to do justice to the Christian idea of revelation is that they understand the revealed God as something existing, whereas all existing things are transcended by act and being. Human beings take all that exists into their transcendental I, which means that

---

36. On how far the substance really is affected, cf. Bartmann, *Lehrbuch der Dogmatik*, 2,101f.,[35] and the references to Aquinas there.

[34.] "habit of being." [MR] Bonhoeffer deliberately stresses the *entitativus*. Cf. Bernhard Bartmann concerning the distinction within Roman Catholicism between the habitus of doing, *habitus operativus*, and that of being, *habitus entitativus* (*Lehrbuch der Dogmatik*, 2:99).

[35.] The citation should have been to 99f.

what exists cannot be genuinely ob-jective [gegen-ständlich],[36] nor encounter human existence, nor finally interpret theologically the revelation of Christ that impinges on Adam's manner of existence. In other words, something that exists, something creaturely, is not able to encounter the existence of human beings, not even the 'You', the 'claim of the neighbor' (Gogarten-Grisebach),[37] unless God takes hold of human beings and turns them around. That this does happen 'through' something which exists is the problem of revelation; everything depends, therefore, on the interpretation of 'through'.

There is no hiding the fact that in the identification of existing things and revelation, genuine ontology did not come to expression. The identification arose at that boundary of thought where, in a manner logic is unable to fathom, the transcendental and ontological paths diverged, and where thought, on the latter path, suspended itself in being so that what exists, too, became transcended by being. Yet the being of what exists remains, in principle, open to demonstration, namely in that which itself exists, which remains ob-jective for demonstration and observation. The decisive problem of critical ontology is, therefore, to show how the being that is spoken of here is to be thought of in distinction from what exists. The position is protected only through the critical suspension of thought in being, even though this permits a variety of approaches (cf. Heidegger, for example, who came to the idealistic system from here).[38]

Demonstrated being is, indeed, being in the manner of that which is [seiendes Sein]; this is not objectionable for ontological thinking, because the basis for transcending that which exists is different in ontology and transcendental philosophy. For transcendental philosophy, what exists, as something objective, is conditioned by the act and is transcended, therefore, through the overcoming of that very objectivity. In ontology, being is amenable to pure demonstration and is brought into pure givenness through something that exists. Thus, for a purely ontological interpretation of revelation, it is as false to define revelation purely as something that is, as it is to evaporate it into something that is not. Rather, it must be seen in a manner of being that includes both of

103

[36.] Bonhoeffer here appeals to the literal meaning of the German word for 'objective': 'standing-against'.

[37.] Cf. above, pages 87–89.

[38.] Cf. above, pages 67–73.

these in itself and, at the same time, 'suspends' in itself the human process of thinking about it (faith).

b) The Knowledge of Revelation

If revelation, as something existing, is an object of knowledge, the result is a positive, immediate knowledge. The system arises on a firm foundation, as the knowledge of revelation that is adequate in itself. To this notion of object corresponds the phenomenological method for which what exists, including the 'existing thing', revelation, is the material a priori of knowing, or, in this case, of faith. But the phenomenological method carries itself forward within the existence of human beings. For they must already bear within themselves the potentialities of perceiving being, or, in this case, knowledge of revelation, and 'discover' being in the manner of something existing, since they already know in principle what 'being' is. From that it follows, however, that Christian revelation cannot be understood when it is perceived as something existing, in the sense of something available at one's convenience. Whether understood transcendentally or phenomenologically and ontologically, revelation seen this way does not lead to contact with the existence of human beings.

And so a *genuine* ontology demands a concept of knowledge which does have to do with the existence of human beings, but which does not remain fixed in pure actualism. Likewise, such ontology demands an object of knowledge that in a genuine sense 'stands over against' the I, in such a way that it challenges and limits its manner of existence, yet without falling victim to being transcended by act and being in the false objectivity of something that exists. In addition, the object of knowledge must so stand over against the I that it is free from becoming known—so that, indeed, knowledge is itself based on and suspended in a being-already-known. The object must in every instance already stand in opposition; it may be said to be something that exists only when it is qualified by being and nonbeing themselves—something existing that underlies or precedes the I in its being and existence. Knowledge cannot have recourse to it as something available at one's convenience, but as that in the presence of which it must suspend itself ever anew in knowledge.

Then the revelation preached to us—of God in Christ, the divine

104

triune person giving itself to us—would, indeed, be the object of our knowing.

c) Human Being as "Being in . . ."

For a doctrine of the human being, the view that intrepets revelation as something that exists implies that human beings can freely and at all times have recourse to this existing something, which one comes across [das Vorfindliche]. It is at their disposal, whether in terms of religious experience, the verbally inspired Bible, or the Catholic church. They know themselves held secure, borne by this something that exists (even though such securing can consist only in that human beings remain by themselves, precisely because the existing something as such is given over into their power). In this way the I arranges a preordained place for that which exists and subjects itself freely to it (*fides implicita*).[39] (The I can subject itself only because that is how it experiences an ultimate securing of itself; it has this experience because it can remain by itself, and it remains by itself exactly because that which exists is kept in sub-ordination to the I!) The I finds itself in every instance under the shelter of this existing thing. It is always 'within the domain' of the sanctuary of the verbally inspired Bible, the factuality of religious experience, and so on. It is 'in' the institutional Catholic church. Yet, even all these cannot, as entities, encounter existence in the sense we have defined it.

The only correct aspect of the description just given is that which a genuine interpretation of the being of revelation also demands, namely the knowledge that the existence of human beings is always already 'being in . . .'. This 'being in . . .' requires two critical qualifications: (1) The existence of human beings must be affected; and (2) it must be possible to think of being in continuity. If we add that the reality of reve-lation is just the sort of existing being which constitutes the being (the existence) of human beings—but that this being [dies Sein] is the triune divine person—our picture is complete, provided that this is understood as 'being in Christ', that is to say, 'being in the church'. Since this being is to affect the existence of human beings, there must be acts of existence

---

[39.] "implicit faith." [MR] This concept was formed in the thirteenth century; it referred to an individual's faith in the faith of the church, the collective subject of faith. The faith of the church contains explicitly what is not known to the faith of the individual. This is developed and supported in Albrecht Ritschl, *Fides implicita.*

that accompany it and constitute this being in the same way as [they][40] are constituted by it.

Here for the first time a *genuine* ontology could come into its own, if only it defined 'being in . . . ' in such a way that knowledge, encountering itself in that which is, suspended [aufheben] itself again and again in face of the being of those existing things and did not force them to be at its disposal.

On this basis it is possible to speak theologically of the essence of human beings, of the knowledge of God that belongs to human beings, and the knowledge of human beings that is God's. From this perspective we gain a glimpse of genuine theological concepts of being.

3. The Church as the Unity of Act and Being

Let us look back first at the decisive questions raised thus far.

1. Where do I obtain understanding of Dasein, of self? It was shown that the existence of human beings can be encountered only from outside, and that it understands itself only in being thus encountered. Only in revelation is there a genuine 'from outside'. 2. How is the mode of being of revelation to be conceived, actualistically or ontologically? What is meant by the freedom of God? How is God's 'being' in revelation to be interpreted theologically? 3. How is the mode of being of the human being to be understood, as decision, or as 'being in . . . '? How is the continuity of the I to be maintained? 4. What consequence does any particular interpretation of revelation have for the concept of knowledge—that is to say, for human knowledge of God, for theological knowledge and the concept of science, or for the system?

In what follows, the attempt will be made to interpret these questions in terms of the concept of church and to answer them in light of it. This suggests the following arrangement: (1) The church as the place where Dasein is understood; (2) The mode of being of the revelation of God within the church, (3) The mode of being of human beings within the church; and (4) The question about knowledge within the church.

a) The Church as the Place Where Dasein Is Understood

The entire foregoing discussion has been directed to, or determined by, one place that has not really come to our attention thus far. The dis-

106

[40.] The word "they" was omitted in earlier versions of Bonhoeffer's text.

cussion becomes intelligible only when brought into the light of thought about the church. It is meaningful to argue that the attempt at an autonomous understanding of Dasein must fail *a priori* only when this is based on the premise that it is not possible for Dasein to place itself into the truth. But such a presupposition is not among the possibilities open to Dasein (hence not doctrine, experience, institution); rather, it is a contingent occurrence that binds us to itself. It is the genuine 'from outside' that gives us an understanding of Dasein, that makes it intelligible that this 'from outside' is what places us into truth. There is no room left in a philosophy of the possibilities of Dasein for the contingency of the occurrence of revelation in the cross and resurrection in the Christian church. Otherwise it would not be genuine contingency, not revelation, not an occurrence originating with God for the atonement of *sinful* humanity [Menschheit].[41] Those who have been placed in the midst of such presuppositions must alone judge to be untruth Dasein's attempts to understand itself out of its own possibilities. But if it is an act of God that draws human beings into the occurrence of revelation, then it is not one among the possibilities of an autonomous philosophy of Dasein. This means that nothing can justify this presupposition save God—which is to say, the presupposition justifies itself.

107

This presupposition, however, needs closer definition. To have been drawn into the occurrence of revelation is understood here as being in the church. It is understood, in other words, through a theological-sociological category, on the basis of which the questions raised earlier are to be discussed and answered with reference to the problem of act and being.

b) The Mode of Being of Revelation in the Church

Revelation should be thought of only in reference to the concept of church, where the church is understood to be constituted by the present proclamation of Christ's death and resurrection—within, on the part of, and for the community of faith. The proclamation must be a 'present' one, first, because it is only in it that the occurrence of revelation happens for the community of faith itself, and secondly, because this is the

---

[41.] Bonhoeffer has not used this term, which is translated with the collective term "humanity," since the statement of "The Problem" at the beginning of *Act and Being*. Normally he uses the much less abstract generic *Menschen*, "human beings." [WF]

only way in which the contingent character of revelation—that is, its being 'from outside'—makes itself known. For contingency is only in the present. What is past, as 'having happened', is essentially caught up 'in its context', unless the proclamation 'coming to' us ('in the future') raises it up into the present. In the concept of contingency, as the occurrence that comes to us from outside, the present is determined by the future. In the system the present is determined by the past, inasmuch as in the system there obtains the principle of the 'priority' of the coherence of reason. The present is always determined by one or the other or both, but it is never 'in itself'. But the decision lies with human beings. It may be said of Christian revelation that the proclamation of cross and resurrection, determined by eschatology and predestination, and the occurrence effective within that proclamation, lift even the past into the present, or paradoxically, into something 'in the future'. It follows from this that the Christian revelation must not be interpreted as 'having happened', but that for those human beings living in the church, in each present, this once-and-for-all occurrence is qualified as future.[37] Christian revelation must occur in the present precisely because it is, in the qualified once-and-for-all occurrence of the cross and resurrection of Christ, always something 'of the future'. It must, in other words, be thought in the church, for the church is the present Christ, "Christ existing as community."[43] In the proclamation of the community of faith for the community of faith, Christ is the 'subject' common to the proclamation (word and sacrament) and the community of faith alike. The proclamation and the community of faith are linked in such a way that each, when considered on its own, loses its meaning altogether. Christ is the corporate person [Gesamtperson] of the Christian community of faith. (Cf. especially 1 Cor. 12:12; 6:15; 1:13; Rom. 6:13, 19; Eph. 2:14. Church as the body of Christ: 1 Cor. 12:12ff.; Rom. 12:4ff.; Eph. 1:23; 4:15f.; Col. 1:18. Christ is in the community of faith as the community of faith is in Christ: 1 Cor. 1:30; 3:16; 2 Cor. 6:16; 13:5; Col. 2:17; 3:11; Community of faith as corporate person that is also called Christ: Gal. 3:28; Col. 3:10f.;

108

---

37. This might be a starting-point for a distinctively Christian philosophy of time in contrast to the concept of time as something reckoned by motion.[42]

[42.] Cf. the philosophy of time that Eberhard Grisebach had developed in the final chapter of his book *Gegenwart*, 511ff.

[43.] In what follows, Bonhoeffer sums up the basic ideas he had developed in *SC* 103–44.

similarly Eph. 1:23. Cf. "Clothe yourselves with the new self," which sometimes takes the form "put on the Lord Jesus": Col. 3:10; Eph. 4:24; Rom.13:14; Gal.3:27.)[38]

For this reason, the Protestant idea of the church is conceived in personal terms—that is, God reveals the divine self in the church as person. The community of faith is God's final revelation as "Christ existing as community [Gemeinde]," ordained for the end time of the world until 109   the return of Christ.[39] Here Christ has come in the closest proximity to humanity. Here Christ has given Christ's own self to the new humanity in Christ so that the person of Christ draws together in itself all whom Christ has won, binding and committing Christ to them and them to one another. The 'church' is, therefore, not a human community [Gemeinschaft] to which Christ then comes or not, nor is it a gathering of such persons as those who (as individuals) seek Christ or think they have Christ and now wish to cultivate this common 'possession'. The church is rather the community of faith created by and founded upon Christ, in which Christ is revealed as the δεύτερος ἄνθρωπος, as the new human, or rather, as the new humanity itself.

Seen in this way, the question of the interpretation of revelation in terms of act and being takes an entirely new turn. God gives the divine self in Christ to the community of faith and to every individual as member of this community of faith. This happens in such a way that the acting subject in the community of faith, proclaiming and believing, is Christ. In the personlike community of faith, but only there, the gospel can be truly proclaimed and believed. Hence, the gospel is somehow held fast here. God's freedom has woven itself into this personlike community of faith, and it is precisely this which manifests what God's freedom is: that God binds God's self to human beings. The community of faith really does have the word of forgiveness at its disposal. In the com-

---

38. Cf. [Ferdinand] Kattenbusch, "Quellort der Kirchenindee," in the *Harnack-Festgabe*, 1921, 143ff., and Traugott Schmidt, *Der Leib Christi*. See further [Max] Scheler, *Formalism in Ethics*, where he develops his position on the corporate person. In my work *Sanctorum Communio: A Dogmatic Inquiry into the Sociology of the Church*, 1930, I have sought to make this idea fruitful for dogmatics.

39. The tension between "Christ existing as community" and the heavenly Christ, whom we await, persists.[44]

[44.] Cf. *SC* 101, and the second of the theological theses stated for Bonhoeffer's final theological examinations in December 1927 (*NRS* 32).

munity of faith the words 'I am forgiven' can be spoken not merely existentially; as the Christian church, the congregation may declare in sermon and sacrament that 'you are forgiven'. Through such proclamation of the gospel, every member of the church may and should 'become a Christ' to the others.

Thus revelation happens in the community of faith; it requires primarily a specific Christian sociology. There is a fundamental difference between thinking of revelation individualistically and thinking of it as something related to community. All that we have examined so far in this study was individualistically oriented. The transcendental attempt of pure actualism as well as that of ontology, which was to establish the continuity of the I, pointed to the individual human being and for that reason failed. In searching for 'reality' it overlooked the fact that in reality human beings are never individuals only, not even those 'addressed by the You'. Human beings, rather, are always part of a community, in 'Adam' or in 'Christ'. The word of God is given to humanity, the gospel to Christ's community of faith. By introducing the sociological category, the problematic of act and being—and with it the problem of knowledge—is stated for theology in an entirely new manner.

110

The being of revelation does not lie in a one-time occurrence in the past, in an existing thing that, in principle at my disposition, has no connection with my old or new existence. But neither can the being of revelation be conceived as the ever-free, pure, and nonobjective act that impinges on individual existence in each instance. The being of revelation 'is', rather, the being of the community of persons that is constituted and formed by the person of Christ and in which individuals already find themselves in their new existence. This warrants three considerations: (1) that the being of revelation can be conceptualized in continuity, (2) that the existence of human beings is really affected, and (3) that the being of revelation can be conceptualized neither as what exists, as something objective, nor as nonexisting, as something nonobjective.

1. The continuity of revelation means that it is always present (in the sense of 'what is in the future'). For that reason, it can be a question today only of the Christ preached in the church, of Christ's death and resurrection. If the individual were the hearer of the sermon, the continuity would still be in danger. But it is the church itself that hears the word of the church, even if I did not hear in each instance. In this manner preaching is always heard. It is outside me that the gospel is pro-

claimed and heard, that Christ 'is' in Christ's community of faith. And so the continuity does not lie in human beings, but rather it is guaranteed suprapersonally [überpersönlich] through a community of persons. In place of the Catholic church as institution there is the community of faith as the transsubjective warrant for continuity and for the 'outside' (cf. point 3 below).

2. But the existence of those human beings who hear in each instance is affected by this community in that they are drawn into it and discover that there they already have been placed into the truth of their old and new existence. But this is founded on the personal character of the community of faith, whose subject is Christ. For only through the person of Christ can the existence of human beings be encountered, placed into truth, and transposed into a new manner of existence. But as the person of Christ has been revealed in the community of faith, the existence of human beings can be encountered only through the community of faith. It is from the person of Christ that every other person first acquires for other human beings the character of personhood. In this way other persons themselves even become Christ for us in demand and promise, in the existential limits they place on us from outside; they become, as such, also the warrant of the continuity of revelation.[45] Were the existence of human beings not affected through revelation in the community of faith, everything said there about the being of revelation in the community of faith would be pointless. A continuity that does not affect existence is not the continuity of Christian revelation; it is not present being, but bygone entity. In other words, the community of faith warrants the continuity of revelation only by the fact that I know myself to be in the community of faith, that I believe. Here the problem of act and being emerges with ultimate clarity in the form of the dialectic of faith and church. But more on that later.

3. If the being of revelation is fixed in what exists, it remains past, existentially of no interest; if the being of revelation is evaporated into nonobjectivity, continuity is lost. The being of revelation must, therefore, have a kind of being that satisfies the two indicated claims. We understand the person and the community to be such a kind of being. Here the possibility of existential encounter is bound up with genuine

111

[45.] Here we see another thread that will lead toward the later, better known writings, in this case "the person for others" of the *Letters and Papers* (381). See also "the service of active helpfulness" in *DBWE* 5:99–100. [WF]

objectivity—in the literal sense of something that concretely stands-over-against, that does not let itself be drawn into the power of the I, because it itself puts limits on existence, since it is the 'outside' per se.[46]

The community in question is visible concretely; it is the Christian church that hears the preaching and believes it. The word of this community is preaching and sacrament; its action is believing and loving. The being of revelation, "Christ existing as community," has to be thought of in this concreteness. That is the only way one can sustain the tension between entity and nonentity in the concreteness of the kind of being that belongs to a true community of persons, one that is founded by Christ.

What is called 'the outside' of personal revelation presents itself as   112
something in correlation with my whole existence, that is to say, in a sociological category. It is essentially different from the category of 'there is'.[47] That category is indifferent to existence. It belongs with individualistic, thing-related epistemology. The kind of being that pertains to revelation is definable only in reference to persons. 'There is' only what exists, the given. It is a contradiction in terms to seek a 'there is', a given beyond what exists. In the social relation of persons the static concept of being that pertains to the 'there is' begins to move. There is no God who 'is there' [Einen Gott, den 'es gibt', gibt es nicht]; God 'is' in the relation of persons, and being is God's being person [das Sein ist sein Personsein].

But all this is comprehensible only for the person who *is* placed into the truth, to whom, through the person of Christ, the other has become

---

[46.] The word "not" in the preceding sentence was inadvertently omitted in the German edition, DBWZ.

[47.] The debate between Erik Peterson and Rudolf Bultmann, beginning in 1926, was one of the guiding influences on *Act and Being*. This, however, has been overshadowed by the attention given the Bonhoeffer-Barth relationship, leaving figures such as Peterson largely unknown in the English-speaking world. Peterson's critique of 'dialectical theology' was governed by the language used here by Bonhoeffer, particularly the phrase, "there is." See, for example, his "Was ist Theologie?" 9–43, and Barth's reply: "Therefore Peterson's often-repeated formula 'there is' (*'es gibt'*) this and that dogma, sacrament, theology, etc., requires at least a very cautious or (if you will pardon the term) a 'dialectical' use. What 'is there' in this context of which it is not essentially true that it 'is there' only as *God*'s gift— that God gives it not once and for all, but keeps giving it repeatedly?" ("Church and Theology," 294). [One might compare Heidegger's claim in his "Letter on Humanism," that even as early as *Being and Time*—itself so influential on *Act and Being*—he had understood *es gibt* to mean not just 'there is', but 'it gives'—'being gives'—as for example in the statement "only as long as Dasein *is* . . . , 'is there' ['gibt es'] being" (*Being and Time*, 255; cf. "Letter on Humanism," 216).] [WF]

a true person. For those people in untruth, revelation remains something that exists, as a person does, a thing, something that 'there is'. Revelation remains that toward which a neutral position can be assumed in which the existence of human beings is unaffected. It is only in the community of faith itself that revelation can be understood in its real, existence-affecting being. That, however, raises the question of the interpretation of the being of human beings in revelation.

c) The Mode of Being of Human Beings in the Church

113   *Prius est enim esse quam operari, prius autem pati quam esse. Ergo fieri, esse, operari se sequuntur* (Luther).[40] [48] In relation to God human beings are in the position of those who suffer, or who are acted upon [die Stellung eines Leidenden]; Luther speaks of this as a *nova nativitas*.[49] Existence is defined as *pati*, as being acted upon; that is, one can speak 'authentically' of existence only as of existence to which things happen. Every concept of existence that is not formed by being encountered or not being encountered by Christ is 'inauthentic' (including Heidegger's 'authentic' existence).[50] This concept of existence was used earlier as the critical standard, measured against which every other concept of existence had to fail. Encountered existence is existence in social context, existence in reference to Christ, which knows itself to be rejected and accepted in its historical totality. Existence, therefore, 'is' only as sinful and as pardoned. We must look to the concept of the church in order to find out how, from the perspective of the problem of act and being, human existence, as determined by *pati*, manifests itself in the community of faith of Christ—or how existentiality and continuity come together in the concept of *pati*.

---

40. [Luther,] *Lectures on Romans*, 105, note 2, and 434. See E. Seeberg: *Luthers Theologie*, 1:67.

[48.] "Thus, being possesses priority over acting; however, being acted upon is before being. Therefore, being created, being, acting follow one on the other" (Luther, *LW* 25:104, note 2, trans. altered [*WA* 56:117]).

[49.] "a new birth" [MR]

[50.] Bonhoeffer's christologically shaped concept of existence intends to provide a clear counterthesis to Heidegger's assertion in *Being and Time* that "the non-relational character of death, as understood in anticipation, individualizes Dasein down to itself. This individualizing is a way in which the 'there' is disclosed for existence. It makes manifest that all being-alongside the things with which we concern ourselves, and all being-with Others, will fail us when our ownmost potentiality-for-being is the issue. Dasein can be *authentically itself* only if it makes this possible for itself of its own accord" (par. 53, 308).

1. In order to 'become' members of the church, human beings must believe, this being understood not as a human possibility but as God's gift. Only in faith do human beings 'have' God. And according to the measure of their faith, human beings 'have' much, little, or nothing at all of God. To that it would appear to correspond, conversely, that God, too, 'is' only in faith and is not where God is not believed. This view, of which at least the first-cited aspect is not infrequent in Luther,[41] was introduced by R. Seeberg into his system as religious transcendentalism.[42] There is no salvation except in faith, no 'being' of reconciliation, as an ascertainable entity in church, doctrine, etc., except in the existential reference of the act to the I. There is 'being' of revelation only in actual faith. Here the *sola fida* seems upheld at its purest.[55]

2. Faith has, as its presupposition, being in the church. Faith invariably discovers itself already in the church; it is there already when it becomes aware of its presupposition. To believe means much the same as to find God, God's grace, the community of faith of Christ already present. Faith comes upon a being that is prior to the act; it clings to this being because it knows itself to be drawn into it as one of the particular expressions of this being. This being is not dependent on faith; on the

114

---

41. [Luther,] *LW* 11:5–6 (*WA*, 3:523);[51] *LW* 26:226–27 (40/1:360);[52] *LW* 12:321f. (40/2:342f.);[53] cited by R. Seeberg and E. Seeberg in their studies on Luther.[54]

42. See above, pages 55ff.

[51.] From Martin Luther, *First Lectures on the Psalms* (1513–1516) on Psalms 75–76, *LW* 11:5–6 (*WA* 3:523).

[52.] Martin Luther, *Lectures on Galatians* (1531): "Fides est creatrix divinitatis, non in persona, sed in nobis. Extra fidem amittit deus suam iustitiam, gloriam, opes etc., et nihil maiestatis, divinitatis, ubi non fides." ("[Faith] is the creator of the Deity, not in the substance of God but in us. For without faith God loses His glory, wisdom, righteousness, truthfulness, mercy, etc., in us; in short, God has none of His majesty or divinity where faith is absent."), *LW* 26:227 (*WA* 40/1:360).

[53.] From Martin Luther, "Psalm 51" [1532], *LW* 12:321 (*WA* 40/2:342f.).

[54.] Cf. Reinhold Seeberg, *Textbook of the History of Doctrines*, 254–55 (*Lehrbuch der Dogmengeschichte* 4/1, par. 81); Erich Seeberg, *Luthers Theologie* 1:102, note 105.

[55.] Among Bonhoeffer's contemporaries, Paul Althaus above all placed the *sola fide*, "by faith alone," at the center of the method and structure of dogmatics: "The *sola fide* can be applied in an all-embracing manner, both as a critical and positive principle. The recovery of systematic theology and, concomitantly, the struggle for Christianity in contemporary spiritual life, would be assisted in no small way were we theologically to take very seriously the *sola fide*, this watchword of humility and freedom" ("Theologie des Glaubens," 118).

contrary, faith knows that this being is wholly independent of faith itself
and faith's own being or nonbeing. Everything hinges on faith's knowing itself not as somehow conditioning or even creating this being, but
precisely as conditioned and created by it.

115   3. The being of revelation, the community of faith of Christ, 'is' only
in faith. Faith knows revelation to be independent of it. These two assertions must be put together in a third, that only in faith do human beings
know the being of revelation, their own being in the church of Christ, to
be independent of faith. The continuity of revelation, like the continuity
of existence, is found only in faith, but truly found there, so that faith is
suspended [aufgehoben] only 'in faith', only in 'the being of the community of faith'. If faith were understood here purely as an act, the continuity of being would be broken up in the discontinuity of acts. But
since faith as act comes to know itself as the mode of being of its being
in the church, the continuity is maintained. Indeed, this occurs only 'in
the believing' but, on account of that, it is truly maintained as being in
the church.

It seems possible, on this basis, to combine and mutually complement
two such highly contradictory views as those of Flacius on *perpetua iustificatio*[56] and those of the Calvinist Zanchi on the *perseverantia sanctorum*.[57] In his teaching about human beings as the *imago Satanae*,[58]

[56.] "perpetual justification" [MR]

[57.] "the perseverance of the saints" [MR]. Bonhoeffer refers to the dispute that
occured in the second generation of the Reformation on the question whether the Christian faith could ever be so sure that, once it has been given, it cannot be lost again (see R.
Seeberg, *Textbook of the History of Doctrines*, 378 [*Lehrbuch der Dogmengeschichte* 4/2:490–96,
527–29]). The Calvinist assertion of the perseverance of faith had been supported by John
Calvin primarily with reference to the faithfulness of the electing God. However, the
father of Calvinist orthodox doctrine, Jerome Zanchi (1516–90), altered it into a subjec-
tively habitual perseverance, during the Dispute of Strasburg in 1561 with the Lutheran
Johann Marbach (Zanchi, *De perseverantia sanctorum*, 92ff.); cf. Jürgen Moltmann, *Prädestination und Perseveranz*. For Luther, on the other hand, the problem of the certainty of election had become less significant than that of the present certainty of salvation. It was the
Lutheran Matthias Flacius (1520–75) who consequently attempted to defend the pure
Lutheran doctrine against Philipp Melanchthon and his disciples in terms of this notion of
perpetua iustificatio [perpetual justification]. When he and Victorin Strigel met at the Disputation of Weimar in 1560, however, he raised the content of the doctrine of original sin
to the level of a thesis about a metaphysical substance, declaring that the sinner "ad imagi-
nem Satanae transformatus" ("had been changed into the image of Satan"). See *Disputatio
de originali peccato et libero arbitrio inter Matthias Flacium et Victorin Strigelium* (1560), N.B.
26f. and 51.

[58.] "in the image of Satan" [MR]

Flacius maintained that *iustificatio* could not become the being of human persons but had to be created anew in each instance. Zanchi, on his part, 116 believed that predestination had established a being of the human person that could no more be affected by acts than ever be lost again. What God has chosen is chosen for eternity. Both theologians have misjudged the central significance of the idea of the church. On the basis of the idea of the church, Flacius would have come to see that his concept of faith was individualistic and one-sided, that individual acts of faith are already within the being of the community of faith of Christ. Zanchi would have understood that the act of faith alone breaks through to being. This being is not something existing that one comes across—no 'there is'—but a being that is to be known and known again in the act, a being that understands itself in the act and whose continuity and true 'outsideness' can be claimed only on the basis of this understanding. Predestination as a doctrine (which comes into consideration for faith only in the historical revelation of Christ) leads to concepts of being that assume the form of what exists, inasmuch as one has the divine knowledge of one's own predestination in one's possession and has access to it any time.[43] Concepts of being that derive from the idea of the church, however, are always formed in reference to acts of faith. Zanchi was undoubtedly correct when he wanted to express the continuity of God's action upon human beings and, as its result, their continuously new being. But so was Flacius when he insisted on a *perpetua iustificatio*. For with that he armed himself against an interpretation of being that understood the being of the new human as a condition, a *habitus*, of the psyche, indeed as something that exists. Against such an interpretation Flacius correctly holds that the act of faith is somehow essentially connected with the new human person's being; only he still thinks of faith as constitutive of being instead of defining faith as something that already understands itself as the mode of being of the new being.

4. The dialectic in the concept of the human being between faith and 'being in . . . ' comes to be concretely interpreted anew through the sociological category. This will figure even more prominently in the final chapter.

Like the being-of-revelation, the being of human beings also is not to 117 be thought of as a reified existing thing nor as having evaporated into

---

43. Not so for Barth, for whom predestination is the mystery lying before and behind everything, thus rendering a 'being' impossible.

nonbeing. Otherwise on both occasions the total existence of human beings would be left unaffected. At issue, rather, are historical human beings who know themselves transposed from the old to the new humanity, who are what they are on account of membership in the new humanity, persons newly created by Christ. All this they 'are' only in referential-act toward Christ. Their being-'in reference to'-Christ ["in bezug auf"-Christus-Sein] is rooted in their being in Christ, in the community of faith, which means that the act is 'suspended' in being just as, conversely, being is not without the act. The person, as synthesis of act and being, is always the two in one: *individual person* and *humanity*.[59] The notion of the individual pure and simple is an unworkable abstraction. Human beings are woven into sociality not only in their general spiritual nature, but also and especially in their existentiality. Touched in their existence (through judgment and grace), they know themselves directed into humanity. They themselves committed the sin of the old humanity; at the same time they know themselves irresistibly pulled by their humanity into its sin and guilt. Through believing, praying, and proclaiming, they bear the new humanity; at the same time they know themselves borne in all their actions by the community of faith, by Christ.[44] [60]

To speak of the human being as individual person and humanity, never in separation but always in unity, is only another way of talking about the human being as act and as being. At no time are human beings one of these alone. But even if their being-humanity could be thought of as an abstraction that is of no concern to existence, such an idea would

118   only break down in face of the historical reality of the community of

---

44. Cf. esp. Luther, "The Blessed Sacrament of the Holy and True Body of Christ, and the Brotherhoods" (1519), *LW* 35. See also Section C below on being in Adam and in Christ.

[59.] In what follows, Bonhoeffer picks up the idea of the 'individual collective person' that he had developed in *SC*, N.B. 50–52, 82–85.

[60.] Martin Luther, "The Blessed Sacrament of the Holy and True Body of Christ, and the Brotherhoods" (1519), *LW* 35/1:49–73 (*WA* 2:742–58). With reference to Bonhoeffer's use of this text by Luther, as well as his use of Luther's "Fourteen Consolations for Those who Labor and are Heavy-laden" (1520), *LW* 42:121–66 (*WA* 6:104–34), cf. below, page 123. For Bonhoeffer's development of the structural togetherness of the community of faith and its members and the members' active way of being for one another in what he calls the principle of vicarious representative action [Stellvertretung], see *SC* 126–36, and *E* 224ff. Bonhoeffer's formulation here foreshadows the debates in political theory later at the end of the century between the individualists and the communitarians. [WF]

faith of Christ and my belonging to it. I hear another human being truly tell me the gospel. Someone offers me the sacrament: you are forgiven. Someone along with the community of faith prays for me. And I hear the gospel, join in the prayer, and know myself bound up in the word, sacrament, and prayer of Christ's community of faith, the new humanity, whether it is here or elsewhere. Bearing it, I am borne by it. Here I, the historically whole human being—individual and humanity—am encountered, and I believe, that is, know myself borne. I am borne (*pati*), therefore I am (*esse*), therefore I believe (*agere*). Here the circle closes. Here even the *agere* is *pati*; but the I is always the historical One, the new, but only in faith. Let it be understood that it is precisely as historical that the I is a member of the new humanity. This humanity presents itself here and there in empirical, individual communities, but precisely in the mode of being that belongs to the being of revelation.

Is not the continuity of the I destroyed again by the fact that the I, as historical, itself fragments into religious and profane life? How are we to judge the fact of 'everydayness'?[61] If we refrain from speaking of historicity, everydayness, as God's punishment, then this difficulty persists at all events only for a form of thinking that sets out from a kind of reflection without faith. Religious acts, after all, are not identical with faith; otherwise being would be interpreted once again as something that exists. The unity of the I 'is' 'only in faith'. Everything points to that conclusion. If being were at hand in continuity for unfaith (perhaps as an everyday psychic datum), the Protestant understanding of faith would have failed and being would have become something that exists.

The unity of the historical I 'in faith' means unity in the community of faith, the historical community of faith that I believe to be the community of faith of Christ. My everydayness is overcome in the community of faith because there humanity—in which I stand, and which I am also myself—quite independently of me prays for me, forgives sins in sermon and sacrament. There, wherever I am, it is always the whole humanity, precisely because I am its member. For only in the community of faith am I embraced as individual and as humanity in existentiality and in continuity—of course, precisely 'in faith' that, however, knows itself to be possible at all in the power of the community of faith, in which faith is brought to life [aufgehoben].

119

[61.] See above, page 101, editorial note 32.

Even while my I crumbles into everydayness, its indivisible unity is guaranteed: ὃ δὲ νῦν ζῶ ἐν σαρκί, ἐν πίστει ζῶ (Gal. 2:20).[62]

Faith is 'in reference to' being (community of faith); it is only in faith that being discloses itself, or 'is' (community of faith). But faith knows this being as independent of itself, while knowing itself to be one of the manners of being [Seinsweise] of being itself. Being transcends something that exists; it is the ground of being of that which exists, as of the I. Thus, act comes from being, just as it proceeds towards being. On its part, being is in reference to act and yet free. The being-of-revelation is 'person', hovering in the tension between the objective and nonobjective, the revealed person of God and the personal community that is founded on God's person. Here the transcendental approach of 'being only in the act' unexpectedly coalesces with the original ontological principle of the freedom of being vis-à-vis the act, of the suspension of the act in being. If, however, being is understood as what exists, with a phenomenological system of autonomous self-understanding as a corollary, the result is as incompatible with the idea of revelation as with Kant's transcendental system of reason.

Since here the transcendental and ontological approaches come together in the sociological category, the existence of human beings is understood to be by nature as much in decision as 'already in Christ (or in Adam)'. Even though faith is act, as an expression of being in the church of Christ it encompasses the totality of Dasein in Christ, just as unfaith, as an expression of being in Adam, encompasses the totality of the old Dasein. Faith knows that it comes upon its decision as one already made. Just as unfaith is no individual psychic act, but rather a mode of being in the old humanity, so on the same basis faith is to be seen as a mode of being in the church of Christ, as it is seen as an act. There is, therefore, a 'standing firm in the faith' (1 Cor. 16:13; 2 Cor. 1:24; Eph. 6:14; 1 Thess. 3:8; 1 Pet. 5:12), as in the decision made without a consciously executed act of faith; this is not a general statement, however, but rather one that can be expressed only in faith.

Just as the being of God is no 'there is', human existence—whether in faith or in sin—is not either. 'There is' no believing one, no sinning one. 'There is' no human existence (as one encountered) in the sense of a 'given'—rather it 'is' through the word of God in the act accomplished in the church, the act in which the unity of existence is also given. Here,

120

[62.] "the life I live now in the flesh I live by faith" [MR]

too, the category of social reference puts the material concept of being into motion.

If in faith the totality of human beings is to be embraced in the community of faith of Christ, sin and death have to be included, for both are intent on disrupting the continuity of the new being. Sin and death, therefore, reach even into the community of faith of Christ. But they do so in such a way that now the community of faith bears my sin and death with me, and I no longer see sin and death in the community of faith, that is, in Christ, but only forgiveness and life. I am in the community of faith as one who bears the old human in me until death. My sin is no longer sin, my death no longer death, because the community of faith is with me. It is temptation which will have me believe that sin takes me away from God's community for good, that death is my eternal judgment: the temptation of σάρξ [63] which endures as long as I live ἐν σαρκί.[45] [64] Temptation comes to naught only in faith. Here it is true: *pecca fortiter, sed fortius fide et gaude in Christo.*[46] In the power of the community of faith—that is, because it bears the entirety of historical human beings—faith can embrace the totality of historical life in its everydayness, sin, and death. For the new being, whose mode of being is faith, seeks to encounter existence and be in continuity.

121

d) The Question of Knowledge and the Idea of the Church

The concept of knowledge that corresponds to the being of revelation and the being of human beings now must be investigated.

1. The attempt to think of revelation as nonobjective and make it thus indirectly the object of knowledge means that when I speak of revelation

---

45. Cf. [Luther,] "The Blessed Sacrament of the Holy and True Body of Christ, and the Brotherhoods" (1519), *LW* 35: 49ff., N.B. 55ff. (*WA* 2:742ff., N.B. 746ff.), and "Fourteen Consolations for Those who Labor and are Heavyladen" (1520), *LW* 42:137ff. (*WA* 6:130ff.).

46. Luther, [*Briefwechsel,* ed.] Enders, 3:208 and 119.[65]

[63.] "the flesh" [MR]

[64.] "in the flesh" [MR]

[65.] The complete citation from Luther's letter to Melanchthon, dated August 1, 1521, is found in Enders's edition of the *Briefwechsel,* 3:208, lines 121ff. (*LW* 48:282, trans. altered): "Esto peccator et pecca fortiter, sed fortius fide et gaude in Christo, qui victor est peccati, mortis et mundi." ("Be then a sinner and sin boldly, but believe and rejoice still more boldly in Christ, who is victor over sin, death and the world.")

I always take into account what God has to say further about that or
against it. It means that I always counter a judgment of knowing with one
of not-knowing, and that any attempt to constrain God is itself limited by
God's freedom, which is beyond anything that could bind it. In other
words, I introduce a factor into my thinking that renders it *a priori* uncertain, a factor that consists in my adding the antithesis to the positive
assertion. This is Barth's dialectic.[47]

Human knowing is not-knowing.[48] Room remains for God's free utter-
ance, and God remains in each instance the subject,[49] only when God *is*
in the divinely wrought, existential act of faith, and never in the reflec-
122   tion on it. That is how the connection among the interpretation of act,
dialectic, and the nonobjective concept of knowledge becomes clear. To
this may be objected: (*a*) The conceptual nexus as shown is conceived
individualistically. If revelation is essentially oriented towards the community of faith, then something must bind God apart from my individual act. (*b*) What binds God to the church is God's freedom. Dialectically
to leave open a freedom of God beyond the occurrence of salvation is to
formalize, to *rationalize*, the contingent positivity of that occurrence. (*c*)
We 'know' of the revelation given to the church from preaching. Theologically this knowing has three forms: as believing,[67] as existentiell,

---

47. That at least is its sense in most general terms. I believe, however, that
when one looks more closely, one will not arrive at an unambiguous concept of
dialectic in Barth. When I compare, for example, [*Die christliche*] *Dogm.*, 456, section b, lines 1–3 and 9; 457, lines 5ff.; and 460, lines 6f., it looks as if three completely different concepts of theological dialectics came together here.[66] They
do not all give expression to the same concerns; rather, they raise doubts as to
whether dialectic for Barth is really only a method, separable from the heart of
the matter (as [Friedrich Karl] Schumann, for example, states; cf. [*Der Gottesgedanke und der Zerfall der Moderne*], 221ff.), or whether Barth's whole case does
not stand or fall with it.

48. Cf. [Barth, *Die christliche*] *Dogmatik*, 61.

49. [Barth, *Die christliche*] *Dogmatik*, 64.

[66.] Cf. Karl Barth, *Gesamtausgabe* (2:579, lines 26–28 and 33f.; 580, lines 6ff.; 583, lines
14ff.). In citing these three places, Bonhoeffer notes that Barth's concept of dialectic
derives its meaning from the kind of conversation known as *dialogue*, from the *paradoxical*
idea of the divine-human and, finally, from the historical antithetic [Antithetik] of human
existence.

[67.] Bonhoeffer's text here says "unbelieving" [ungläubig]. We follow the German
editor in assuming this to be in error; thus we change it to "believing," as in the *DBW* 2
text. Whichever way one translates the term, there is a lack of parellelism between the triad

and as ecclesial; this is to be explained later. It is wrong to suggest that to the 'knowing' of revelation there corresponds quite generally a not-knowing that has been derived from idealistic-rationalistic anthropology. If we believed, we would know without not-knowing. There must, therefore, be a knowing in faith, that is, in the community of faith. We can know what has been given to us (1 Cor. 2:12). How such knowing becomes a scholarly discipline is a question for another time. (*d*) It is a fateful mistake on Barth's part to have substituted for the concept of creator and lord that of the subject. It means, in the first place, that I have God always at my back, with the result that in place of the direct attention to Christ there is the ongoing reflection of dialectical theology on one's own faith. God's nonobjectivity is thereby sealed. This has the further consequence of defining God virtually as the subject of my new existence, of my theological thinking, instead of as the creator and lord of both. In the latter case, the transcendental understanding of act, which is directed prospectively and retrospectively 'in reference to' the transcendent, is supported just as well, if not better, by the notion of the creator and the lord than by the concept of the subject. But the ultimate reason for the inadequacy of this definition lies in the fact that it finally fails to understand God as person. From such an inadequate definition of the being of revelation arises an inadequate concept of knowledge. Whether or not it is justified to defend the understanding of the act that underlies a nonobjective concept of knowledge depends on the defini-   123
tion of the being-of-revelation as the being-of-a-person—with all the subsequent consequences for the concept of knowledge itself.

2. If, contrary to the foregoing, the being of revelation is understood as what exists, then revelation is, on account of its false objectivity, delivered fully into the power of human beings. Knowledge here finds no limitations placed on it by revelation. Even though revelation is bound, it is no longer *God's* revelation.

3. To the being of revelation, defined as the being of the person of Christ in the community of persons of the church—defined, that is, in terms of sociological categories—there must correspond a concept of

---

of believing, existentiell, and ecclesial forms of 'knowing' (which here are said to be given to the church from preaching), and his statement below that there are three forms of thinking corresponding to three functions of the church: believing-, preaching-, and theological-knowing. Bonhoeffer's precise meaning remains unclear. Cf. below, pages 126ff. [WF]

knowledge that is also framed in sociological categories. In order to understand this, we must first distinguish among three distinct ways of knowing and the concepts that correspond to three sociologically different functions of the church: the *believing*, the *preaching*, and the *theological* ways of knowing, of which the first may be called *existential* and the other two '*ecclesial knowing*'.

The concept of a *believing way of knowing* is a matter of basic sociological epistemology. A believing way of knowing means to know oneself overcome and pardoned by the person of Christ in the preached word. The question of the possibility of such knowing[50] can no longer be raised because it arises, posed as it is, from the isolation of unfaith and must logically be answered with an Impossible! (*incapax!*).[68] Behind such questioning lies a concept of existence in terms of potentiality. But faith is a God-given *reality*, whose 'how' but not 'that' can be called into question. The object of faith is the person of Christ preached in the community of faith. This object resists any inclusion into a transcendental I, or any nonobjectification; it stands as person over against human beings as persons. The person is a unity over and above 'entity' and nonentity; it is objective, that is, knowable and recognizable. And yet, on account of its true, qualified *ob*-jectivity, and by virtue of its freedom from the knower and its freedom not to be, it never falls into the power of the knowing I. The person gives itself to the I through the word in the act of faith, which on its part acknowledges the freedom of the self-giving person, testifying thereby to its being absolutely 'from outside'. If the person so turns in upon itself, however, all that remains is the 'word' in 'memory'. It becomes something that exists, to which only the person can restore the power over human existence not to be, that is, the power of what is 'from outside'. If the I as person is encountered by the person of Christ in judgment or in the incorporation into the community of faith, then that I cannot conceive this necessary suffering (*pati*) as derived from itself, but only as coming from outside. In this lies the peculiarity of the sociological-theological category.

124

---

50. Cf., for example, Barth, [*Die christliche Dogmatik,*] section 6, 2, "Die Möglichkeit des Hörens" (The possibility of hearing), and section 17, "Die subjektive Möglichkeit der Offenbarung" (The subjective possibility of revelation).

[68.] An allusion to "finitum non est capax infiniti" ("the finite is not capable of the infinite"). Cf. above, page 84, editorial note 7.

The 'outside' sought in individualistic epistemology is a given reality here in the community of faith, a reality which, as a contingent presupposition, can no longer be called into question, which cannot be stabilized by means of a 'there is' and turned into something one 'comes across' for cognition. The exteriority of the person of Christ by nature transcends existence and yet, it *is* only in its action on human existence. It is not the exteriority of the external world but that of the person of Christ, claiming my whole personal existence both as guilty and as pardoned, the 'outside' of the sociological-theological category, which is known as a genuine *outside* only where human beings are *in* Christ.

Through the person of Christ other human beings, too, are moved out of the world of things—to which they, as still something-existing, continue to belong—and into the social sphere of persons. Only through Christ does my neighbor meet me as one who claims me in an absolute way from a position outside my existence. Only here is reality utterly pure decision. Without Christ, even my neighbor is for me no more than a possibility of self-assertion through 'bearing the claim of the other' (Grisebach).[69]

So it is that through the outside of the person of Christ the *external world* appears in a different light. But even the external world, as mediator of the spirit of Christ—such as the empirical church—should not be included in the sphere of 'there is'. The 'there is' presupposes the kind of observation associated with disinterested noticing. With regard to the being of revelation, such disinterest does not exist even in the external world, that is, in creation, precisely because the being-of-revelation is the very basis of my being-a-person. The judgment, therefore, that 'there is' this person, is a reflection that has already fallen away from direct reference and has further concern only with the existing thing that remains. We must be constantly mindful that *being* is the mode both of being-a-person and of 'there is' and that, though the point may be left open for now, the first mode is the foundation of the second.

Thus in faith is disclosed a new sphere of knowledge and objects, that of existence in social reference, which replaces other concepts of knowledge. The 'outside', the 'limit', is redefined by the sociological category (cf. above, page 45). Dilthey had already attempted to deal with the prob-

125

[69.] Cf. Eberhard Grisebach, *Die Grenzen des Erziehers*, 54: "The law of the community is the relationship of conflicting claims and duties, which are borne according to the concrete, ethical law of conflict."

lem of transcendence in terms of the historical problem of the
encounter of two personal wills (cf. above, page 55, footnote 26). But
even this attempt can succeed only when it sets out from the person of
God who encounters human beings in revelation.

Now this sociological category that we have discovered here proves
to be the point of unity of the transcendental and the ontological
approaches to knowledge. The person 'is' only in the act of self-giving.
Yet, the person 'is' free from the one to whom it gives itself. It is through
the person of Christ that this understanding of person is won; it has
validity only for the personal community of the Christian church, which
is based in Christ. The Christ preached in the community of faith gives
himself to the member of the community of faith. Faith is "to know oneself to be in reference to this." In faith I 'have' Christ in his personal
objectivity, that is, as my Lord who has power over me, reconciles, and
redeems me. There is no not-knowing in faith, for Christ bears witness to
himself in it.

In faith Christ is the creator of my new being, a person and at the
same time the lord, 'in reference to' whom—εἰς αὐτόν—the person is
created. Thus, Dasein is determined by transcendence both retrospectively and prospectively; it 'is' 'amidst' transcendence. Christ, by being
the one who creates within me the act of faith by granting me the Holy
Spirit who hears and believes within me, thereby proves to be also the
free lord of my existence. Christ 'is' only 'in faith', and yet 'is' Lord of my
faith. Christ is the absolute 'outside' of my existence, and for that very
reason, Christ meets it and makes Christ known to it.

The movement of faith, understood as the concrete event of being
taken hold of by Christ, in time ceases to occur; it cannot be pointed to
in a here-and-there open for exhibit. God alone knows whether I have
believed; this is not accessible to my reflection. Faith rests in itself as
actus directus (cf. above, page 99f. and Section C below). Nothing could
be more mistaken than—on the basis of the fact that everything is accessible to reflection only in reflection and that, therefore, faith is accessible only as 'credulity'[70] or 'religiosity'—to dispute that there is an *actus*

[70.] In his work *Erfahrung und Glaube*, H. M. Müller distinguishes between "credulity"
[Gläubigkeit] and "faith" [Glauben] in the precise sense of the word (N.B. 159ff.): "Faith
and experience [Erfahrung] are one, but not so faith and credulity. Credulity stands
between *Erfahrung* and *Erfahrung*, just as it stands between temptation [Anfechtung] and
temptation" (161). Cf. the text of Bonhoeffer's seminar from the winter term of 1932–33,

directus which takes place in time. Reflection has by nature no right to do so; it discovers itself always to be already in reflection, and this very reflection must become the reminder that immediate reference to the act has been interrupted. This is the fundamental problem of everydayness. Even though my faith, as a temporal act, embraces by nature the whole of my Dasein and though my faith (that is, my existence) is suspended in being in the community of faith (see above, page 120f.)—all of which can be asserted only in faith—there remains for *reflection* only the word of Christ spoken in the past as a general proposition, as 'meaning' in 'remembrance'. Person and word have separated and we are left with the situation of preaching and theological knowing.[71]   127

The *preachers*, as preachers of the community of faith, must 'know' what they preach: Jesus Christ the crucified (1 Cor. 2:2). They have been given authority to proclaim the gospel to the hearers, to forgive sins in preaching and the sacrament. There may be no uncertainty here, no notknowing; everything must be made plain from the given word of God, from the bound revelation. For in the sermon, which creates faith, Christ lets himself be proclaimed as the 'subject' of the words spoken. I preach, but I preach in the power of Christ, in the power of the faith of the community of faith, not in the power of my faith. For, supposing that in the course of preaching I could in the act of faith overcome temptation, then the existential declaration, 'I have been forgiven', would not be capable of supporting the ecclesial declaration, 'you have been forgiven'. Rather this latter statement depends on the community whose office preaching is. For that reason preaching is in principle always heard.

But preachers themselves must reflect on the 'what' about which they preach, on the word concerning the crucified, and bring it to expression. Thus for them the 'how' of preaching also makes the 'what' of preaching problematic. For only general 'assertions', 'words' taken 'from the memory' of divine happenings stand before their reflection. These they can repeat over and over again, but the living, creative word of the person of Christ they cannot speak.

"Probleme einer theologischen Anthropologie" (The problem of a theological anthropology), *GS* 5:340–58, N.B. 348–52.

[71.] Cf. Bonhoeffer's student paper "Luthers Anschauungen vom Heiligen Geist" (Luthers view of the holy ghost) in connection with the distinction between preaching and theology in Luther's writings (*DBW* 9:398ff.) discussed below.

Preaching, as an office of the community of faith, has been given the promise that when preachers faithfully utter the 'words' and 'assertions' (pure doctrine! *'recte docetur'*),[72] the living person of Christ declares itself in them by disclosing itself to the hearer. But how can preachers speak 'faithfully', when all they can do is put forth 'assertions'?

This raises the problem of *theological knowing* and, hence, the question: how is the theological scholarly discipline possible?

128   Theology is a function of the church.[73] For there is no church without preaching, nor any preaching without remembrance. But theology is the memory of the church. As such, theology helps the church to understand the presuppositions of Christian preaching; it helps it, in other words, to form dogmas. To this end it must have knowledge of the subject matter of Christianity. How is such knowledge possible?

In theological reflection I am removed from the intentionality of the faith that overcomes temptation. Therefore, theological knowledge is not existential knowledge. Its object is all the happenings held in remembrance in the Christian community of faith; in the Bible; in preaching and sacrament, prayer, confession; in the word of the person of Christ, which is preserved as something that exists in the historical church. Theology is, therefore, the scholarly discipline that has its own presuppositions as its subject matter, that is to say, it stands between past and future preaching. Theology is to make the connection between past preaching and the real person of Christ, as Christ preaches in, and is preached by, the community of faith. Future preaching is to have before it the dogmas on the basis of which it preaches in Christian faithfulness. It follows that, logically, dogma is not the aim but the presupposition of preaching.

It seems that, in light of what we have said, theological thinking is in principle indistinguishable from profane thinking. Dogmatic knowledge is positive knowledge reflecting on entities and is, therefore, to be

---

[72.] Bonhoeffer alludes to the seventh article of the Augsburg Confession. It states, in part: "Est autem ecclesia congregatio sanctorum, in qua evangelium pure docetur et recte administrantur sacramenta." ([The church, moreover, is] "the assembly of all believers among whom the Gospel is preached in its purity and the holy sacraments are administered according to the Gospel."), *The Book of Concord*, 32.

[73.] Bonhoeffer proposed this formula obviously at the same time as Karl Barth; whether he did so independently of Barth is another question. Cf. K. Barth, "Die Theologie und der heutige Mensch," 375; *Die christliche Dogmatik*, 422; and from later, *Church Dogmatics* 1/1 (1932):3. Cf. also Bonhoeffer's "Das Wesen der Kirche," *GS* 5:234ff.

understood as fundamentally systematic. Even the reference to the living person of Christ remains a reference in thought, and, as such, systematic. Any genuine reference, however, is not made possible by a theoretical method, but by holding fast in humility to the word that has been heard. Here, not in its method of thinking, but rather in the obedience of thinking, the scholarly discipline of theology does differ fundamentally from everything profane. The dialectical method of 'the proviso' is as such no humbler than any honorable systematic thinking. For that reason, dialectical thinking as such is certainly not yet existential thinking. As long as theology claims that its assertions are 'existential' or represent the thinking of faith (which in the end amounts to the same), humility is not possible for it. Theological thinking and knowledge is possible only as *ecclesial thinking and knowledge*. Because theology turns revelation into something that exists, it may be practiced only where the living person of Christ is itself present and can destroy this existing thing or acknowledge it. Therefore, theology must be in immediate reference to preaching, helping its preparation, all the while humbly submitting to its 'judgment'. Theology is a positive science [Wissenschaft],[74] for it has its own given object, the *spoken* word of Christ in the church. By reason of this fact, it has power to make general pronouncements; the aim it pursues is the system, that is, dogma. But it is only in the community of faith that all this acquires its special meaning. Only the community of faith knows that the word which is addressed to it, and which theology has for its subject matter, is always uttered anew beyond theology. Only the community of faith knows that theology is merely the remembrance of this word, taking care and ordering it. The community of faith knows that making general pronouncements makes sense only where Christ confirms it in each instance—it knows that the very dogma on which preaching builds is 'judged' by preaching. It knows that when theology declares 'God forgives sins', neither God nor sin in themselves are affected, but that a general proposition has been formed of both. For only when Christ himself speaks these words *hic et nunc*[75] are they really about God and about sin—that is, about my sin, in a truly existential way. This is why theology cannot speak creatively; but when

129

[74.] The characterization of theology as a 'positive science' goes back to Friedrich Schleiermacher, based albeit on different theoretical presuppositions. Cf. his *Brief Outline of the Study of Theology*, section 1.

[75.] "Here and now" [MR]

130 the community of faith is aware of these limitations to its theology, it can and should do theology courageously. Then it may 'know' even as Paul 'knew' (Rom. 6:9; 1 Cor. 2:2, 2:12; 2 Cor. 4:14, 5:1; Eph. 1:9), not as existential or as speculative knowing, but as *ecclesial knowing*. The community of faith may be assured of the faithfulness of God, who stands by the word God has given to the it, so that theology, if it locates itself earnestly within the community of faith, can never go wholly astray. For the community of faith needs theology.

It is true that theology is never able to overcome the real temptation of faith with its assertions. The issue here is the concrete struggle between Christ and Satan effected in the direct consciousness of human beings, from which time and again we must first escape. We may recite as many theological assertions about forgiveness of sin and redemption as we wish. But they all become our temptation unless Christ himself in person speaks to us his new word, the word that creates our Dasein again and again—unless the general assertion becomes a living occurrence.

Here lie the limits of theology; they are known by the community of faith in which it is practiced. It would appear that what [Wilhelm] Herrmann calls 'intellectual works-righteousness'[76] can be overcome in theology only in the knowledge of its limitations, including the limitations of its legitimacy and necessity. Dialectical theology takes its method more seriously than is consonant with its presuppositions only because, in the final analysis, it thinks individualistically, that is, abstractly. The fact is that, as a theologian, I cannot resist the lure of intellectual works-righteousness except by locating my theology within the community of faith (which is the theologian's humility), allowing the community of faith to allocate its place and bestow meaning upon it. Thinking, includ-

131 ing theological thinking, will always be 'systematic' by nature and can, therefore, never grasp the living person of Christ into itself. Yet there is obedient and disobedient thinking (2 Cor. 10:5). It is obedient when it does not detach itself from the church, which alone can 'upset' it as 'systematic' thinking, and in which alone thinking has meaning.

[76.] The term does not appear as such in Wilhelm Hermann's works. It is found in Karl Barth's description of one of the basic motifs of Herrmann's theology: "the ghost of intellectual works-righteousness against which Wilhelm Herrmann struggled tirelessly" (*Die christliche Dogmatik*, 3, in *Karl Barth Gesamtausgabe*, 2 [1927]:14, 54, N.B. note 42). The actual focus of Herrmann's critique was Roman Catholic and Protestant orthodox dogmatics that place assent to faith-statements ahead of confidence (*fiducia*) in the person of Jesus as the ground of faith. Cf. Wilhelm Herrmann, *The Communion of the Christian with God*, 216–18.

For preaching it follows that preachers must be theologians. The way of knowing of preaching differs from theological knowing because of the particular situation in which preachers have to speak the word to the just-now-gathered historical community of faith. The object of the way of knowing of preaching is no longer the already spoken word but the one to be spoken just now to this community of faith. This word is not spoken from the pulpit as existential confession, nor as theologically pure doctrine; everything depends on the office. Preachers who know that—just here, just now, precisely through them—Christ seeks to speak to the community of faith, proclaim the gospel by the full power of the authority of the community of faith. And for the hearers this word is a word of decision. As isolated individuals, preachers cannot cease praying the fifth petition: "forgive us our trespasses." But for themselves, as ordained to the preaching office of the community of faith, they offer it no longer. As a way of knowing of individuals, the way of knowing of preachers, too, is reflexive; but as the one borne by the office, it is productive and authoritative. Only the office, but that is to say, only Christ and the community of faith themselves, can make the claim of the church: 'you are forgiven'. Individuals may pronounce it because they must pronounce it, because the community of faith desires to hear it.

Viewed sociologically, preachers are by nature in the community of faith, and secondarily individuals, whereas dogmaticians are by nature individuals, and secondarily in the community of faith. Believers, however, are, by nature, equally individuals and 'in the community of faith'.

In summary, in the believing way of knowing there is simply no reflection. The question about the possibility of faith can only be answered through its reality. But since this reality is not amenable to the manner of exhibition of what exists, any reflection proves to be destructive. Faith looks not on itself, but on Christ alone. Whether faith *is* faith can neither be ascertained nor believed; but the faith that believes *is* faith.

It is as certain that such faith carries itself forward in 'direct consciousness' as that it cannot be reflectively reproduced in its qualified, actual reality. Wherefore one can never say: I believed at such a time and place. | 132

If the object of the believing way of knowing is the living word of Christ, then that of theological knowing is the word already spoken, and that of the preaching way of knowing is the word of proclamation to the community of faith. As an activity of individuals, the preaching way of knowing is as reflexive as is the theological way; but in the office of the community of faith, to whom they are to proclaim the forgiveness of sins, preachers see their knowledge as that of the community of faith and, on account of that, appropriate for its edification.

In recalling the original course of our inquiry, it becomes clear that the general part of the investigation must conclude with the problem of a theological doctrine of human self-understanding in its connection with the 'being-placed-into-the-truth' of revelation. 'In faith' people understand themselves as in the church of Christ in their new being, in an existential reality that was not included in their deepest potentiality. They see their existence to be founded solely by the word of the person of Christ. They live in God's sight and in no other way. Being is being in Christ, for here alone is unity and wholeness of life; thus they discover their old being as being in Adam. There is no formal, metaphysical, psychological definition of the being of human beings that is not comprehended in the statement that human beings are either 'in Christ' or 'in Adam' (see next section).

Human beings are 'in reference to' truth because they 'are' in the truth. This truth is no longer the self-imposed boundary of the self-transparent I (to the 'truth' of which, too, there was reference because one was in it). This truth is revealed, bestowed truth; it is Jesus Christ himself, and the relation of Dasein to Christ a granted relation (*iustitia passiva!*).[77]

133   Because it is 'in Christ', Dasein is 'in reference to' Christ. But because here untruth is placed into truth, unlike is known by unlike (cf. above, page 53). The mediator remains the 'meaning', the 'clear' word, but not as if the meaning, as something 'given', could be turned by human beings into the possibility of autonomous self-understanding. But through this medium of 'meaning', unlike gives itself to be known by unlike: Christ, the crucified and risen one, gives Christ's own self to be known by human beings, who live to themselves. It is in being known by God that human beings know God. But to be known by God means to become a new person. It is the justified and the sinner in one who knows God. It is not because the word of God is in itself 'meaning' that it affects the existence of human beings, but because it is *God's* word, the word of the creator, reconciler, and redeemer. Yet it is in 'meaning' that this

---

[77.] Luther speaks of "*iustitia dei passiva*" when referring to the righteousness of God bestowed on us as distinct from that we have earned; e.g. see *LW* 26:4 (*WA* 40/1:41).

word carries itself forward, even if that meaning is absurd. Thus human beings, when they understand themselves in faith, are entirely wrenched away from themselves and are directed towards God.

This self-understanding 'in faith', which arises when Christ assails my existence, is preserved for theology only in 'remembrance'. To view self-understanding as possible only through self-understanding-in-remembrance gives rise to a twofold reflection on what it means to understand-oneself-in-faith. It is the reflection of theologians on themselves. They know that their doctrine of human self-understanding is limited by their own self-understanding, and that their own situation is limited as one that 'understands itself only in remembrance'. They cannot go beyond themselves unless Christ assails them and overcomes them, in which case they are no longer only theologians. And so their anthropology remains a doctrine like any other, as does the concretely developed doctrine of self-understanding in revelation; it remains system, autonomous self-understanding. Only in the church itself—where the word of Christ is 'held in remembrance' and his living person is at work—is it understood that a theology which wants to serve the concrete church in reality also serves, as autonomous thinking, the law of Christ. A theological self-understanding no longer is defined as a 'self-understanding that has been placed into the truth'—which is what it is in faith—but as 'reflexive thinking that has been placed in the service of the church'. *Reflecte fortiter, sed fortius fide et gaude in Christo*, to adapt Luther's words and apply them to theologians.[78]

134

Nothing of this justifies any particular theology. Instead, the enterprise of theology is found to be based in the structure of the church and is justified only in that context. Which particular theology is right is something for dogma to judge; but dogma is judged by the preaching of the living Christ.

[78.] "Think boldly, but more boldly still, believe and rejoice in Christ." Cf. above, page 123. Cf. also "The Theology of Crisis, " *NRS* 372 (*GS* 3:124), where Bonhoeffer has Karl Barth repeat this expression of his own. Cf. *GS* 3:545.

C. The Problem of Act and Being in the Concrete Teaching concerning Human Beings 'in Adam' and 'in Christ'

1. Being in Adam

a) Definition of 'Being' in Adam

Sola fide credendum est nos esse peccatores.[1][[1]] 'Being in Adam' is a more pointed ontological, and a more biblically based (1 Cor. 15:22; cf. 15:45; Rom. 5:12–14), designation for *esse peccator*. Were it really a human possibility for persons themselves to know that they are sinners apart from revelation, neither 'being in Adam' nor 'being in Christ' would be existential designations of their being. For it would mean that human beings could place themselves into the truth, that they could somehow withdraw to a deeper being of their own, apart from their being sinners, their 'not being in the truth'. Being in Adam would, consequently, have to be regarded as a potentiality of a more profound 'possibility of being in the truth'. It would rest on a being untouched by sin. In theological terms, it would mean that the sinner remains creature, that being-'there' ['Da'-sein] as creature lies at the foundation of 'how' ['Wie'] one ontically is as sinner. If one disputes that being a sinner involves all of the being

---

1. Luther, *Lectures on Romans*, 25:215 [Ficker II:69, lines 12ff.].

[1.] "By faith alone we know that we are sinners." Cf. Bonhoeffer's comment on Luther's lectures on Romans in *DBW* 9:324. In relation to the knowledge of sin, see also "Sünde und Verfehlung" (Sin and transgression), *GS* 3:164–65, and the piece by the same title in *GS* 5:354–56, both dating from 1932–33.

of human beings, then the danger of semi-Pelagianism, the ontological teaching of *causae secundae,*[2] is unavoidable. Seen in this light, the words of Luther cited above become intelligible: we can never comprehend our existence as a whole, because it is entirely founded on God's word—and God's word demands faith. Only to faith, in revelation, do we have access to the knowledge that we are sinners in the wholeness of our being, since it is only then, by God's word, that the wholeness of our being can be placed into the truth. 136

This is knowledge from revelation, which can never be had apart from it, that is, precisely, in Adam. For 'in Adam' means to be in untruth, in culpable perversion of the will, that is, of human essence. It means to be turned inward into one's self, *cor curvum in se.*[3] Human beings have torn themselves loose from community with God and, therefore, also from that with other human beings, and now they stand alone, that is, in untruth.[2] Because human beings are alone, the world is 'their' world, and other human beings have sunk into the world of things (cf. Heidegger's '*Mitsein*', 'being-with').[4] God has become a religious object, and human beings themselves have become their own creator and lord, belonging to themselves. It is only to be expected that they should now begin and end with themselves in their knowing, for they are only and utterly 'with themselves' in the falsehood of naked self-glory.

Ontologically this means that sin is the violation of Dasein (created

---

2. H. Fr. Kohlbrügge, *Das 7. Kapitel des Briefes Pauli an die Römer,* 1839, 52: (Human beings) "did not lose the image of God, they lost — God; after they had become disobedient, God called them 'flesh' and their deeds 'evil', 'sin'. — And what are human beings doing ever since? They make use of the nature in which God had created them as if they had not become transgressors through the disobedience of one. They act as if they themselves, as they are and live, were not fallen; they act as if all of their heart, inclination, thought, and deliberation were not perverted and false. . . . They make use of *life* so as to deny their death; they make use of *righteousness* so as to set up their own righteousness, and to pronounce thereupon that they disclaim their own righteousness. . . . They make use of the *truth* so as to make God a liar, to break loose from God where they are bound to God, and to bind God to themselves with a word which—as they interpret it—did not come to them."

[2.] See above, page 74, editorial note 83.
[3.] "the heart turned in upon itself" [MR]
[4.] Cf. Martin Heidegger, *Being and Time*, par. 26, N.B. 162–63.

being) by its concrete being-how-it-is [Wie-sein].[5] It means that in face of
the concept of sin, this ontological distinction between human existence
and the form in which one actually exists [Da- und Wiesein] becomes
meaningless, because the I is its own master now and has itself taken possession of its Dasein. Furthermore, this knowledge is not possible within
the state of sin, because here Dasein is still in the power of how-it-is [Wie-
sein] as sinner; rather, it is knowledge that has to be deduced from reve-
137   lation, in which creatureliness and sin are separated in a manner yet to
be described. Therefore, the ontological designation of human beings
as being sinners, as existing in sin 'in reference to' God, remains correct.
Every attempt to utilize the idea of creature in a fundamentally ontological fashion, when speaking of the human being 'in Adam', leads directly to the Catholicism of the *analogia entis*, to a pure metaphysics of
being. As long as it will not allow revelation to drive it into the historical
church of Christ, the thinking and philosophizing of human beings in
sin is self-glorifying, even when it seeks to be self-critical or to become
'critical philosophy'. All knowledge, including particularly γνῶθι σε-
αυτόν,[6] seeks to establish the ultimate self-justification of human
beings. Under the heavy burden of being both creator and bearer of a
world, and in the cold silence of their eternal solitude, they begin to be
afraid of themselves and to shudder. Then they arise and declare themselves their own final judges and proceed to their own indictment—
couched in the language of conscience. But the response of the indicted

---

[5.] Throughout this third section of *Act and Being*, Bonhoeffer contrasts *Da-sein* (literally "there-being," or the distinctive form of human existence) with *Wie-sein* (literally "how-
being," the form in which Dasein at any moment actually exists). *Wie-sein* has been
translated as Dasein's "being-how-it-is" or as "the form in which it actually exists." It is
unclear where Bonhoeffer got this precise terminology; despite its Heideggerian sound, it
may have come most directly from Rudolf Bultmann. Cf. above, Section A, footnote 89. It
is not clear whether Bonhoeffer intended a parallel between the prominent use of the *Wie*
here in Section C of *Act and Being* and the *Wie?* of the Christology lectures, which is rejected for the sake of the *Wer?* ("Who?") of authentic christological inquiry (see *CC* 29ff.).
[WF]

[6.] "know thyself" [MR]. This inscription in the Temple to Apollo in Delphi is ascribed
to Thales of Miletus or Chilon. G. W. F. Hegel discusses the interpretation of that statement in contemporary philosophy (with reference to Socrates) in his *Encyclopedia of the
Philosophical Sciences*, section 377, and in *Hegel's Lectures on the History of Philosophy*, 1:447f.;
cf. Søren Kierkegaard, *The Concept of Irony* (1841), in *Kierkegaard's Writings*, 2:177–78. Cf.
also Bonhoeffer's sermon for "Sonntag nach Trinitatis, 21. Oktober 1928" (Sunday after
Trinity, October 21, 1928), *GS* 5:469.

human being is repentance (*contritio activa!*).[7] The conscience and repentance of human beings in Adam are their final grasp at themselves, the confirmation and justification of their self-glorifying solitude.[3] Human beings make themselves the defendant, they appeal to their better selves. But the cries of conscience only dull the mute loneliness of a desolate 'with-itself' ['Bei-sich']; they ring without echo in the world that the self rules and explains. Human beings in Adam are pushed to the limits of their solitude but, misunderstanding their situation, "they seek themselves in themselves" (Luther),[4] hoping that in being repentant they may yet save their sinful existence.[5] As sinners they keep their sins with them, for they see them through their conscience, which holds them captive in themselves and only bids them to look at sin over and again. But "sin grows and gets bigger also through too much[10] looking and

138

---

3. On the other hand, cf. [Friedrich] Brunstäd, [*Die Idee der Religion,*] ". . . The value of the reality of that which is unconditionally personal manifests itself in conscience" (226).

4. *LW* 42:106 (*WA* 2:690).[8]

5. *LW* 35:16 (*WA* 2:719): "There are those who believe that this is possible if one has all the world's repentance. But it would be no more than Judas's repentance, which angers rather than placates God."[9] Luther continues: "I have no objection to people being asked during confession, or to their examining themselves, about whether or not they are truly contrite. But people should not offend God by insisting that they have all the contrition that is needed, for that is presumptuous and mendacious since no one has sufficient contriteness for sins" (*LW* 35:18 [*WA* 2:720], trans. altered MR).

[7.] In post-Tridentine Catholicism the 'substance' of the sacrament of penance is the graded set of acts—repentance (*contritio*), confession (*confessio*), and satisfaction (*satisfactio*). Cf. Bernhard Bartmann, *Lehrbuch der Dogmatik*, 2:383. According to the understanding of the justification of the sinner in Reformation thought, the faith wrought by the gospel has to supplement the repentance aroused by the law. Bonhoeffer differentiates between these diverse interpretations of repentance by speaking of *contritio activa* [active repentance], on the one hand, and *contritio passiva* [passive repentance], on the other (see below, page 141). Cf. Reinhold Seeberg's exposition of this matter in his *Textbook of the History of Doctrines*, vol. 2—see the index under *contrition, penance, penitence*, and *repentance*. See also Bonhoeffer's student paper, "Luthers Anschauungen vom Heiligen Geist" (Luther's view of the holy spirit), *DBW* 9:367ff.

[8.] From Martin Luther, "A Sermon on Preparing to Die" (1519): "Search for yourself only in Christ and not in yourself, and you shall find yourself for ever in him" (*LW* 42:99–115, trans. altered [*WA* 2:685–97]).

[9.] From Luther's "The Sacrament of Penance" (1519), *LW* 35:9–22 (*WA* 2:714–23).

[10.] Luther actually says "too deeply," not "too much."

thinking on it, aided by the foolishness of our conscience, which is ashamed before God and sorely punishes itself."[6] For this reason, such conscience is of the devil,[7] who leaves human beings to themselves in untruth; for this reason this conscience must be mortified when Christ comes to human beings. Conscience can torment and drive to despair; but it cannot of itself kill human beings—it cannot because it is their final grasp at themselves.[8] Human beings are unable to will their own death,

---

6. *LW* 42:102, 104 (*WA* 2:687, 689). "Therefore, you should not look on the sin in sinners nor in your conscience. . . ."[11]

7. *LW* 26:330–31 (*WA* 40:511).[12] Cf. *LW* 26:26 (*WA* 40/1:74) on the *duo diaboli* [the two devils].[13]

8. This was already expressed with admirable clarity by H. Fr. Kohlbrügge, [*Das siebente Kapitel des Briefes Pauli an die Römer in ausführlicher Umschreibung*]: "For sin does not lurk behind evil only; even more, it lurks behind good. . . . When we do good, sin lets us renounce evil before God, helps us to pray and weep, strive and struggle, till we are exhausted; it does this in order to drive and goad us in that very activity to maintain our wretchedness before God. . . . For such piety and holiness is well-pleasing to the flesh. There is penance, absolution, and never-ending forgetting by means of the washing away of former sins; and yet, human beings remain stuck fast in the death of the flesh. Only to assert themselves therein do they will the good . . . , so that they can obtain for themselves rest in their unrest. . . ." (27f.). Kohlbrügge continues: "A thousand times have I protested against all evil desires, sundered myself from my flesh, armed myself with tears, exercises of penance and incessant prayer. I cried out for the Spirit of God, that it might sanctify me through and through. I believed, I acted; but I did all this as one pressed by necessity, not from love of the law. I shunned the will of God while I endeavored to live according to it. . . . And so I did good, out of enmity against God . . ." (29). "Then it plagued me with sin and let me feel remorse soon after, so that I might not become conscious that I fall short of the glory of God. . . ." (37). "This is the sin of us all; this is the high priest in the

[11.] From Luther, "A Sermon on Preparing to Die" (1519).

[12.] Martin Luther, *Lectures on Galatians* (1535) [1531]. The citation given by Bonhoeffer should read *WA*, 40/1:511: "Legis theologia est mortificare, reos facere et conscientia dem Teufel zugehoret. . . ." ("The theological use of the law is to kill, to indict, and conscience is of the devil. . . .") The translation of this passage in *LW* 26/1:330–31, has been altered so signficantly as to make this quotation unrecognizable in the published English text [WF].

[13.] Luther, *Lectures on Galatians* (1535) [1531]. The correct citation should be: "Duo diaboli nostri qui nos excruciant, sunt Peccatum et Conscientia, Vis legis et stimulus peccati. Haec duo monstra Christus vicit et conculcavit in hoc saeculo et futuro" (*WA* 40/1:73) . ("The two devils who plague us are sin and conscience, the power of the Law and the sting of sin [1 Cor. 15:56]. But Christ has conquered these two monsters and trodden them underfoot, both in this age and in the age to come" [*LW* 26:26].)

even in conscience.[9] Here is their limit: human beings cling to them- 139
selves, and thus their knowledge of themselves is imprisoned in
untruth.[10] To be placed into truth before God means to be dead or to
live; neither of these can human beings give themselves. They are con- 140
ferred on them only by the encounter with Christ in *contritio passiva* and
faith. Only when Christ has broken through the solitude of human
beings will they know themselves placed into truth. It matters not
whether, in the offense that the cross causes the sinner, human beings
die forever and remain in solitude, or whether they die in order to live
with Christ in the truth (for die they must, as Christ died). In both cases,
true knowledge of themselves is given here only through Christ. If
"thinking that knows itself to be lord of its world" previously corre-
sponded to the situation of solitude, it is now recognized in its true
nature as guilt toward Christ. That is to say, it is recognized really only in
the moment when Christ breaks through the solitude. When conscience
is said to be an immediate relation to God, Christ and the church are
excluded, because God's having bound the divine self to the mediating
word is circumvented.[11]

temple of the religiosity of all flesh who, making use of the very worship of God,
kills everything that is under the sun" (40).

9. *LW* 33:106 (*WA* 18:664).[14]

10. *WA* 18:674: "Caeca est enim natura humana, ut nesciat suas ipsius vires
seu morbos potius, deinde superba videtur sibi nosse et posse omnia . . . scrip-
tura autem definit hominem esse corruptum et captum, tum superbe contem-
nentem et ignorantem suae corruptionis et captivitatis." ("Human nature is
struck with blindness, so that it does not know its own strength or, rather, its
morbid passions. Furthermore, it haughtily imagines that it knows everything
and can do everything. . . . But Scripture states that human beings are corrupt
and in captivity, that they in haughtiness dismiss their corruption and captivity
as untrue" [*LW* 33:121, 122, trans. altered]).[15]

11. It is no coincidence that Holl both defines Luther's religion as a religion
of conscience and admits to the possibility of finding God without Christ in the
first commandment. Cf. his *Luther*, 70.[16]

[14.] Luther's polemics here derives from *The Bondage of the Will* (1525), where he
opposes Erasmus's description of the will as a power that wills the word and work of God
on its own. Luther writes against that view: "Since the works of God which lead to salvation
include death, the cross, and all the evils of the world, the human will must be able to will
both death and its own perdition" (*LW* 33:106).

[15.] From Luther, *The Bondage of the Will* (1525).

[16.] Karl Holl writes that the highest stage of Luther's experience of temptation

Even temptation [Anfechtung], which leads to death, is the work of
Christ, for human beings die of the law only because Christ died
through the law or—this applies to the time before Christ—was to die
141   through it. The temptation that comes through the death of Christ as
the end is the most severe temptation of the law, of the *deus in sua majestate*.[12] [17] In principle it is impossible to draw the distinction between
real temptation by Christ and temptation as the final grasp for oneself,
a distinction analogous to the relation between faith and credulity.
Wherever the I is truly at the end, where it truly reaches out of itself, and
where this reaching is no final 'seeking the self in oneself', there Christ
is at work. However, certainty about this is never won by reflecting on the
act—psychologically we remain opaque to ourselves—but only in each
case in pure regard to Christ and Christ's action for us. Hence Luther's
countlessly repeated admonition not to look upon one's own repentance,
one's own faith, but precisely upon the Lord Christ. For, in order to find
Christ, as long as I still reflect on myself, Christ is not present. If Christ
is truly present, I see only Christ. Conscience can be termed the voice of
God only insofar as conscience is the place where Christ, in real temptation, kills human beings in order to give them life or not.[13] It is crucial

---

12. Luther uses this term essentially to speak of God's not being bound by the
word of grace. It is not intended to imply an impossibility of encountering the
deus in sua majestate in Christ.

13. In relation to the current discussion about conscience, cf. Holl, *Luther*;

[Anfechtung] was "that even Christ disappeared from his view, that Satan . . . changed into
Christ himself. For Christ was also God, he was *also* . . . law-giver and judge; so how could
he be of use to Luther against 'God'? . . . Truly, there were situations when he felt himself
directly and all alone before God. . . . What upheld Luther in such extreme affliction was
something surprisingly simple. It was *the first commandment*" (*Luther*, 69–73). Cf. Hans
Michael Müller, *Erfahrung und Glaube*, 90, note 1, concerning the debate on this position.
Cf. Holl's *Luther* on the characterization of Luther's religion as "religion of conscience."
What is presupposed here is the understanding of conscience as "receptivity for obliga-
tion," as a "feeling of responsibility," and as a "sense of commitment" (35–37). Cf. Holl's
"Gogartens Lutherauffassung," 308, where citations are given.

[17.] "God in God's majesty" [MR]. See Holl, *Luther*, 38f.

that self-understanding is possible only where the living Christ ap-

Hirsch, *Jesus Christus der Herr;*[18] and Brunstäd, *Die Idee der Religion.*[19] Luther's religion is a religion of conscience for all three of them. On the opposite side stands Gogarten's critique of Holl in the journal *Christliche Welt,* 1924 ("Theologie und Wissenschaft: Grundsätzliche Bemerkungen zu Karl Holls 'Luther'"), and his later works *Ich glaube an den dreieinigen Gott,* 1926, and *Theol. Tradition und theol. Arbeit,* 1927.[20] See Grisebach, *Gegenwart,* 1928, e.g., "Limits are placed upon me, therefore, through the experience of conscience, from myself and never but through myself, but I never am provided a genuine limit from without. That is [. . .] just the astounding thing about conscience, that human beings hear only themselves in an ultimate and frightful isolation and therefore believe that they are hearing themselves . . . as God" (564f.). "It would be overestimating oneself to maintain that one hears the voice of the actual basis of ethical reality in one's essence" (475). H. M. Müller evinces a large measure of agreement with Grisebach in his *Erfahrung und Glaube bei Luther,* 1929.[21] Cf. also Heidegger, *Being and Time,* 311–46;[22] G. Jacob, *Der Gewissensbegriff in der Theologie Luthers,* 1928, a work that is influenced by Heidegger and Tillich;[23]

[18.] Emanuel Hirsch's lectures on Christology, *Jesus Christ der Herr,* introduce the concept of conscience in connection with the critique of the ancient church's Christology. "We reject the notion that human and divine life could ever be combined except in personal community; we reject the notion that God could be present to us in a material form; in Jesus, however, we see a word that encounters us in conscience" (48). For Hirsch, Luther's teaching of "the omnipresence of Jesus Christ according to his humanity" is taken up wherever Christ is said to have power "to act as one present upon our conscience" (60). Cf. also E. Hirsch, *Die idealistische Philosophie* (Idealist philosophy), 39, 80f., 83.

[19.] Friedrich Brunstäd, *Die Idee der Religion,* builds upon the critical-idealist concept of knowledge, rather than upon Luther, in developing his concept of conscience. He defines conscience as "the unconditional form of the I" of the transcendental unity of apperception, which is posited within us as "inwardness" and "personality" (102).

[20.] Cf. Friedrich Gogarten, "Theologie und Wissenschaft" (N.B. 39–42, 71–76). Also see *Ich glaube,* where he distinguishes the judging conscience from that discussed in idealism (chap. 8, N.B. 190–96). In relation to Gogarten's critique of Emanuel Hirsch's understanding of conscience, see Gogarten's *Theologische Tradition,* 119f., as well as his "Ethik des Gewissens oder Ethik der Gnade?"

[21.] Cf. Hans Michael Müller, *Erfahrung und Glaube,* 21–24, 45f., 111f.

[22.] In *Being and Time,* Heidegger says that conscience "manifests itself as the call of care" (322). This call "discloses Dasein's most primordial potentiality-for-being as being-guilty. Thus conscience manifests itself as an attestation which belongs to Dasein's being—an attestation in which conscience calls Dasein itself face to face with its ownmost potentiality-for-Being" (334).

[23.] In his work *Gewissensbegriff,* Günter Jacob contests the methodological propriety of asking "what Luther understands by conscience in the sense of a human capacity and phenomenon of consciousness." Conscience, he says, is a relational concept for Luther: "The concept of conscience is made clear only when it is shown which relations determine conscience and how it is determined by them" (5f.).

proaches us, only in beholding him. αὐτοὶ ἐν ἑαυτοῖς ἑαυτοὺς μετροῦντες καὶ συγκρίνοντες ἑαυτοὺς ἑαυτοῖς οὐ συνιᾶσιν[26] (2 Cor. 10:12).

But because the attempt to understand oneself from oneself remains in sin, the designation of human existence in Adam as the being-of-a-sinner is correct at the formal ontological level and sufficient. To being-in-sin,[27] there corresponds an act of sin—the act of misconstruing the self that takes place when Dasein is violated by its being-how-it-is [Wie-sein] as one who falsely claims to possess full power over the self. How act and being are related 'in Adam' remains to be seen.

b) 'Adam' as I and as Humanity

Sin is the inversion of the human will (of human essence) into itself. Will has no reality save as free and conscious, and thus sin must be understood as act. Every decision made in a self-seeking sense is to be judged as a sinful act. The seriousness of this definition of sin lies in the fact that it does not seem otherwise possible to maintain the guilt-character of sin; the experiential base for this definition is the verdict of conscience, according to which one is responsible only for decisions of the self against God taken willfully. One may well then differentiate between sin and guilt, as between being and act. But to understand sin *qua* guilt as the being of human beings appears untruthful in light of the experience of one's own conscience and seems to minimize the gravity of the concept of guilt. Sin, therefore, is act. Underlying this view is a concept of conscience as the unmediated voice of God in human beings. But this

---

and R. Seeberg's article "Gewissen" in R.G.G., 2. ed.[24] Cf. Stoker, *Das Gewissen,* 1925, which is of relevance to the phenomenology of conscience.[25]

[24.] The reference is to the article by Reinhold Seeberg, "Gewissen" in *Die Religion in Geschichte und Gegenwart*: "Conscience is the activity of the consciousness of self in relation to moral action. It consists primarily in assuring that what human beings will and do freely are so placed into their consciousness that they judge it at the same time" (1166).

[25.] Hendrik Gerhardus Stoker, a pupil of Max Scheler, had developed an emotive theory of conscience. According to his book *Das Gewissen,* the origin of conscience is the "moral emotion" as "the genuine experience of the contrast between good and evil within us" (48). This is where the "moral urge" for involvement in the good arises, as do our "moral knowledge" and "moral consciousness" (222).

[26.] "But when they measure themselves by one another, and compare themselves with one another, they do not show good sense."

[27.] Hyphenation added for clarity of meaning; not originally in Bonhoeffer's text. [WF]

argument breaks down before the different interpretation of the experience of conscience that was given above. The attempt of conscience to limit sin to the act must be understood as a human attempt at self-deliverance. The knowledge of what sin is comes solely through the mediation of the Word of God in Christ; and that knowledge overrules the dissenting conscience. _Sola fide credendum est nos esse peccatores._[28]

If sin were no more than a free act of the particular moment, a retreat to sinless being would in principle be possible, revelation in Christ having become redundant. The death of Christ reveals that the whole human must die to the law, because the totality of the old human is in sin. The continuity of the human being in Adam is judged by the death   144
of Christ. Thus it is necessary to understand sin in some way as being.

There are two possibilities for understanding sin as having the form of the being of entities.

1. We may historicize, psychologize, and naturalize the doctrine of original sin. Somehow sin clings to human nature as humanly generated. _Non posse non peccare_ holds true for this tarnished nature.[29] The concept of nature is intended to warrant the continuity and existentiality of sin.

2. Sin may be understood as a pretemporal deed that gave rise to sin in the present (a view proposed lately by Julius Müller).[30] All speculative dualisms, as well as the metaphysical theory of satanic revolt, subscribe to this view. In undialectical fashion, something ontologically prior—something in the sense of entity with all the implacability of the 'there is'—is being placed here ahead of the act of sinning. Yet sin as entity cannot touch me existentially. It is transcended within me; I remain its lord even when it overpowers me. Sin understood as entity is the exoneration of human beings. A mode of being must be ascribed to sin which, on the one hand, expresses the fully unexcusable and contingent character of sin that breaks forth anew in the act and which, on the other hand, makes it possible to understand sin as the master into whose hands human beings are utterly delivered. The New Testament itself provides

[28.] "By faith alone we know that we are sinners." See above, page 136, editorial note 1.

[29.] "Not able not to sin" was the phrase Augustine coined in his debate with Pelagius about the meaning of sin for the free will ("A Treatise on Nature and Grace," chap. 57, in _Saint Augustine: Anti-Pelagian Works_, 140).

[30.] Julius Müller (1801–78), professor of dogmatics in Halle and advocate of the union of Protestant churches. In relation to sin, cf. his major work _The Christian Doctrine of Sin_.

the concept of being that is sought: Adam as I and as the being-of-the-person-of-humanity.

In the judgment brought upon me by the death of Christ, I see myself dying in my entirety, for I myself, as a whole, am guilty as the actor of my life, the decisions of which turned out to be self-seeking ever and again. I made false decisions and, therefore, Christ is my death; and because I alone sought to be the master, I am alone in my death as well. But the death of Christ kills my entire being human, as humanity in me, for I am I and humanity in one. In my fall from God, humanity fell. Thus, before the cross, the debt of the I grows to monstrous size; it is itself Adam, itself the first to have done, and to do again and again, that incomprehensible deed—sin as act. But in this act, for which I hold myself utterly responsible on every occasion, I find myself already in the humanity of Adam. I see humanity in me necessarily committing this, my own free deed. As human being, the I is banished into this old humanity, which fell on my account. The I 'is' not as an individual, but always in humanity. And just because the deed of the individual is at the same time that of humanity, human beings must hold themselves individually responsible for the whole guilt of humankind. The interrelation of individual and humanity is not to be thought of in terms of causality—otherwise the mode of being of the entity would once again come into play; rather, it is a knowledge given the individual in God's judgment—given in such a way that it cannot be used, in detachment from that judgment and in theoretical abstraction, for purposes of exoneration. On the contrary, because everyone, as human being, stands within the humanity of Adam, no one can withdraw from the sinful act to a sinless being; no, the whole of one's being a person is in sin. Thus, in Adam act is as constitutive for being as being is for act; both act and being enter into judgment as guilty. The structure of Adam's humanity should not be conceived in terms of theories of psychological-historical interpretation; no, I myself am Adam—am I and humanity in one. In me humanity falls. As I am Adam, so is every individual; but in all individuals the one person of humanity, Adam, is active. This expresses both the contingency of the deed and the continuity of the being of sin. Because sin is envisaged through the concept of 'Adam', in the mode of being of 'person', the contingency of conduct is preserved, as is the continuity of the person of humanity, which attests itself in action—the person that I also am.

This perspective agrees with Luther's view of sin, which wishes to define it equally as original sin and as one's own act and guilt: sin as ego-centricity [Ichsucht], as the seeking of one's own person after itself. The being of sin is being-a-person. In the knowledge of my being-a-sinner as an individual, I see that my Dasein is in the power of the form in which I actually exist [Wiesein]; I cannot know it in its creaturely being. In the knowledge of my being a sinner as humanity, I see my sinful Dasein as the basis of the form in which I actually exist, yet never as an exoneration—never, that is to say, as if from the position of a neutral observer who looks at an entity. On the contrary, I see this only in the judgment in which I must die as 'Adam'.

c) Everydayness, Knowledge of Conscience, and Temptation

The *everydayness*[31] of human beings in Adam is guilt. It is the decision for solitude which, because it has already been taken, is being taken all the time. It is a *coercive* seeking after pleasure in the creature and, for that reason, always in flight from that the right knowledge of which sets pleasure within its proper limits: from death and the self. But the flight is hopeless,[14] for human beings are to be revealed before the tribunal of Christ, if not today, then certainly in death (2 Cor. 5:10). Because this is so, the wilder the flight and the less human beings are conscious of that hopelessness, the more desperate is everydayness in Adam. Superficiality masks solitude; it is oriented toward life, but its ground and end is death in guilt.

---

14. *LW* 25:401.[32]

[31.] See above, page 101, editorial note 32.

[32.] Martin Luther, *Vorlesung über den Römerbrief* (2:236, lines 31–33): "Hec est enim pena damnatorum et inquies sine fine, quod fugiunt Deum et tamen effugere non possunt, quod etiam omnis conscientia mala Christum oblita facit. . . ." ("For this is the punishment of the damned and their torment without end, that they flee from God but cannot escape, which is what every bad conscience does that has forgotten Christ" [*Lectures on Romans, LW* 25:401]). The reader should note the way in which Bonhoeffer, at a decisive point in his argument, can turn his attention *both* toward his theological forebears such as Luther *and* his philosophical contemporaries such as Heidegger. We need only notice that the very notion of 'flight' occurs at the beginning of a section titled 'everydayness'—a term Bonhoeffer has borrowed from *Being and Time*. And the *angst* that Heidegger describes there—the anxiety of "Dasein's falling into the 'they' and the 'world' of its concern, . . . a 'fleeing' in the face of itself" (230)—is the anxiety over the finitude of human existence that Bonhoeffer's own next footnote addresses. [WF]

Conscience, in which desperation and solitude become-conscious-of-themselves, seeks thereby to overcome them. Solitude is not grasped in its authentic sense. There arises merely a general consciousness of being-left-alone, and this is what conscience is to eliminate by restoring human beings once again to themselves. In conscience, the powers of this world, law and death, fall upon human beings and make them anx-
147   ious; here, anxiety in the face of oneself erupts from life, because it neither knows the future nor holds it in its power. Yet there is in this anxiety an inability to break free of oneself, a final perseverance of the I in itself. In conscience death steps within the horizon of the I, but only as an entity, as an event that conscience can conquer. Human beings think themselves immortal and remain alone.

Temptation, in which Christ assails human beings through the law, discloses that this solitude has the character of guilt. All that has gone before becomes deadly serious [wird . . . zum Ernst] here.[33] Here human beings are detained from their ultimate flight, which conscience makes possible for them, and are forced to recognize that their guilt and death are the ground and end of their flight. Moment by moment their guilt brings death near. Death is no longer an entity to be conquered. Rather, the moment guilt and the curse of death are recognized, human beings see that they are already in death. They are dead before they die and they die every moment anew.[15] Their knowledge and volition come

---

15. On this point, cf. Heidegger's analysis of 'being towards death' as the 'own-most potentiality for being' that makes possible 'the whole of Dasein'. Heidegger's concept of death is metaphysical and utterly insincere, for he includes death in the dialectical process of the spirit ('Dasein') finding itself. Inasmuch as 'being towards death' is for him an ontological structure of Dasein, rather than an ontic-existentiell experience, death has already been incorporated into living Dasein.[34] The Christian understanding is very different. In death, into whose power human beings in Adam already know themselves to have fallen, existence finds its real end and not its wholeness, its 'completion'. Only in the metaphysi-

[33.] The term *Ernst,* here translated as "deadly serious," is an allusion to a major concept in the work of Søren Kierkegaard. In Kierkegaard scholarship it is often rendered as "ernest(ness)," but this lacks the same force in English as in German. See Kierkegaard's *The Concept of Anxiety,* N.B. 146–54, and Erik Peterson's examination in his "Was ist Theologie?" (N.B. 13ff.). See also Bonhoeffer's remarks from 1930 in relation to Heidegger (*NRS* 55ff. [*GS* 3:71]). And, from the time of Barcelona in 1928, see *GS* 5:116, 454f. Also, selections from *GS* 5:135f. are translated in *TF* 52–56. [WF]

[34.] Cf. Martin Heidegger, *Being and Time,* section 53.

from death, for they do not come from the life of God. This perennial
dying is accompanied by anxiety and uneasiness. Guilt, death, and the
world press in upon human beings and make the world too 'narrow'[16]
('narrowness' ['Enge'], 'anxiety' ['Angst'] , and 'uneasy' ['bange'] have a   148
common root). Here, human beings are no longer alone; everything
now speaks to them, becomes their accuser, and yet they nonetheless
remain alone and without defense. In this temptation human beings die
of Christ; they die of the law that is of the spirit.[17] In the death of the sinner, however, predestination takes its course: for one, eternal death, for
another, eternal life. Temptation itself is part of being human in Adam
and must lead to death. It brings with it ever anew the horrors of eternal
death. In it sin, guilt, and the law obscure the cross and resurrection and
seek to be accepted as definitive. Whether Christ will give himself to the
tempted one in grace and faith ever and again remains in the balance,
for which reason temptation must never be regarded as a dialectical
point of transition toward faith.[18] Temptation is, indeed, the real end of
sinners, their death. That life should come from death is God's free gift
to God's community, free also for those who 'are' in the community—
that is to say, find themselves believing. God can let human beings die of
the knowledge of their sin and can lead them through this death into
community. For then God turns one's eyes away from oneself, and gives
them God's own orientation (the pure intentionality of the *actus directus*)

---

cal system can 'end' and 'wholeness' or 'completion' be identified. Death is eternal death, unless Christ wake human beings from the dead (Eph. 5:14).

16. *LW* 42:99, 100 (*WA* 2:685f.): "Just as a child is born in fear and peril from
the small dwelling place of its mother's womb into this wide heaven and earth of
this world, so human beings go out of this life through the narrow gate of death.
However full and great and wide appear the heaven and the earth where we now
live, yet all is far narrower and smaller against the heaven to come than is the
mother's womb against the heaven we see. . . . Thus, in dying also one must resist
fear and know that a great spaciousness and joy will be thereafter" [trans. altered
MR].[35]

17. On this point also Fr. H. Kohlbrügge has written unusually perceptive
things, *Das siebente Kapitel des Briefes Pauli an die Römer in ausführlicher Umschreibung.*

18. Holl is inclined toward this view; see his *Luther*, 67ff., and elsewhere.

[35.] Luther, "A Sermon on Preparing to Die" (1519).

towards Christ, the crucified and risen one who is the overcoming of the temptation to death.

149   **2. Being in Christ**

a) The Definition of 'Being' in Christ

"Seek yourself only in Christ and not in yourself, and you will find yourself in him eternally."[19] Here, the person *in se conversus* [turned in upon itself][20] is delivered from the attempt to remain alone—to understand itself out of itself—and is turned outwards towards Christ. The person now lives in the contemplation of Christ.[21] This is the gift of faith, that one no longer looks upon oneself, but solely upon the salvation that has come to one from without. One finds oneself in Christ, because already one is in Christ, in that one seeks oneself there in Christ. If in Adam Dasein was violated by the form in which it actually exists [Wiesein]—through the encapsulation of human beings in themselves—then the solution to this problem comes as humanity reorients its gaze towards Christ. Dasein becomes free, not as if it could stand over against its being-how-it-is [Wiesein] as autonomous being, but in the sense of escaping from the power of the I into the power of Christ, where alone it recognizes itself in original freedom as God's creature.

---

19. *LW* 42:106 (*WA* 2:690).[36]

20. *WA* 40/1:282, lines 21 ff.: "Sed hic oportet Christum et conscientiam meam fieri unum corpus, ita ut in conspectu meo nihil maneat nisi Christus crucifixus et resuscitatus. Si vero in me tantum intueor excluso Christo, actum est de me . . . ibi in me conversus et considerans qualis ego sim vel esse debeam, item quid mihi faciundum sit, amitto ex oculis Christum, qui solus est iustitia et vita mea." ("But here Christ and my conscience must become one body, so that nothing remains in my sight but Christ, crucified and risen. But if Christ is put aside and I look only at myself, then I am done for. . . . By paying attention to myself and considering what my condition is or should be, and what I am supposed to be doing, I lose sight of Christ, who alone is my Righteousness and Life" [*LW* 26:166]).[37]

21. *LW* 26:167 (*WA* 40/1:283, line 2); or see Gal. 2:20: "that means 'non ego': non inspicio me ('not I': not I who is looking upon myself)".[38]

[36.] From Luther, "A Sermon on Preparing to Die" (1519).
[37.] From Luther, *Lectures on Galatians* (1531).
[38.] Ibid.

Only in Christ do human beings know themselves as God's creatures; in Adam they were creator and creature all at once.[22] In order to know itself as a creature of God, the old human being has to have died and the new one arisen, whose essence it is to live in disregard of self and wholly in contemplation of Christ. As those living in Christ, the new human beings know themselves in identity with the old human beings that have passed through death—as God's creatures. That sinners too are still creatures is something that can be expressed only by a believer; as long as this is an insight of sinners, it stays an idea in untruth.

It well may be objected that the ontological definition of being human as being-the-sinner [Sünder-Sein] and being-in-Christ [in-Christus-Sein] needs to be undergirded by a general ontology of being-a-creature [Geschöpf-Sein].[23] That would take us into Catholicism. Being-a-creature is only 'in faith'; it is the Dasein of the one who believes, which cannot be divorced from how-one-is [Wiesein] in faith. Being-a-creature is not something in the manner of 'there is'; being-a-creature is in the agitation of being in faith. Ontologically this means that God is at once the creature's ground of being and lord; transcendentally it means that Dasein is 'amidst' and 'in reference to' transcendence. There is no ontological specification of that which is created that is independent of God being reconciler and redeemer, and human beings being sinners and forgiven. In the Christian doctrine of being, all metaphysical ideas of eternity and time, being and becoming, living and dying, essence and appearance must be measured against the concepts of the being of sin and the being of grace or else must be developed anew in light of them. For only on this basis was it also possible to define the being of sin, grace, and revelation as a being that was described as the unity of act and being, as personal being. In the idea of the creature, however, the personal-being [Person-Sein] of God and revelation manifests itself as creative-being [Schöpfer-Sein] and lordly-being [Herr-Sein] over my human personal

150

151

---

22. The possibility of forming the idea of a Creator-God, which naturally also obtains in the *status corruptionis*,[39] is another matter. It is, however, only an idea, which the individual cannot understand as reality, precisely because individuals postulate themselves continually as their own creator.

23. The other possibility for a foundation, through a phenomenological interpretation of the existentiality of Dasein, has been already rejected in another context.

[39.] "the state of corruption" [MR]

being. And the second of these is the more encompassing of the two latter designations.

Even though I am able through faith alone to know myself as God's creature, I know, nonetheless, that I have been created by God in my entirety, as an I and as humanity, and that I have been placed into nature and history. I know, therefore, that these factors, too, have to do with creatureliness. The faith of the creature, however, refuses to call the 'world' that has become its own—which has been defined in the form in which it actually exists [Wiesein] by sin and death and has been violated in its Dasein—the creation of God. Nevertheless, God remains lord even of this world. In view of the hope offered in the resurrection of the historical Christ and in the life I live with him—a hope to which has been promised a new heaven and a new earth—faith must believe that the world is God's creation, despite its falling away. It follows that an ontology that conforms to the so-called 'pure creative being' ends up transforming itself into a definition of being apart from the revelation in Christ, since it is only in Christ that authentic faith in creation arises.

If one desired to discover the ontological boundaries of the being-of-the-creature, the being assumed in being-the-sinner and being-justified, it is to be found in the structure of its being-there [Dasein]—as it is violated in sin and liberated in grace—as well as in the structure of its being-how-it-is [Wie-sein] as 'directed-towards-being'. The 'there' ['Da'] of human beings is not to be defined independently of the 'how' ['Wie']. No metaphysical deductions or distinctions (*existentia, essentia, ens* [existence, essence, being]), and no ontological structures of existence can reach up to the 'there' as created. Creaturely-being is what Dasein is called by means of and for God in faith—that is to say, being touched by revelation. This very general definition indicates already that in the concept of the creature, too, the 'there' and 'how' belong indissolubly together.

Creaturely Dasein is 'there' only in being directed towards revelation; conversely, being-directed is an ontological definition of the 'there'—which is to say, 'there' and 'how' are grounded solely in revelation, inseparable from one another. Here alone is the understanding of the 'there' and 'how' protected against interference from extraneous categories.

Likewise, it is only in revelation itself that being-a-creature can be defined in terms of being-a-person, insofar as it is the person whose existence has been encountered, judged, or created anew by Christ. Thus, all ontological definitions remain bound to the revelation in Christ; they are appropriate only in the concretions of being-the-sinner and being-justified. This does not do away with the idea of the creature; it is preserved and expressed, rather, in the concretion of "what Dasein is called by means of and for God." Nor is the possibility of reflecting theologically on such 'creaturely' categories as individuality, being in history, in nature, being and becoming, and so forth, eliminated. But this can be done only on the presupposition of existence touched by revelation.

The objection that categories of a general metaphysical kind also have been employed in these proceedings overlooks the necessity of a certain formal 'preunderstanding'[40], on the basis of which alone questions—even if wrong ones—can be raised, whose answer is then surrendered by revelation, together with a fundamental correction of the question.

And so, the idea of creation is unable to provide a basis for the ontological definition of the human being in Christ. The human being only 'is' in Adam or in Christ, in unfaith or in faith, in Adamic humanity and in Christ's community; God only 'is' as the creator, reconciler, and redeemer, and that being as such is personal being. The world of entity is transcended and qualified by this personal being. That world 'is for' human beings in Adam their own, violated, 'interpreted'[41] world under the curse of death; and it 'is for' human beings in Christ the world set free from the I and, yet, given anew by God into their dominion, in the hope for the new creation (Rom. 8:19ff). It is ultimately the world utterly for God, who remains its Lord. There is no more general definition of its being.

Being in Christ, as being directed towards Christ, sets Dasein free. Human beings are 'there' for and by means of Christ; they believe as long as they look upon Christ. In the depiction of faith in terms of pure intentionality, one must avoid every attempt, on the one hand, to freeze the temporality of faith by exhibiting it—which is what the theology of consciousness had done and which, in my view, is repeated again by H. M. Müller.[24] And, on the other hand, one must avoid every attempt to

---

24. Cf. [H. M. Müller,] *Erfahrung und Glaube bei Luther*, 1929. The 'times of

[40.] Cf. Rudolf Bultmann, "The Significance of 'Dialectical Theology' for the Scientific Study of the New Testament," 156; also "The Historicity of Man and Faith," in *Existence and Faith*, 99ff.

[41.] Friedrich Gogarten attacked such 'interpretation' in *Ich glaube an den dreieinigen Gott*, 17ff.

incorporate into the act of faith itself the reflection that meets with faith merely as 'credulity'. This is the danger in Barth. Faith and 'credulity' lie together in the same act. Every act of faith is credulous insofar as it is an event embedded in the psyche [im Psychischen] and accessible to reflection; it is 'faith' in its intentionality towards Christ, which is grounded in being in the community of Christ. A faith that grows doubtful of itself because it considers itself unworthy, stands in temptation. Faith itself knows that it is Christ who justifies and not faith as *opus;*[43] it requires no reflection to find this out, particularly since reflection declares something quite different, as it brings faith into temptation. The theological right with which Barth reproached Schleiermacher for his "grand confusion" of religion and grace[25] is compromised when one allows reflection to enter into the act of faith itself, thereby casting doubt on Christ right along with faith. This is the penalty paid for the inadequate distinction between theological knowing and that of faith. Doubt is cast when one forgets that Christ is apprehended in believing faith; it is in such forgetfulness that all the ominous terms such as enthusiasm, experience, piety, feeling, and conversion of the will recur by necessity. It must be stated clearly that in the community of Christ faith takes form in religion and that, consequently, religion is called faith—that seen in light of Christ I may and must calmly confess, "I believe," only to add, of course, with a view to myself, "help my unbelief."[44] For reflection, all praying, all searching for God in God's Word, all clinging to promise, every entreaty in the name of God's grace, all hope with reference to the cross is 'religion', 'credulity'. But in the community of Christ, even though it is always the work of human beings, it is faith, given and willed by God, faith in which God may truly be found. Were faith to inquire about its own sufficiency, it would have fallen already from intentional-

---

distress' in which faith overcomes temptation[42] should be open to exhibition; but where do we get the criterion for distinguishing 'times of distress' from exaggerated experiences, if not from a perhaps particular intensity of 'experience'? But does this truly avoid psychologism? The only ones who 'know' of the reality of faith, as distinct from credulity, are those who in faith no longer ask questions about this, and Christ.

25. [Barth, *Die christliche*] *Dogmatik*, section 18, 301ff.

[42.] Cf. Hans Michael Müller, *Erfahrung und Glaube*, 44f.
[43.] "work" [MR]
[44.] Cf. Mark 9:24. "Immediately the father of the child cried out, 'I believe: help my unbelief!'"

ity into temptation. Rather, faith only assures itself of its contents by laying hold of them, relating them to itself, and in so doing, abiding in an undisturbed contemplation of Christ that can be destroyed only by self-reflection. Being-in-Christ is being directed towards Christ, and that is possible only through 'being already in the community of Christ' (in the sense presented above). And so, the transcendental and ontological points of departure again find themselves brought together.

If this, as it were, is only a formal definition, then being in Christ, as historical, is also defined by past and future (see above, pages 110f.). Here the concrete manner of being pertaining to being directed towards Christ, and pertaining to being in the community, clearly emerges for the first time.

b) The Definition of Being in Christ through the Past: The Conscience

"Whoever is without conscience is Christ or the evil Spirit" (*Theologia deutsch*).[45] The historical human being has conscience, not only in Adam as a protection against God's assault, but also in the church of Christ. Conscience is only where sin is. But since the human being in Christ is no longer governed by sin, conscience is something defined by the past in Adam. Human beings have conscience by and in themselves; it does not belong to the things 'to come'. It is the reflection on one's self beyond which human beings in Adam cannot advance. Conscience primarily is not God's but the human being's own voice. If being-in-Christ means being oriented towards Christ, reflection on the self is obviously not part of that being. Here lies the problem of Christian conscience.

A distinction has to be made between two forms of conscience that pertain to the human being in Christ.

1. Conscience interposes itself between Christ (the community of faith) and me, and either obscures my view of Christ or shows Christ to me as my judge on the cross, thereby pointing relentlessly to my sin. The spiritual law has arisen against me. I hear only my accuser, see myself rejected; death and hell grasp for me. Truly, this is temptation[26] and

¹⁵⁵

---

26. Cf. Luther's entire "A Sermon on Preparing to Die" (1519), *LW* 42:99–115 (*WA* 2:685ff.).

[45.] An ascetic-mystical tract, the first writing of which is dated circa 1430 and attributed to Johannes de Francfordia, professor of theology at Heidelberg. Cf. Willo Uhl: "Whoever now is without conscience is Christ or the evil spirit" (*Der Franckforter*, 45).

rebellion against Christ, since it is disregard for the grace offered in Christ. In this temptation even those in Christ's community stand in real danger of losing Christ if this very one does not come forward to kill their conscience, declare Christ's self anew to human beings, and give them back their faith. In faith, however, human beings find themselves once again already in the community of faith. They know that through faith, for those who stand in the community of faith, temptation through sin and death is overcome. The belief that such temptation is required in order to come to faith turns evil into a necessary stage on the way to the good, as in Hegel's dialectics. This temptation belongs entirely to the righteousness of the flesh, and this conscience is itself defection from Christ.

2. The other form of conscience, that of reflection on the self, is included within the intention towards Christ. It is the 'look of sin' within faith. Those who seek themselves in Christ see themselves always in sin; but now this sin can no longer distort their contemplation of Christ (it is, after all, the basis on which I, ἐν σαρκί,[46] can look upon Christ and him alone). I see my sin within the forgiveness through Christ. "You may, therefore, safely look upon your sin without your conscience (!), as sins are no longer sins there; they are overcome and swallowed up in Christ . . . If you believe that, they can do you no harm."[27] Repentance, too, is now no longer the last grasp for oneself, but rather repentance within the belief in forgiveness[28] (*contritio passiva*).[48] This is the meaning of daily penance and repentance. It is not the loss of oneself to the self; rather, it is finding oneself in Christ. True, even the reflection of repentance presupposes life ἐν σαρκί,[49] the sin of falling away from the intention towards Christ. If there were no sin, repentance could have become thanksgiving. This final barrier put up by sin against the pure contemplation of Christ is conquered by the faith, which sees its sin only within the context of Christ's forgiveness, within the community. This faith is called penitence. Reflection as such can no longer break the

27. *LW* 42:105 (*WA* 2:690).[47]
28. Cf. Luther, "The Sacrament of Penance," *LW* 35:9ff. (*WA* 2:713ff.).

[46.] "in the flesh" [MR]
[47.] From Luther, "A Sermon on Preparing to Die" (1519), *WA* 2:689f., pagination corrected.
[48.] "passive contrition" [MR]
[49.] "in the flesh" [WF]

intentionality towards Christ. And yet, intentionality is caught again and again in struggle, as it is not yet in the pure form of 'being defined by the future alone'. (See below.)

The self-reflection of sinful human beings in face of Christ and in Christ is the death of human beings ἐν σαρκί, just as the self-reflection of human beings in Adam was the death of spiritual human beings. Because Christ died, and because we, too, died that death with Christ in baptism (Romans 6), death is concealed in faith; for that reason the faithful must daily die that death. The strength to die is not given by asceticism or focusing on the self—that is a work of natural human beings who cannot desire cross and death; rather, they die solely in faith. They do not give themselves death but, in faith, see themselves given into death by Christ. They see themselves in the daily death throes of σάρξ,[50] drawn into the agony of the old human being; believing, they see Christ fighting with death in them. They believe in Christ's victory and, yet, are subject in body and soul to the power of death. The death of the old human is guilt, the future's recompense to the past for having snatched the new human from its clutches. Those over whom the future of Christ has triumphed in faith must daily die the death of that past anew with open eyes. The more forcefully death assails human beings, the mightier the power of the past over them. Thus being in Christ— which when defined by the past is the reflection, taking place in faith, of repenting and dying— is taken up and determined by the future; and this future is holiness and life.

c) The Definition of Being in Christ by Means of the Future: The Child

Future means: the definition of being by something outside 'yet to come'. There is a genuine future only through Christ and the reality, created anew by Christ, of the neighbor and creation. Estranged from Christ, the world is enclosed in the I, which is to say, already the past. In it life is reflection. What is 'yet to come' demands immediate acceptance or rejection, and reflection signifies refusal, as the one absolutely yet to come, Christ demands faith directed towards Christ without reflection.[51]

[50.] "the flesh" [MR]
[51.] See above, pages 99–100, 111, and 131–32.

Here, the second stage of reflection is also superseded—not only self-reflection outside of Christ, but also the reflection of the 'Christian' conscience. As long as there is sin, there is also Christian conscience. In the pure orientation towards Christ there is no sin, and consequently there is no reflection of repentance in faith. In their definition by the future, human beings are wholly detached from themselves into contemplation of Christ. Of course, this is no mystical self-dissolving contemplation; no, I behold Christ as 'my Lord and my God'.[52] But that is no longer a reflection upon the I. Rather, it expresses the personality in relation, which, even in the position of intentionality, remains a personality in relation.

158   Classical Protestant dogmatics spoke of *fides directa* to describe the act of faith which, even though completed within a person's consciousness, could not be reflected in it.[29] The act of faith rests on the objectivity of the event of revelation in Word and sacrament. Clinging to Christ need not become self-conscious; rather, it is wholly taken up by completion of the act itself. Human beings are in Christ, and as there is no sin and death in Christ, human beings do not see their sin or death, nor do they see themselves or their own faith. They see only Christ and their Lord and God. To see Christ in Word and sacrament means to see, all in one

---

29. On this point see Franz Delitzsch, *A System of Biblical Psychology*: "The *Actus Directi* and *Reflexi* of the Life of Grace" (407ff.). "This *actus directus* as such already has God's promise. The *actus reflexi* of divine assurance, joyful self-confidence, perceptive sight and taste do not belong to the essence of justifying faith, but, as our forebears used to say, it is that *actus directus* which is the *forma fidei essentialis*" (413, trans. altered).[53] "The processes named and promised by the Word (such as rebirth) themselves happen to us in the depth of the unconscious, and only now and then do reflexes thereof enter into consciousness" (403, trans. altered). "If the fact of rebirth did take place in the sphere of our consciousness, why would there possibly be such diversity of views about the difference of the effects of Word and sacrament among the enlightened spirits?" (404, trans. altered).[54] Here, of course, a theological interpretation has to take the place of the psychological one.[55]

[52.] Cf. John 20:28. "Thomas answered him, 'My Lord and my God!'"
[53.] "the essential form of faith" [MR]
[54.] Delitzsch's text has "the most enlightened Christians."
[55.] It must be noted, however, that Delitzsch himself asserts that "by its nature, faith itself is *actus directus*, namely, a line, drawn from us to Christ and God in Christ. It is a desire that reaches out to the salvation offered in word and sacrament, gazing away from our native, natural condition directly at Christ; open to his grace, faith longs and grasps for that grace and, in the unity of all its powers, takes hold if it" (*A System of Biblical Psychology*, 413, trans. altered).

act, the crucified and risen one in the neighbor and creation. Here alone does that future reveal itself which in faith determines the present. In the definition of being in Christ by means of the future, the dialectic of act and being recurs. In faith the future is present; but inasmuch as faith suspends itself before the future (knowing itself to be its mode of being, but not as productive), the human being 'is' in the future of Christ—that is, never in being without act, and never in act without being.

To-let-oneself-be-defined by means of the future is the eschatological possibility of the child. The child (full of anxiety and bliss) sees itself in the power of what 'future things' will bring, and for that reason alone, it can live in the present. However, they[56] who are mature, who desire to be defined by the present, fall subject to the past, to themselves, death and guilt. It is only out of the future that the present can be lived.

Here the child becomes a theological problem. *Actus directus* or *reflexus*, infant baptism or religiosity? *Actus directus*, as an act directed solely by and on Christ, and infant baptism, as the paradoxical occurrence of revelation without the reflexive answer of consciousness, as brought together in classical Protestant dogmatics,[30] are the eschatological prelude under which life is placed. Both can be understood only in connection with the last things. Baptism is the call to the human being into childhood, a call that can be understood only eschatologically.[57]

---

30. Cf. Hollatz, *Examen* [*theologicum universam theologiam theticopolemicam complectens*], in the chapter "De Gratia Regenerante" (On regenerative grace): "Habent infantes fidem non reflexam aut discursivam, sed directam et simplicem a Spiritu Sancto, cui malitiose non resistunt per baptismum accensam." ("Children possess a faith that does not reflect and is not given to discursive reasoning; rather, it is immediate and simple, kindled through baptism by the Holy Spirit whom they (as opposed to adults) do not maliciously oppose.") Also see Delitzsch, *A System of Biblical Psychology*, 407. Cf. above, page 158, footnote 29.

[56.] This is one of only two times Bonhoeffer uses *Mann* (man) rather than *Mensch* (human being) in all of AB. [WF]

[57.] In relation to the theological weight of Bonhoeffer's discussion of the child, see his student essay, "Das jüdische Element im ersten Clemensbrief" (The Jewish element in the first letter of Clement), *DBW* 9:231; from the Barcelona period see "Rein bleiben und reif werden" (Remain pure and become mature), *Predigten – Auslegungen – Meditationen: 1925–1945*, 1:133–37; "Jesus Christus und vom Wesen des Christentums" (Jesus Christ and the essence of Christianity), *GS* 5:145 ff. (selections from this are translated in *TF* 53–56); "Grundfragen einer christlichen Ethik" (Basic questions of a Christian ethics), *GS* 5:61ff.; the sermon on 1 Cor. 12:27, *GS* 5:439–46; and finally, his inaugural lecture, "Man [*sic*] in Contemporary Philosophy and Theology," *NRS* 64 (*GS* 3:84).

160 The meaning of infant baptism is something about which only the community of its members can speak.[58] The child is near to what is of the future—the eschata. This too is conceivable only to the faith that suspends itself before revelation. Faith is able to fix upon baptism as the unbreakable Word of God, the eschatological foundation of its life.

Because baptism lies temporally in the past and is, nonetheless, an eschatological occurrence, the whole of my past life acquires seriousness and temporal continuity. It lies between eternity and eternity, founded by means of and 'in reference to' God's Word. And so, my past and that of the Christian community in general is founded, defined, and 'directed' by means of the future that is called forth from it by the Spirit.

Our discussion of the *actus directus*—as something that can never be captured in reflection (I cannot capture the act in myself, not to mention in someone else)—and of infant baptism—as of faith that excludes itself—allows a perspective to open up in which not all roads appear blocked to the eschatology of apocatastasis.[31] [60] And yet, this very talk of apocata-

---

31. Luther states that the *actus directus* can be hidden also under the guise of blasphemies: "cum tales blasphemie, quia sunt violenter a diabolo hominibus invitis extorte, aliquando gratiores sonent in aure dei quam ipsum Alleluja vel quecunque laudis iubilatio" (*Röm. Komm.* 2:227). ("For such blasphemies shall once sound more pleasant in God's ear than even the Hallelujahs or any other hymn of praise, because they have been forced out by the devil against the will of people" [*Lectures on Romans, LW* 25:390, trans. altered]).[59] "Now there are many who have truly laid hold of Christ, even though they do not feel that they have done so; but they are no less justified" (Pontoppidan, [*Der*] *Helle Glaubenspiegel* [*und die Kraft der Wahrheit*], 1726 and 1768,[61] cited in Delitzsch, *A System of Biblical Psychology*, 413).

[58.] This positive inclusion of the child's '*fides directa*' repeals what Bonhoeffer had maintained in *SC* 172. It reverts to something he had come to know from Luther; cf. his student essay, "Luthers Auschauungen vom Heiligen Geist" (Luther's view of the holy spirit), *DBW* 9: 396f.

[59.] Eberhard Bethge relates the following incident in connection with Bonhoeffer's first encounter with Karl Barth in July 1931: "According to the story current among Bonhoeffer's later students, he had quoted at Barth's seminar Luther's saying that the curses of the godless sometimes sound better in God's ear than the hallelujahs of the pious; at this the delighted Barth inquired: 'who had made this contribution?'" (*Dietrich Bonhoeffer: Man of Vision, Man of Courage*,132). Cf. also *GS* 5:225, 265f. and *E* 100.

[60.] "the doctrine of the 'recapitulation of all', the salvation of all" [MR]

[61.] Erik Pontoppidan, 1698–1764, was the founder of the moderate pietism of Denmark and Norway.

stasis may never be more than the sigh of theology whenever it has to speak of faith and unfaith, election and rejection.

In pure orientation towards Christ, there-being [Dasein] and how-being [Wiesein] are restored to their right status. The 'there' is delivered from the violation wrought by the 'how', while conversely the 'how' finds itself anew in the 'there' appointed by God. The echoless cries from solitude into the solitude of self,[62] the protest against violation of any sort, have unexpectedly received a reply and gradually melt into the quiet, prayerful conversation of the child with the father in the Word of Jesus Christ. In the contemplation of Christ, the tormented knowledge of the I's tornness finds 'joyful conscience',[63] confidence, and courage. The servant becomes free.[64] The one [Mann][65] who became an adult in exile and misery becomes a child at home.[66] Home is the community [Gemeinde] of Christ, always 'future', present 'in faith' because we are children of the future—always act, because it is being; always being, because it is act.

This is the new creation of the new human being of the future, which here is an event already occurring in faith, and there perfected for view. It is the new creation of those who no longer look back upon themselves, but only away from themselves to God's revelation, to Christ. It is the new creation of those born from out of the world's confines into the wideness of heaven, becoming what they were or never were, a creature of God, a child.

[62.] Cf. the subsequent use of this motif in "Man [*sic*] in Contemporary Philosophy and Theology," *NRS* 66 (*GS* 3:82); *GS* 5:241; *CF* 72; and *DBWE* 5:155.

[63.] Cf. Luther, "The Large Catechism," *The Book of Concord*, 433 (*WA* 30/1:208); "Psalm 118," *LW* 14:102–3 (*WA* 31/1:176f.) in relation to this term.

[64.] Bonhoeffer will again speak of the connection between the child and Christian freedom in his sermon of July 24, 1932, at the close of the academic year in Berlin, taking as his text John 8:32: "The truth will make you free" (*GS* 4:79–87). Here Bonhoeffer speaks of three "knights of truth"—the child, the fool, and the sufferer. "The child," according to Bonhoeffer, "is able to speak the truth because it is unaware or oblivious [ahnungslos] of what the truth does to people. The child speaks the truth, laughs and is free" (trans. Michael F. Möller). One also might compare his remarks on the child and truth in *E* 363–72. [WF]

[65.] This is only the second time this term, rather than *Mensch* (human being), has been used in *AB*.

[66.] An allusion to Luke 15:11–32.

HANS-RICHARD REUTER

EDITOR'S AFTERWORD
TO THE GERMAN EDITION

I

Act and Being may well be among the least known and understood of Dietrich Bonhoeffer's works. The bewildered reader who takes up this book after having studied his writings of the 1940s—for example, the *Letters and Papers from Prison* or the *Ethics*—may well ask whether we are dealing with one and the same author. Indeed, this very reader, whom Bonhoeffer had impressed as the theological writer of those better known works, may well have the sense when reading *Act and Being* of visiting another planet. Is this the same author who is so capable in his later writings of communicating the terse reality of contemporary Christian existence—which takes place and is borne in suffering—in an unpretentious, precise, authentic language saturated with experience?

This book is a treatise about the problem of method in theology as it had been raised by the movements of theological renewal after World War I, most acutely by 'dialectical theology'. The intelligibility of revelation, faith, and history had once again come to be discussed, following not only the demise of the *homo religiosus*[1] as a species of a disappearing bourgeois world, but also the humiliation of Christianity as a humanizing cultural force, as well as the historical-critical relativization of the documents relating to its origin. Bonhoeffer diagnosed the core of the controversies and the source of theology's conceptual divergencies as originating in the struggle for a *form of thinking* appropriate to revelation, a struggle that, for his part, he traced back to the conflict between

---

[1.] "religious human being" [WF]

interpreting revelation in terms of act or in terms of being. In naming revelation as the crisis of all human exercises of thought, Bonhoeffer showed himself to be a decisive adherent of the new theology of the Word of God. But contrary to Karl Barth's disinterest in clarifying theo- 164 logical concepts philosophically, Bonhoeffer held firm to the belief that theology cannot leave behind general philosophical forms of thought. And, in so doing, he remained the heir to liberal theology that he had always seen himself to be.[2] He wanted to sustain the freedom of theology from philosophy in such a way that theology would not be left fixated negatively on philosophy and left to fall prey to it once again—but this time unawares.

In Bonhoeffer's effort in the present book, which discusses nearly all of the prominent positions of his contemporaries, the reader looks over the shoulder of a young university teaching assistant from Berlin, who treats his demanding material with a mixture of geniality and chutzpa. What is presented—altogether in the style of the sovereign independent thinker—is a philosophical *tour d'horizon*, followed by a theological *tour de force*.[3] It leads us into the rarified air of conceptual abstraction and through the compact, abbreviated formulae of the language of philosophical-theological theories and schools. Whoever tries to replicate these stylized and extremely compressed lines of thought cannot help— as Bonhoeffer himself conceded—but occasionally push against the limits of assured understanding, which no amount of commentary can entirely remove. The free-wheeling, discursive development of Bonhoeffer's thinking is always constrained by the systems that he presents: in rapid succession an apodictic assertion follows on a citation from the literature; argumentative passages of varying stringency are interrupted abruptly by meditative interjections. One may with good reason ask whether the limits of intelligibility of the text are to be blamed solely on the reader's lack of understanding or on the author's unwillingness or inability to convey his subject matter in more detailed arguments as well.

No injustice is done to Bonhoeffer, just twenty-four years old when he completed the manuscript, if one considers now and then the latter possibility. This in no way lessens the respect due to an exercise in thought which, at second glance, is striking because of the sure intuition with 165

[2.] Cf. *LPP* 381.
[3.] As Thomas Day puts it in his *Dietrich Bonhoeffer on Christian Community and Common Sense*, 32.

which the author finds something that is true, or at least worth discussing, even where the supporting argument leaves something to be desired. *Act and Being* justifiably has been characterized as an example of the sort of writing "that one must compose in one's youth if ever one is to have the courage to do it at all."[4]

II

The thematic focus of this study strikes one as downright daring, since, according to its title, it places itself programmatically into the conceptual arena within which the metaphysical outline of the entirety of Western philosophy is to be debated. *Act and Being* shows Bonhoeffer in search of a theological form of thought that would free theology from the remaining hidden premises of metaphysics. According to the scholastic philosophy of the High Middle Ages, God was just act (*actus purus*),[5] nothing but pure being. Thomas Aquinas translated the Aristotelian term for actuality (ἐνέργεια) as *actus purus*. And, as pure reality, pure act was by no means the concept opposite to being, but rather the concept opposite to potentiality as unrealized possibility. As *actus purus* God was first being (*primum ens*) in the sense of the prime mover, because God contains no unrealized possibilities whatsoever—because to realize them God would be dependent on another being. German idealism, in contrast, understood *actus purus* as the free activity of reason [Vernunft] and placed it vis-à-vis being as necessarily existing substance. In Friedrich Schelling's *System des transzendentalen Idealismus*,[6] dating from 1800, we find portrayed the attempt to contrapose the absolute understood as a free act over against Baruch Spinoza's absolute thought of in terms of substance. Transcendental philosophy and ontology were differentiated in that opposition, as were act and being. And act, defined now as the activity of the absolute in the intellectual intuition of self-producing self-consciousness, became a new ontological basic concept.[7]

[4.] Carl Friedrich von Weizsäcker, "Gedanken eines Nichttheologen zur theologischen Entwicklung Dietrich Bonhoeffers" in *Der Garten des Menschlichen*, 465.

[5.] "pure act" [WF]

[6.] "System of transcendental idealism" [WF]

[7.] For the philosophical-historical background and a detailed examination,

It would appear that Bonhoeffer, at least at the time of writing *Act and* 166
Being, had gained his understanding of the basic conceptual constella-
tions of the European tradition from secondary sources. But he fully
understood, as can be seen also from the direction his work takes, the
renewed transformation of idealism into ontology that always places the
ontological point of departure after the transcendental: "Act pointed to
being. Hegel again honored the ontology Kant had dethroned" (59).[8]
In the ascent from the historical dialectic of rest and movement, of act
and being, to the unity of an absolute, a God *an sich*[9] who ultimately
devours time and history, Bonhoeffer sees, in no way unjustly, the sure
criterion for the basic metaphysical form of thinking in which classic
ontology and modern idealism are bound together. Bonhoeffer seeks to
make the thematic of act and being fruitful anew for the interpretation
of reality, which, this time, is not understood metaphysically. He finds
this reality in God's self-binding to the historical revelation in Jesus
Christ; hence Bonhoeffer consistently has repudiated the preeminence
of the category of 'possibility' in theology as a rebirth of the nominalist
potentia Dei absoluta (85).[10]

One should not, therefore, be deceived by the bipolar, systematic
structure of *Act and Being* to think that Bonhoeffer's own reflections are
intended to raise anew the question of legitimate concepts of being in
theology on the basis of a 'genuine ontology'. For example, his characterization of 'genuine transcendentalism' in terms of the concept of act
as 'pure intentionality' makes clear that Bonhoeffer approaches this task
from convictions—inspired by the phenomenological movement—that
are not otherwise immediately apparent (Cf. above, pages 34f., 28–29).
The philosopher Hinrich Knittermeyer, on whose interpretation of Kant
Bonhoeffer had built his case in *Act and Being* against Neo-Kantianism
and idealism, immediately referred to this critically in his review of Bon- 167
hoeffer's book.[11] Bonhoeffer's interest in attaining theologically
responsible concepts of being was likely inspired by two contemporary
authors.

---

cf. Wolfhart Pannenberg, *Akt und Sein im Mittelalter,* as well as Georg Picht, *Akt*
und Sein bei Schelling.

[8.] The numbers in parentheses indicate pages in Bonhoeffer's text above.
[9.] "in itself" [WF]
[10.] "the absolute power of God" [WF]
[11.] Hinrich Knittermeyer, "Rezension," 179f.

The first was the Jesuit father Erich Przywara, whose *Religionsphiloso-phie katholischer Theologie*[12] and its program of the *analogia entis*[13] had created a stir, particularly in the camp of dialectical theology. After an address on "Das katholische Kirchenprinzip,"[14] delivered in February 1929, Przywara laid himself open to discussion in Karl Barth's seminar in Münster. His address appeared immediately in *Zwischen den Zeiten*,[15] the journal of dialectical theology. Przywara was, according to Barth's testimony at the time, "the only truly serious opponent whom I have to fear, . . . a little man who knows how to respond considerately to everything—yes to everything—one says to him, with an answer that somehow is always clever and in some way pertinent to the matter at hand." He was one, in Barth's words, who explained in detail "how, according to his teaching, the loving God, at least within the Catholic church, so inundates human beings with grace that the formula 'God in-above human being from God' constitutes the signature of this man's existence. And this formula signals, at the same time, the resolution of all Protestant and modernistic, transcendentalistic and immanetistic stupidities and distortions into the peace of the *analogia entis*."[16] Bonhoeffer took Przywara's essay "Drei Richtungen der Phänomenologie"[17] as the basis for his presentation of the 'ontological attempt' (59–80). And those who let themselves be affected by the claim of integration made by Przywara in his *Religionsphilosophie*, and presented there with all the virtuosity of sagacious combination,[18] might conclude that Bonhoeffer in *Act and* 168   *Being* had intended to present a similarly constructed project or, at least, intended to contribute to the elaboration of a "philosophical terminol-

---

[12.] (The philosophy of religion of Catholic theology) [WF]

[13.] "analogy of being" [WF]

[14.] (The catholic principle of the church) [WF]

[15.] (Between the times) [WF]

[16.] Karl Barth and Eduard Thurneysen, "Briefwechsel," 2:638, 652.

[17.] (Three trends in phenomenology)

[18.] Which one watches—according to the inimitable portraiture of Barth—"like a squirrel leaping from one treetop to the next, with the Tridentine and Vatican Councils always at hand, Augustine, Thomas, Duns Scotus, Molina, etc. inside and out, and always the church, the church, the church, but precisely the church that revolves full of life and in manifold ways around the fixed pole of the increasingly manifest dogma, the church whose visible unity he himself seems to represent" (Barth and Thurneysen, "Briefwechsel," 652).

ogy proper" to Protestantism,[19] a contribution that could compete with the heritage of Catholic theology.

There was, above all, Martin Heidegger, whose unfinished work, *Sein und Zeit*, published in 1927, intended to raise first and foremost the question that classic ontology had left unanswered, namely the question of the meaning of being. Heidegger posed anew the question of being—led to it by the existential analysis of Dasein[20] as the mode of being of human beings—in order to show time to be the unreflected ground of metaphysics. Presumably Bonhoeffer first familiarized himself with *Sein und Zeit* while he was in Barcelona, at the insistence of his cousin Hans-Christoph von Hase, who was studying in Marburg. Bonhoeffer recognizes that Heidegger succeeded in "forcing together act and being in the concept of Dasein" (71). Heidegger understood his program of philosophy, however, as "universal phenomenological ontology, [which] takes its departure from the hermeneutic of Dasein, which, as analytic of existence, has made fast the guiding-line for all philosophical inquiry at the point where it *arises* and to which it returns."[21] On this basis Bonhoeffer can see himself authorized to critique every way of doing philosophy that leads back to an "autonomous understanding of Dasein," yet without subjecting to this verdict the self-referentiality of the hermeneutic of Dasein expounded in Heidegger's program. Bonhoeffer justly regards as a failure the attempt to expose the temporality of every understanding of being through the analysis of the historicity of Dasein. He takes Heidegger seriously in his fundamental-ontological claim and does not misconstrue him—as did many in those days—as an anthropologist. Whether it was 'consciously atheistic' or not, Bonhoeffer had reason to see in *Sein und Zeit* a 'philosophy of finitude' (72), and to affirm that a "distinctively Christian philosophy of time," capable of distinguishing the present of what is past from the present of what is to come (110f.), would have to be developed from the encounter of the concrete human being with revelation.

169

[19.] Bonhoeffer, "The Theology of Crisis and its Attitude toward Philosophy and Science," *GS* 3:118 [composed in English].

[20.] "human existence" [WF]

[21.] Martin Heidegger, *Being and Time*, 62, 487.

III

Bonhoeffer took a gamble in choosing the genre of an academic qualifying thesis in order to show his colors in the theological discussion of the day by means of a systematic essay that took a definite position. At that time, as well as today, theses of this kind tended to the contrary to elaborate their own interests in the medium of research, reconstruction, and the interpretation of major conceptions of the history of theology. One must concede, however, that the book's chances of a charitable reception were lessened because of its monograph form. Controversies about theoretical foundations were carried out in the theology of that time primarily in lectures, essays, and reviews, which promptly and in rapid succession filled the columns of influential journals. The *Christliche Welt, Theologische Blätter, Zeitschrift für Theologie und Kirche,* and above all, of course, *Zwischen den Zeiten,* had been since the mid-1920s the arena of the sort of fast-moving debate in which Bonhoeffer wanted to intervene. His contemporary from the Grisebach circle in Jena, Hans Michael Müller, characterized the situation in 1928 accurately when he said that "'the' dialectical theology is a phantom. Barth called it into being some time ago. But today its leading proponents are less in agreement in method than the political generals of China."[22] But a book such as *Act and Being,* published a year and a half after its composition and clearly bearing the marks of a flash in the pan, could not place Bonhoeffer among those who on their part could influence the course of the discussion.

If with regard to Barth it could be said aptly that Bonhoeffer "was aiming at a moving target,"[23] then the same holds for his debate with Rudolf Bultmann. The restricted angle of vision that Bonhoeffer brought as a young scholar to the writing of *Act and Being* made it difficult for him to see and explain the extent to which both of these theologians, in their own way, were beginning to correct the initial, actualistic-existentialistic themes of their theology—Barth provoked by discussion with Przywara, and Bultmann stimulated by contact with Heidegger.

Bonhoeffer sensed the danger that Barth's early Neo-Kantian and Platonizing dialectic of time and eternity could dissolve the historicity of human beings as *simul iustus et peccator*[24] into the imperceptible

[22.] Hans Michael Müller, *Credo, ut intelligam,* 175.
[23.] Franklin Sherman, "Act and Being," 105.
[24.] "at the same time justified and sinful" [MR]

supratemporality of a "heavenly double" (99) who endures before God.[25] Accordingly, in his doctoral study, *Sanctorum Communio*, Bonhoeffer had still defended the criticism of Barth that "the dialectic of the so-called dialectical theology" and its antithetical and paradoxical manner of speaking was a theological method that has "a logical, not real character."[26] What was decisive for Bonhoeffer here was that Barth seemed—in thought—to emphasize the singular divinity of God at the expense of the sociality of human beings.[27] Prompted by the publication of Barth's *Christliche Dogmatik im Entwurf* [28] in 1927, Eberhard Grisebach and his school had pushed the methodological critique of Barth to the point of saying that he was "an identity-thinker . . . of a higher order," who presupposes the revelation of God as a principle of cognition in order to be able nonetheless to develop a quasi 'catholic' knowledge of revelation as a system, indirectly within the frame of a self-made dialectical proviso.[29] Although Bonhoeffer notes the unclarity of Barth's concept of dialectic (124, footnote 47), he finds himself in *Act and Being* with the still unresolved doubt as to whether a critique of Barth should best be formulated as a critique of method. A lecture series Barth delivered in the spring of 1929 was of decisive significance here. Under the impact of the discussion with Przywara and his own study of Thomas, Barth in his essay "Schicksal und Idee in der Theologie"[30] was moved to address the subject-object-relation as the "basic problem of all philosophy . . . expressible in a variety of tongues."[31] Bonhoeffer was able to discover his own mode of questioning in this essay. Above all, the

171

[25.] Cf. Bonhoeffer's student paper on "Luthers Anschauung vom Heiligen Geist" (Luther's view of the holy spirit) (*DBW* 9:377), where it is connected with a critique of Luther.

[26.] *DBW* 9:478.

[27.] Cf. *SC* 226, note 47, which refers the reader to Karl Barth, *The Epistle to the Romans*, 451ff. and 492ff.

[28.] (Christian dogmatics in outline)

[29.] Cf. Müller, *Credo, ut intelligam*, 172; also see above, "The Problem," page 25, editorial note 1.

[30.] "Fate and Idea in Theology."

[31.] "I might just as well have said 'reality and truth', or 'nature and spirit', or 'the particular and the general', or 'the given and the non-given', or 'the objective and the non-objective', or 'the conditioned and the unconditioned', or 'being and thinking', or 'heteronomy and autonomy', or 'experience and reason'. I might also have said 'realism and nominalism', or 'romanticism and idealism'" (Barth, "Fate and Idea in Theology," 25).

point to be taken from this work of Barth's was—as Bonhoeffer now concedes—that the "proviso made by dialectical theology is not a logical one that might be canceled by the opposite but, in view of predestination, a real one in each case" (86). For Barth did not let the subject-object dialectic collapse into a conceptually demonstrable third (tertium) but, rather, he allowed it to emerge from "free divine election."[32] This removed him, in Bonhoeffer's eyes, from the accusation that he was engaged in a catholicizing thinking in terms of systems. But it did not clear him of the suspicion that in going behind ontology and idealism he was left with a merely formal understanding of the freedom of God, an understanding which—heavily favoring the side of the concept—places the living God of the Bible once again into the role of the absolute subject (124–25). Bonhoeffer counters by saying that "God is free not from human beings but for them. Christ is the word of God's freedom" (90–91).

In a confrontation with Erik Peterson in 1926, Rudolf Bultmann addressed the task of "deriving genuinely theological concepts from the quest for concepts of being."[33] As compared to the enduring interest shown in the relation between Barth and Bonhoeffer, the systematic affinity of Bonhoeffer to Rudolf Bultmann's theological thought—which in *Act and Being* is hard to deny—has not as a rule had much exposure. In general, this affinity consisted in the fact that Bonhoeffer could completely agree with Bultmann's basic premise that "to speak of God means at the same time to speak of the human being." In *Sanctorum Communio* Bonhoeffer had already appealed to Bultmann against Barth in order to take concrete historical existence seriously.[34] What must have impressed Bonhoeffer in Bultmann's early works was the latter's attempt to differentiate 'the intentionality of faith' towards revelation[35] from the self-reference of the reflecting I, and to do so in such a way that God can be thought of as "the reality which determines our existence."[36] In *Act and Being* Bonhoeffer is convinced that Bultmann suc-

172

[32.] Barth, "Fate and Idea in Theology," 58.

[33.] Rudolf Bultmann, "The Question of a Dialectic Theology: A Discussion with Peterson," 261f.

[34.] *SC* 227, note 47, where Bonhoeffer quotes from Bultmann's *Jesus and the Word*, 115.

[35.] Bultmann, "On the Question of Christology," 119f.

[36.] Bultmann, "What Does It Mean to Speak of God?": "If, looking backward

ceeds through his "concept of historicity" in "conceiv[ing] the continuity of the new I with the total I" (100). Yet it is difficult for Bonhoeffer to reconcile this insight into the limited legitimacy of Bultmann's approach with his own endeavor to keep it firmly within an interpretation of revelation purely in terms of act. The more sharply Bultmann after about 1928 defined his concept of existence and opened it to philosophical discussion, the more apparent became his connection with Heidegger's analysis of Dasein. This in turn had to evoke Bonhoeffer's critique not of the transcendentalistic but of the existential-ontological version of the dominance of the concept of possibility (97, 98, 101). Once again it was a student of Grisebach, the young philosopher and theologian Gerhardt Kuhlmann, who made it necessary for Bultmann to state the relationship between philosophy and theology more precisely, in other words, the relationship between the existential analysis of natural Dasein and the   173
interpretation of faithful existence.[37] The 1930 essay "The Historicity of Man and Faith,"[38] in which Bultmann conclusively lays out his position without giving in to his critics, can have come to Bonhoeffer's attention only when he was revising his manuscript in the United States. Throughout *Act and Being*, however, Bonhoeffer follows the incisive critique of Kuhlmann who, like Karl Löwith,[39] had contested vehemently Bultmann's and Heidegger's view that there could be an existentially-ontologically neutral, that is to say an existentially and ontically unaffected, interpretation of Dasein. As an exegete, Bultmann was not interested in the question of being as such, but in an interpretation that rendered the biblical tradition contemporaneous. He attempted on that basis to ground the possibility that past texts could be understood in a manner foreign to their original setting by appealing to a 'preunderstanding' which was framed as an ontic life-relationship to the subject of which the text speaks. At the same time he wanted to make Heidegger's

---

or forward, I rely on myself, then I split my personality. The relying self is my existential self; the other self on which I rely, taking it as something objective, is a phantom without existential reality. And the existential self, who looks around, who questions, is proved by this very questioning, this looking around, to be godless" (83).

[37.] Cf. Gerhardt Kuhlmann, "Zum theologischen Problem der Existenz."
[38.] Literally, "Faith and the historicity of human existence."
[39.] Karl Löwith, "Phänomenologische Ontologie und protestantische Theologie."

existential analysis fruitful for the methodology of a hermeneutics of the New Testament. In letting 'preunderstanding' hover between ontic experience and ontological analysis, Bultmann consciously kept ontological preconceptions open for correction by existential affects; but in so doing, he ignored the closedness of the existential analysis of Dasein of *Being and Time*, which remains under the spell of metaphysics.[40]

To see the critique of metaphysics as a task of theology does not mean for Bonhoeffer the dismissal of philosophical thought-forms from theological discourse. Thus, the act-being theme not only provides the categories for a critical presentation of metaphysical residues in theology but also points the direction toward the horizon of genuinely Christian thinking. Bonhoeffer tries to retain Bultmann's concerns through his 174 notion of the "necessity of a certain formal 'preunderstanding'." But he relates this entirely to the conceptual-categorical refinement of a question that has to be raised in the context of 'being in Adam', but which must be corrected by revelation and given "an entirely new form" (79, 153). Bonhoeffer attempts to demonstrate in the problem of act and being the continuum of a questioning that is "brought together, surmounted and transcended in an original fashion" (79) only in what the question seeks, only in revelation itself; in this he comprehends—as one might say—the task of philosophy theologically in the *usus elenchticus*.[41]

IV

The young postdoctoral student demonstrated his courage not least of all before the thrones of the learned scholars of Berlin. This holds for the decisiveness with which he announced his intention in *Act and Being*, but even more so for the consistency with which he carried it out. Bonhoeffer indeed incorporated some of the basic positions of his systematics teacher, Reinhold Seeberg, into the flow of the course of his thinking. But while he did so in such a way that Seeberg did not feel that he had fallen entirely by the wayside in respect to the protagonists from Münster, Marburg, and Jena (55ff., 101ff.), Bonhoeffer actually radicalized Seeberg's and Lütgert's semi-critique of idealism. He may have done the latter of his teachers—who took the author of *Being and Time* to be a neo-

---

[40.] Cf. Bultmann, "The Significance of 'Dialectical Theology' for the Scientific Study of the New Testament," and "The Historicity of Man and Faith."

[41.] "use for the purpose of refutation" [WF]

Thomist[42]—a favor, in that he at least placed Heidegger in the perspective of Przywara. But nowhere in the book does Bonhoeffer present himself as the docile pupil; nowhere can one claim that he gleaned sustaining elements for his own reflections from the store of his Berlin teachers' theological thoughts. He used the works of Karl Holl and Seeberg essentially as a treasure trove of quotations, but in order to contradict them radically. Given all the peculiarities attributable to writings of one's youth, the Bonhoeffer of *Act and Being* shows a heightened independence of theological thinking as compared to the author of *Sanctorum Communio*. The swift and sharp critical judgments of *Act and Being* read like a distillation of the contentious spirit that his fellow students observed with a good deal of fascination in Dietrich Bonhoeffer in the course of their studies together.[43] To the extent, however, that the doctoral thesis, *Sanctorum Communio*, itself had still been conceived in the basic categories of Berlin theology, Bonhoeffer's second work signifies a further development of his own approach, which is marked with thoroughly clear accents of self-correction. 175

Certainly the basic idea of the book, namely to identify the joining of act and being in the church as the concretion of revelation, had been prepared in detail in *Sanctorum Communio*. In a combination of phenomenological (Max Scheler) and dialogue-philosophical (Eberhard Grisebach) motifs, Bonhoeffer had developed, on the basis of the concept of person, a theology of sociality that was intended to overcome the constraints on thought imposed by the epistemological schema of subject-object, in favor of a more adequate understanding of reality. Like the concept of spirit, the concept of person was and remained appropriate to the task of joining together the individual and collective aspects of

---

[42.] Cf. Bethge, *Dietrich Bonhoeffer*, 94.

[43.] Cf. the reminiscence of Helmut Goes: ". . . What drew me powerfully to Bonhoeffer was the recognition that here not only was one who learned and took the *verba* (words) and *scripta* (writings) of any of the *magistri* (teachers) into himself, but also here was someone who thought for himself and who already knew what he wanted and quite likely also wanted what he knew. I experienced . . . a young blond student contradicting the revered polyhistorian, his excellency von Harnack, politely but definitely on objective theological grounds. Harnack replied but the student contradicted again and again. I . . . still recall the secret enthusiasm which I sensed for free, critical and independent thinking in theology" (quoted in Bethge, *Dietrich Bonhoeffer*, 45).

human beings. At the same time the concept of person—unlike that of spirit—allowed him to hold on to the boundary that the external other—the You—poses to the I. Similar to Reinhold Seeberg's voluntaristic understanding of God, Bonhoeffer's basic concept of person in the first dissertation, however, still evidenced certain decisionistic and actualistic features as well.[44] And the problem of original sin—for Bonhoeffer presumably the nexus of discovery of the simultaneity of (individual-) act and (species-) being—was still treated in the schema of a monadic representation of the "whole act" in the "individual act."[45]

176

Bonhoeffer begins the movement toward an implicit self-revision of his earlier position through a systematic differentiation of *actus directus* and *actus reflexus*.[46] It permits him to think of the new I in continuity with the old, without making them identical. The theological innovation here consists in no way in the differentiation of the intentionality and reflexivity of faith as such; this also had been taken up—as had been mentioned—by Bultmann in connection with motifs of his teacher Wilhelm Herrmann. Bultmann, however, had developed that distinction in terms of the conceptual pair of *fides qua* and *fides quae creditur*,[47] which had gained prominence in classic Protestant orthodoxy, and thus settled it immediately in the relationship of faith and theology. Bonhoeffer himself reaches back to the equally classic Protestant distinction of *actus directus* and *actus reflectus*, which stems from the doctrine of baptism (158–59). In doing so, he from the beginning (28) points us in the direction he intends to take—the location of the question of the relationship between faith and theology more principally in the relationship of faith and *church*. Bonhoeffer wants to show that the *true* historicity of existence can be identified only in the social context of word and sacrament, in the *concretissimum*[48] of the *actual* church. From such a perspective, Bonhoeffer radically redefines the function of theology as a scholarly discipline, thereby overcoming an individualistic narrowing of the question of the certainty of faith.

Bonhoeffer sees the only chance for theology to escape the Scylla of the circle of reflection and the Charybdis of the madness of objectifica-

---

[44.] *SC* 29f.
[45.] Ibid., 72ff.
[46.] "direct act and reflexive act" [WF]
[47.] "the faith which we believe" and "the faith by which we believe" [WF]
[48.] "utter concreteness" [WF]

tion—and yet remain λόγος τοῦ θεοῦ[49]—in the uncompromising submission of theological knowledge under the authority of the church as *Christus praesens* (125ff.).[50] The presence of Christ in the church's word and sacrament is the present of something always still 'to come', which— precisely when the intentional relation to the one who approaches turns itself into reflexive re-presentation— becomes the present of something always already past (110ff.). Dogmatics, understood as an endeavor of thought, can candidly admit that up to a certain degree it can be nothing but a form of reflection and objectification, if it places itself as "obedient thinking" into the space of the church (132f.), in which alone it can be "placed" "into truth" and "into actuality" (87f., 114–15, 135). Bonhoeffer construes knowledge "in terms of sociological categories" (125) that constrain one to distinguish sharply between believing, preaching, and theological knowledge. In this way Bonhoeffer seeks to avoid the danger that he discerned in Barth's identification of the act of faith with reflection (154) and in Bultmann's identification of faith with the enactment of existence (100f.). The real social relation of the *communio sanctorum*[51] thus replaces all self-establishment and self-relativization by means of methodological prolegomena. "Because theology turns revelation into something that exists, it may be practiced only where the living person of Christ is itself present and can destroy this existing thing or acknowledge it. Therefore, theology must be in immediate reference to preaching, helping its preparation, yet all the while humbly submitting to its 'judgment'" (131). It is clear, of course, that Bonhoeffer wanted his earlier statement that "every Protestant Christian is a theologian" to be understood in a wholly different sense from Emanuel Hirsch's similar assertion.[52] But it is equally clear that the sentence he put forth in *Act and Being*, that "theology is a function of the church" (130), has a thoroughly different meaning than Karl Barth's identical statement.[53] In his

---

[49.] "the word of God" [WF]

[50.] "the present Christ" [WF]

[51.] "communion of saints" [WF]

[52.] Cf. Emanuel Hirsch, *Jesus Christus der Herr*, 42: "Thus it is true what has lately been said mockingly against Protestant Christianity, namely that we Protestant Christians are all theologians."

[53.] Karl Barth, "Die Theologie und der heutige Mensch," 375; cf. *Church Dogmatics*, 1/1:1: "As a theological discipline dogmatics is the scientific *self-examination* of the Christian Church with respect to the content of its distinctive talk about God" [trans. altered, emphasis added].

178 lectures on the church, Bonhoeffer specified the difference: "Theology is a function of this empirical community of God and not of the 'eternal' one."[54] He locates the relativization of all theological thought in the authority of the present community and not, as Barth does, in God's pretemporal choice of grace.

The new concept of theology also leads, however, to a self-distancing from the social-metaphysical and primal-theological premises of the design of *Sanctorum Communio*. Now we read that "There are in theology no ontological categories that are primarily based in creation and divorced" from sin and grace (32). "And so, the idea of creation is unable to provide a basis for the ontological definition of the human being in Christ" (153). Bonhoeffer had made known quite early, and of all places in a seminar study for Karl Holl, his reservations about conscience as the locus where faith is experienced psychologically.[55] In *Act and Being* he radically puts the problem of the certainty of faith back into the sociality of the church's basic processes. Luther's tracts on the sacraments from 1519 are his predominant source of appeal. Here Bonhoeffer relies on the Luther who drew comfort in despair from the remembrance of baptism rather than from the self-examination of subjectivity. On this basis, Bonhoeffer denies in *Act and Being* the self-reflexive certainty of faith that he had still asserted in *Sanctorum Communio* (94, esp. editorial note 20)[56] and retracts the critique stated there of the acceptance of a *fides directa*[57] of the recipient of baptism (158f.).[58] He succeeds thereby also in leaving behind the voluntaristic interpretation of personal relationships in favor of an intentionality understood antecedent to the will. Just as the distinction of 'being in Adam' from 'being in Christ' represents for Bonhoeffer the means for the social interpretation of the justification of the godless, so he perceives in the distinction between *actus directus* and *actus reflexus* the key to a temporal

179 interpretation of the process of faith, which alone allows faith "to rest

---

[54.] *GS* 6:237ff.

[55.] *DBW* 9:34, 391f: "Here conscience, which, to be sure, is 'good' for the Christian, also fails. But is a good conscience not a highly ambiguous phenomenon? Certainly, it remains the basis for everything else, but it is nonetheless not capable of 'sensing' faith." Cf. also *SC* 69ff.

[56.] Cf. *SC* 124.

[57.] "direct, unmediated faith" [WF]

[58.] Cf. *SC* 166–67.

not on psychic experiences but on itself."[59] The temporality of faith is its pure ability "to-let-oneself-be-defined by means of the future" (159). In an ultimate step of reduction, of the "exclusion" (160) of 'consciousness', 'conscience', 'devoutness', and 'religiosity' as anthropological domains of the power of the self and of temptation, *Act and Being* reaches the projected goal which is to clarify "the problem of the child in theology."[60] In his fascination with the figure of the child, Bonhoeffer may have been inspired by ideas of the philosophy of life[61] and Friedrich Nietzsche.[62] As the climax of *Act and Being*, 'the child' is the adoption of a metaphor of the gospel for eschatological existence, mirrored in a social ontology of not-yet-being. It is a symbol of the paradoxical return to the homeland that never was: a new creation.

V

Bonhoeffer's postdoctoral thesis, *Act and Being*, was his second and, at the same time, last publication in the realm of professional academic theology. There followed a "turning from phraseology to reality," according to his own retrospective testimony in the prison letters; yet at the same time Bonhoeffer asserts that he perceived the continuity with his own past as "a great gift."[63] Both comments need to be taken seriously for the interpretation of his work. A few indications must suffice to

180

[59.] *DBW* 9:478, cf. 324.

[60.] *NRS* 38–39 (*GS* 1:53), which Bonhoeffer in 1928 says he would like to pursue "in connection with the problem of consciousness" (39). [WF]

[61.] Cf., for example, Ellen Key, *The Century of the Child*.

[62.] According to Zarathustra's "Discourse on the Three Metamorphoses," it is characteristic of the metamorphoses of the spirit that the spirit, in taking upon itself burdens, turns into a 'camel', in self-liberation from duty into a 'lion' and, in playful innocence, into a 'child'. "But say, my brothers, what is yet possible for the child that was not so even for the lion? Why must the predatory lion still turn into a child? The child is innocence and forgetting, a new beginning, a game, a wheel rolling on its own, a first movement, a holy yes. Yes, my brothers, the game of creation needs the holy yes: the spirit now wills *its* will, the one lost to the world wins *its* world for itself" (Friedrich Nietzsche, *Thus Spoke Zarathustra*, 27, trans. altered). Cf. Nietzsche *Werke in drei Bänden*, 1:212, where in the second of the "Untimely Meditations" Nietzsche speaks of the child, "who plays between the hedges of the past and the future with a blindness that transcends bliss" [trans. WF].

[63.] *LPP* (April 22, 1944), 276.

mark the significance of *Act and Being* for the continuities and changes in Bonhoeffer's theological existence.

Bonhoeffer hardly understood the ecumenical breadth of his theological thought as a contradiction to his self-understanding as a Lutheran theologian. Thus, he can relate without reservation to Hermann Kohlbrügge of the Reformed Church in his attempt at a reformation-like self-cleansing of theology of all remnants of neo-Protestant semi-Pelagianism while, at the same time, depicting his objection against Karl Barth as a classic theological debate on the controversy over *finitum capax seu incapax infiniti*.[64] At the end of his lectures on the history of systematic theology in the twentieth century[65] Bonhoeffer poses the question: "where do we stand?" in a manner specific to his denomination. There, characterizing succinctly what *Act and Being* intended to say, he answers: "It is a matter of shame for today's Lutherans that they do not know at all how to express the Lutheran understanding of revelation by distinguishing it, on the one side, against the substance-thinking of the Catholics and, on the other side, against the actualism of the Reformed tradition."[66] However, Bonhoeffer soon grasps how little substance dogmatically rigid statements of limits—that is to say, phraseology—can actually bear. For if mistaken as a statement about the nature of human beings, the *capax* as well as the *incapax infiniti* both would fall prey to the critique of the concept of possibility.[67] It is, characteristically, the Christology lectures in which Bonhoeffer brings together the illusory opposition in the statement: "*Finitum* capax *infiniti, non per se sed per infinitum!*"[68] However, he does take the liberty later, at the conclusion of his reading of the songs of Nicholas Ludwig von Zinzendorf, to confess: "One dreads the consequences of the *finitum capax infiniti*."[69]

181   In *Act and Being* Bonhoeffer is still preoccupied by the attempt

---

[64.] "whether or not the finite is capable of sustaining the infinite" [WF]. On the discussion among Bonhoeffer's contemporaries, see also Hans Asmussen, "Finitum capax infiniti."

[65.] "Die Geschichte der systematischen Theologie des 20. Jahrhunderts" (The history of systematic theology in the twentieth century), *GS* 5:181–227.

[66.] *GS* 5:226.

[67.] Cf. Bonhoeffer's inaugural lecture, "Man [*sic*] in Contemporary Philosophy and Theology," *NRS* 64ff. (*GS* 3:81).

[68.] "The finite is *capable* of taking up the infinite, not through itself, but through the infinite," *C* 93 (*GS* 3:222).

[69.] Bonhoeffer *WF* (July 31, 1936), 73 (*GS* 2:278).

through criticism and logical argumentation not to provide for, but certainly to point to, revelation in the medium of the philosophical concept. The 'method' of *Act and Being* is one of deconstruction, a procedure which itself has at its root that constructivistic style that can so irritate the reader: all concepts must first be posited in an ambiguous generality (29), with the intention that as things progress they will be made more specific. For his North American audience Bonhoeffer still depicted the relationship between theology and philosophy in a way that may well be read as a description of his own experiment.[70] Yet having returned to the University of Berlin, where as a young instructor he introduced German students to Barth's theology in a comprehensible format during the winter term 1931–32,[71] he declared that "the relation between philosophy and theology requires a new clarification."[72] *Act and Being* seems not to have spoken the last word on this issue but to have pointed out the direction. For Bonhoeffer the transition from the phraseological to the real is at hand. Thus the future director of a preachers' seminary of the Confessing Church begins to inquire about the institutional consequences of his understanding of theology: "Ought it (i.e., theology) separate itself from the association with the university and pursue its subject in its own scholarly-ecclesial schools?"[73]

But above all Bonhoeffer is led by the implications of *Act and Being* toward a christological concentration of his theology, a transition from the "boundary at the margin" to the "boundary at the center."[74] Bon-   182

[70.] "It (i.e. philosophy) must try to think truth with regard to the real existence of man and must see that it is itself an expression of the real existence of man and that by its own power it not only cannot save man, but it cannot even be the crisis of man. By doing so it gives room, as far as it can, for God's revelation, which indeed makes room for itself by itself," *NRS* 372 (*GS* 3:124).

[71.] Before his North American audience, Bonhoeffer had let his own position merge in part indistinguishably into that of Barth. Cf. "The Theology of Crisis and its Attitude toward Philosophy and Science," *GS* 3:110–126 (written by Bonhoeffer in English).

[72.] Bonhoeffer, "Die Geschichte der systematischen Theologie des 20. Jahrhunderts" (The history of systematic theology in the twentieth century), *GS* 5:226; cf. "Thesenfragmente für systematische Seminare" (Fragments of theses for a seminar in systematic theology), *GS* 3:160f.

[73.] Bonhoeffer, "Die Geschichte der systematischen Theologie des 20. Jahrhunderts" (The history of systematic theology in the twentieth century), *GS* 5:226.

[74.] For the first reference on this see *CF/T* 52ff.

hoeffer acquired the thought-construct of 'becoming-other' from Grisebach's dialogism, that is, the overpowering objectification of the I by the
You, both in *Sanctorum Communio* and *Act and Being*, in order to localize
the change of law into gospel at the point where the concrete I, at the
boundary of its autonomy, experiences itself as being placed into truth
and actuality (87f.). But how can the You be protected from fixation as a
heteronomous superpower (89)? And how is 'boundary' permanently
guarded from the misunderstanding that it is merely an invented category that would have to fall prey to the Hegelian argument that it is as
such always mediated and sublated in thought (89)?[75] This can succeed,
obviously, only when 'boundary' is simultaneously thought of as *ground*—
that is to say, when it is no longer *thought of* as ground but is *presupposed*
as true *center*. Taking the concrete You seriously as 'boundary' had
helped Bonhoeffer to an ecclesiological bracketing of theology within
the empirical church. Now the discovery of the boundary as 'center'
leads not only to the sharper distinction between the church and Jesus
Christ, but also allows for a new solution to the problem of how the
human logos of theology might correspond to the divine logos. In his
Christology lectures of 1933, Bonhoeffer discovers in the themes of the
person and work of Jesus Christ the classic case of a question that "can
only be posed scientifically in the setting of the church."[76] Behind this
question, however, there is concealed at the same time—as the question
about the 'counter-logos'[77] to human reason—"scholarly pursuit *kat'*
exochen,"[78] namely the thematization of the basic problem of ontology.
Bonhoeffer now sees the problem of *Act and Being* suspended in the
paradoxical statement of Chalcedon about the divine and human nature
of Jesus Christ ("without confusion, without change," "without division,
without separation"). The philosophical propaedeutic of *Act and Being*
183   can be replaced by the acknowledgment of a conciliar decision of the
church in which the metaphysical form of thought is already destroyed
in nuce and a view on the center of reality is opened up. "The mystery is
left as a mystery and must be understood as such."[79]

[75.] Cf. Bonhoeffer, "Man [*sic*] in Contemporary Philosophy and Theology,"
NRS 59ff. (*GS* 3:73f.); "The Theology of Crisis and its Attitude toward Philosophy and Science," *GS* 3:121f.; and *CC* 29f.
[76.] Bonhoeffer, *CC* 32.
[77.] Ibid., 29.
[78.] Ibid., 28: "*the* scholarly pursuit."
[79.] Ibid., 87–88.

The constant in the development of Bonhoeffer's theology remains—as his subsequent writings bear out—the understanding of faith as *actus directus*, as immediate, intentional orientation.[80] The differentiation of the *actus directus* from the *actus reflexus* manifests itself from now on as a structural principle rich with consequences, which Bonhoeffer retains, albeit in changing terminological instrumentation. It recurs in the "simple obedience" of the disciple in *The Cost of Discipleship*, who sees "always Christ only" and "not Christ *and* the world."[81] It is also in "the new knowledge, fully taken up into the doing, of the reconciliation accomplished in Jesus," which overcomes the splitting of knowledge into good and evil, as one of the *Ethics* fragments puts it.[82] It recurs as well in "the man of the undivided heart," who, in another sketch of the *Ethics*, is set against "the man with two souls."[83] Finally, it is in the "unconscious Christianity" of the prison correspondence, the characteristic of which is "partaking in God's suffering in the life of the world" which calls for a "non-religious interpretation of biblical concepts."[84] Bonhoeffer's life-long foundational theological-hermeneutical objection to Karl Barth—in spite of their growing convergence, particularly in the matter of the christological concentration of theology—is to be explained from this adherence to the original insight of *Act and Being*. Barth's definition of the epistemological bases of his theology in his book on Anselm's argument did, indeed, appear at the same time as *Act and Being*,[85] and it helped Barth cast off the "peculiar crust of Kantian-Platonic concepts,"

184

[80.] Cf. the citations in their chronological sequence: "Man [*sic*] in Contemporary Philosophy and Theology" (1930), *NRS* 65f. (*GS* 3:80f.); "Concerning the Christian Idea of God" (1931), *GS* 3:102; "The Theology of Crisis and its Attitude toward Philosophy and Science" (1931), *GS* 3:124; "Probleme einer theologischen Anthropologie" (The problems of a theological anthropology) (1932/33), *GS* 5:343, 349, 353f.; *TP* (1942), 154 (*GS* 3:443); *LPP* 373. Ernst Feil was the first to point out the persistent difference between *actus directus* and *actus reflexus* in his *The Theology of Dietrich Bonhoeffer*.

[81.] *CD* 87ff., 192; cf. 175ff. (*DBW* 4:69ff., 167; cf. 153ff.).

[82.] *E* 34 (*DBW* 6:320).

[83.] Ibid., 68 (*DBW* 6:67).

[84.] On "unconscious Christianity" see Bonhoeffer's letter (July 27, 1944), *LPP* 373; cf. 380. On "partaking of God's suffering" see Bonhoeffer's letter (July 18, 1944), *LPP* 361–62; cf. 348–49. On "the nonreligious interpretation of biblical concepts" see Bonhoeffer's letter (July 8, 1944), *LPP* 344; cf. 362.

[85.] Karl Barth, *Anselm: Fides quaerens intellectum*.

which had clung to the second edition of his commentary on Romans and the first edition of the *Dogmatics*.[86] And yet, Bonhoeffer finds that "nothing of course in fact has become any less questionable."[87] His respect for Barth's authority was always directed to the man "over and beyond his books,"[88] from which Bonhoeffer gratefully gleaned important insights but before which he consistently maintained the independence of his own theological approach. Although Bonhoeffer seeks to deploy the human forms of thought in a theology of the hidden, so as to protect the *mysterium*, he sees Barth in his theology of revelation as primarily occupied with the attempt to make the human logos into an instance of the divine logos's self-explanation, so as to satisfy still the claims of the age of reflection. Theology is to lead toward the divine mystery as the self-withdrawing center of reality[89] without babbling out its eternally given truth in ways that belong to the playground of logic. Given this basic difference between Bonhoeffer and Barth, however it is assessed, the later verdict on Barth's "positivism of revelation" is anything but surprising.[90]

When one sees the continuity by which Bonhoeffer manifests the structural principle developed in *Act and Being*, the change in his horizons of interpretation and experience, through which the principle becomes manifest, show up so much more clearly. This change is more

185 than a mere variation of terminology; it is also something other than the changeable development of a principle that itself always remains the same. In this change there is mirrored, in the medium of theological reflection, the enactment of Dietrich Bonhoeffer's own historical existence in the interplay of biography and contemporary history. In his critique of the omnipotence of consciousness, Bonhoeffer proves himself to be not only a modern Lutheran revisionist who reformulates Luther's problem of the existence of the heteronomous, moral conscience into a

---

[86.] Karl Barth *Credo*, 185. In the great *Dogmatics*, which began to appear in 1938, Barth criticized himself for moving from "the subjective possibility of revelation to the description and valuation of its reality" instead of, conversely, having understood revelation "simply in its reality, and only then, and on that basis, in its possibility" (*Church Dogmatics* 1/2:205f).

[87.] Bonhoeffer, *NRS* (December 25, 1931), 141 (*GS* 1:26).

[88.] Bonhoeffer, *NRS* (July 24, 1931), 121 (*GS* 1:19).

[89.] "God is transcendent in the midst of life" (*LPP* 282, trans. altered). "The God who is with us is the God who forsakes us" (*LPP* 360).

[90.] *LPP* 280, 286, 329.

fundamental critique of conscience itself as an autonomous function of the I. One may well inquire whether in his struggle against the solipsistic claim of autonomy on the part of subjectivity Bonhoeffer did not also work against a temptation which he had himself experienced as a representative of just this autonomous form of consciousness, and which is to be regarded as the subjective factor in his merciless destruction of all philosophical self-understanding.[91] But that is not where it finally ended. Of course, the individualistic striving for the dominance of the self-empowered subjectivity is broken in the "obedience" of "discipleship"; but the socially related, responsible self discovers its "strength"—in "resistance" up to the point of "surrender." The "I" becomes the "child," the "child" becomes the "disciple" and the "disciple" experiences liberation into "maturity." That Bonhoeffer carried out this dialectic of modern self-consciousness not in a system but rather in life as a Christian and a contemporary—therein lies the compelling seriousness of his existential theology.

[91.] On the psychodynamic aspect of the development of Bonhoeffer's theology, see Clifford J. Green, *The Sociality of Christ and Humanity*.

CHRONOLOGY OF
ACT AND BEING

4 February 1906
Dietrich Bonhoeffer and his twin sister, Sabine, born in Breslau, Germany

1912
Dietrich's father, Karl Bonhoeffer, called to the Friedrich Wilhelm University, Berlin

1913
Bonhoeffer begins gymnasium studies

28 April 1918
Dietrich's brother, Walter, dies in World War I

1921
Bonhoeffer is confirmed at Grunewald Church, Berlin

1922
Publication of the second edition of Karl Barth's *Der Römerbrief*

Summer semester 1923
Bonhoeffer begins year of theological study at the University of Tübingen; attends lectures by Karl Groos on logic and the history of modern philosophy and joins Groos's seminar on Kant's *Critique of Pure Reason*

June 1924–July 1927
Bonhoeffer's theological studies at the University of Berlin

Summer 1924
Bonhoeffer attends Heinrich Maier's lectures on epistemology

1924
Publication of Eberhard Grisebach's *Die Grenzen des Erziehers und seine Verantwortung*

February 1926
Bonhoeffer's student essay, "Luthers Anschauungen vom Heiligen Geist"

1927
Publication of Karl Barth's *Christliche Dogmatik im Entwurf,* Rudolf Bultmann's "Zur Frage der Christologie," Erich Przywara's *Religionsphilosophie katholischer Theologie,* and Martin Heidegger's *Sein und Zeit*

17 December 1927
Bonhoeffer receives licentiate in theology; *Sanctorum Communio,* his doctoral dissertation, is accepted by Reinhold Seeberg at the University of Berlin

1928
Publication of Erich Przywara's "Drei Richtungen der Phänomenologie," Hans Michael Müller's "Credo, ut intelligam. Kritische Bemerkungen zu Karl Barths Dogmatik," and Eberhard Grisebach's *Gegenwart: Eine kritische Ethik*

15 February 1928–February 1929
Bonhoeffer serves as curate for German congregations in Barcelona; he first reads Heidegger's *Sein und Zeit*

February 1929
Erich Przywara's lecture, "Das katholische Kirchenprinzip"

Spring 1929
Karl Barth's lecture series, "Schicksal und Idee in der Theologie"

1929–1930
Bonhoeffer serves as *Voluntärassistent* to Wilhelm Lütgert at Berlin; *Act and Being* written during summer semester 1929 and winter semester 1929–1930

February 1930
Bonhoeffer's deadline at Berlin to finish *Act and Being*

Summer 1930
Bonhoeffer's oral *Habilitation* examinations at Berlin and his church examinations leading toward ordination

12 July 1930
Acceptance of *Act and Being,* Bonhoeffer's *Habilitationsschrift* or qualifying thesis, at the University of Berlin

31 July 1930
Bonhoeffer's inaugural lecture at Berlin, "Humanity in Contemporary Philosophy and Theology"

September 1930
Publication of *Sanctorum Communio*

5 September 1930–1931
Post-graduate year at Union Theological Seminary, New York; Bonhoeffer reads Rudolf Bultmann's "Die Geschichtlichkeit des Daseins und der Glaube" (1930); publication of Paul Tillich's *Religiöse Verwirklichung*

1931
Bonhoeffer's essay "Concerning the Christian Idea of God" and his lecture "The Theology of Crisis and its Attitude toward Philosophy and Science"

July 1931
Bonhoeffer meets Karl Barth for the first time in Bonn

1 August 1931
Bonhoeffer begins his post as lecturer on the theological faculty of the University of Berlin

September 1931
Publication of *Act and Being* by C. Bertelsmann Verlag

October 1931
Bonhoeffer appointed chaplain at Technical College in Charlottenburg

11 November 1931
Bonhoeffer's ordination at St. Matthias Church, Berlin

Winter semester 1931–1932
Bonhoeffer's Berlin lectures on "Die Geschichte der systematischen Theologie des 20. Jahrhunderts" and his seminar "Die Idee der Philosophie und die protestantische Theologie"

Winter semester 1932–1933
Bonhoeffer's Berlin lectures on "Schöpfung und Sünde" and his seminar, "Probleme einer theologischen Anthropologie"

30 January 1933
Adolf Hitler made chancellor of Germany

1933
Reviews of *Act and Being* by Heinz Erich Eisenhuth in *Theologische Literaturzeitung* and by Hinrich Knittermeyer in *Zwischen den Zeiten*

Summer 1933
Bonhoeffer's final lecture course at Berlin on "Christologie" and his final seminar on "Hegel"

1956
Publication of *Act and Being* by Christian Kaiser Verlag

BIBLIOGRAPHY

1. Literature Used by Bonhoeffer

Barth, Karl. "Bemerkungen zu Hans Michael Müllers Lutherbuch" (Comments on Hans Michael Müller's Luther book). *Zwischen den Zeiten* 7 (1929):561–70.

——. *Die christliche Dogmatik im Entwurf* (Christian dogmatics in outline). 1: *Die Lehre vom Worte Gottes: Prolegomena zur christlichen Dogmatik* (The doctrine of the Word of God: Prolegomena to Christian dogmatics). Munich, 1927. *NL* 3 B 9. Also published in *Gesamtausgabe* (Collected works), 2 (1927). Edited by G. Sauter. Zürich, 1982.

——. *Der Römerbrief.* 2d ed. of the new, rev. ed. of 1922. Munich, 1923. English translation: *The Epistle to the Romans.* Translated from the 6th German ed. by Edwin C. Hoskins. London, 1933, 1960.

——. "Schicksal und Idee in der Theologie." *Zwischen den Zeiten* 7 (1929):309–48. Also published in his *Theologische Fragen und Antworten*, 54–92. Vol. 3 of his *Gesammelte Vorträge*. Zollikon, 1957. English translation: "Fate and Idea in Theology." In *The Way of Theology in Karl Barth: Essay and Comments*, 25–61. Edited by H. Martin Rumscheidt. Allison Park, Pa.: Pickwick Publications, 1986.

——. "Das Schriftprinzip der reformierten Kirche" (The scriptural principle in the Reformation church). *Zwischen den Zeiten* 3 (1925):215–45.

Bartmann, Bernhard. *Lehrbuch der Dogmatik* (Textbook of dogmatics). 2 vols. Freiburg in Breisgau, 1923. *NL* 6 B 3.

Brunstäd, Friedrich. *Die Idee der Religion: Prinzipien der Religionsphilosophie* (The idea of religion: Principles of the philosophy of religion). Halle, 1922.

Bultmann, Rudolf. "Die Bedeutung der 'dialektischen Theologie' für die neutestamentliche Wissenschaft." *Theologische Blätter* 7 (1928): 57–67. *NL* 3 A 2. Also published in his *Glauben und Verstehen*, vol. 1, 114–33. Tübingen, 1933. English translation: "The Significance of 'Dialectical Theology' for the Scientific Study of the New Testament." In *Faith and Understanding*, 145–64. Edited by Robert W. Funk, translated by Louise Pettibone Smith. Philadelphia: Fortress Press, 1987.

———. "Die Frage der 'dialektischen' Theologie. Eine Auseinandersetzung mit Erik Peterson." *Zwischen den Zeiten* 4 (1926): 40–59. Also published in *Anfänge der dialektischen Theologie*, vol. 2, 72–92. Edited by Jürgen Moltmann. *Theologische Bücherei* (Theological library), vol. 17. Munich,1967. English translation: "The Question of a Dialectic Theology: A Discussion with Peterson." In *The Beginnings of Dialectic Theology*, 257–74. Edited by James M. Robinson, translated by Keith R. Crim and Louis De Grazia. Richmond: John Knox Press, 1968.

———. "Zur Frage der Christologie." *Zwischen den Zeiten* 5 (1927): 41–69. Also published in his *Glauben und Verstehen*, vol. 1, 85–113. Tübingen,1933. English translation: "On the Question of Christology." In *Faith and Understanding*, 116–44. Edited by Robert W. Funk, translated by Louise Pettibone Smith. Philadelphia: Fortress Press, 1987.

———. "Die Geschichtlichkeit des Daseins und der Glaube. Antwort an Gerhardt Kuhlmann." *Zeitschrift für Theologie und Kirche*. New series 11 (1930): 339–64. Also published in *Heidegger und die Theologie*, 72–94. Edited by G. Noller. *Theologische Bücherei* (Theological library), vol. 38. Munich, 1967. English translation: "The Historicity of Man and Faith." In *Existence and Faith: Shorter Writings of Rudolf Bultmann*, 92–110. Edited by Schubert M. Ogden. Cleveland: World Publishing Company, 1960.

———. "Welchen Sinn hat es, von Gott zu reden?" *Theologische Blätter* 4 (1925):129–35. Also published in his *Glauben und Verstehen*, vol. 1, 26–37. Tübingen, 1933. English translation: "What Does It Mean to Speak of God?" In *Faith and Understanding*, 53–65. Edited by Robert W. Funk, translated by Louise Pettibone Smith. Philadelphia: Fortress Press, 1987.

Cohen, Hermann. *Logik der reinen Erkenntnis* (The logic of pure knowledge). Vol. 1 of *System der Philosophie* (System of philosophy). Berlin, 1902.

Delitzsch, Franz. *System der biblischen Psychologie*. Leipzig, 1855. English translation: *A System of Biblical Psychology*. Translated by Robert Ernest Wallis. Edinburgh: T. & T. Clark, 1890.

Dilthey, Wilhelm. "Beiträge zur Lösung der Frage vom Ursprung unseres Glaubens an die Realität der Außenwelt und seinem Recht" (1890) (Contributions to the solution to the question of the origin of our faith in the reality of the exterior world and its legitimacy). In his *Gesammelte Schriften* (Collected works) 5/1:90–138. Leipzig/Berlin, 1924.

Ehrlich, Walter. *Kant und Husserl: Kritik der transzendentalen und der phänomenologischen Methode* (Kant and Husserl: A critique of transcendental and phenomenological method). Halle, 1923.

Fichte, Johann Gottlieb. *Sämmtliche Werke* (Collected works). Edited by I. H. Fichte. Berlin, 1845/1846; reprinted 1965.

Geyser, Johannes. *Max Schelers Phänomenologie der Religion nach ihren wesentlichen Lehren allgemeinverständlich dargestellt und beurteilt* (Max Scheler's phenomenology of religion, according to its essential teachings as understood, portrayed, and assessed for the general reader). Freiburg in Breisgau, 1924.

———. *Neue und alte Wege der Philosophie: Eine Erörterung der Grundlagen der Erkenntnis im Hinblick auf Edmund Husserls Versuch ihrer Neubegründung* (New and old ways of philosophy: A discussion of the fundamentals of knowledge in view of Edmund Husserl's search for new foundations). Münster i. W., 1916.

Gogarten, Friedrich. *Ich glaube an den dreieinigen Gott: Eine Untersuchung über Glauben und Geschichte* (I believe in the triune God: An investigation into faith and history). Jena, 1926. *NL* 3 B 29.

———. "Das Problem einer theologischen Anthropologie" (The problem of a theological anthropology). *Zwischen den Zeiten* 7 (1929): 493–511.

———. "Theologie und Wissenschaft: Grundsätzliche Bemerkungen zu Karl Holls 'Luther'" (Theology and science: fundamental comments to Karl Holl's 'Luther'). *Christliche Welt* 38 (1924):34–42, 71–80.

———. *Theologische Tradition und theologische Arbeit: Geistesgeschichte oder Theologie?* (Theological tradition and theological work: History of ideas or theology?). Leipzig,1927.

Grisebach, Eberhard. *Gegenwart: Eine kritische Ethik* (The present: A critical ethic). Halle, 1928.

——. *Die Grenzen des Erziehers und seine Verantwortung* (The boundaries of teachers and their responsibility). Halle, 1924.

Hartmann, Nicolai. *Grundzüge einer Metaphysik der Erkenntnis* (Basic features of a metaphysics of knowledge). Berlin/Leipzig, 1925.

Hegel, Georg Wilhelm Friedrich. *Enzyklopädie der philosophischen Wissenschaften im Grundrisse* (1830). Edited by G. Lasson. Leipzig, 1905. English translation: *Encyclopedia of the Philosophical Sciences in Outline.* Translated by Steven A. Taubeneck. In *Encyclopedia of the Philosophical Sciences in Outline, and Other Philosophical Writings.* Edited by Ernst Behler. Continuum, 1990.

——. *Vorlesungen über die Geschichte der Philosophie. Werke,* vols. 13–15. Edited by K. L. Michelet. Berlin, 1833–36. English translation: *Hegel's Lectures on the History of Philosophy.* 3 vols. Translated by E. S. Haldane and Francis H. Simon. London: Routledge and Paul, 1968.

Heidegger, Martin. *Sein und Zeit.* Halle, 1927. English translation: *Being and Time.* Translated by John Macquarrie and Edward Robinson. London: SCM Press, 1962.

Hirsch, Emanuel. *Die idealistische Philosophie und das Christentum: Gesammelte Aufsätze* (Idealist philosophy and Christianity: Collected essays). *Studien des apologetischen Seminars in Wernigerode* (Studies of apologetical seminars in Wernigerode), vol. 14. Gütersloh, 1926. *NL* 3 B 37.

——. *Jesus Christus der Herr: Theologische Vorlesungen* (Jesus Christ the Lord: Theological lectures). Göttingen, 1926. *NL* 3 B 39.

Holl, Karl. "Gogartens Lutherauffassung: Eine Erwiderung" (Gogarten's view of Luther: A reply). *Christliche Welt* 38 (1924): 307–14.

——. *Luther.* Vol. 1 of *Gesammelte Aufsätze zur Kirchengeschichte.* Tübingen, 1923. English translation: *What Did Luther Understand by Religion?* Edited by James Luther Adams and Walter F. Bense, translated by Fred W. Meuser and Walter R. Wietzke. Philadelphia: Fortress Press, 1977.

Hollatz, David. *Examen theologicum acroamaticum universam theologiam theticopolemicam complectens* (1707) (A consideration of theological issues including polemical theology). Leipzig, 1763; reprinted in Darmstadt, 1971.

Husserl, Edmund. *Ideen zu einer reinen Phänomenologie und phänomenologischen Philosophie: Allgemeine Einführung in die reine Phänomenologie.* Halle, 1922. *NL* 7 A 31. English translation: *Ideas: General Introduction to Pure Phenomenology*. Translated by W. R. Boyce Gibson. New York: Collier Books, 1962.

——. *Logische Untersuchungen*. 2 vols. Halle, 1922. English translation: *Logical Investigations*. 2 vols. Translated by J. N. Findlay. New York: Humanities Press, 1970.

Jacob, Günter. *Der Gewissensbegriff in der Theologie Luthers* (The concept of conscience in the theology of Luther). In *Beiträge zur historischen Theologie* (Contributions to historical theology), vol. 4. Tübingen, 1928.

Kattenbusch, Ferdinand. "Der Quellort der Kirchenidee" (The origin of the idea of the church). In *Festgabe von Fachgenossen und Freunden: A. von Harnack zum 70. Geburtstag dargebracht* (Commemorative volume from faculty colleagues and friends: For Adolf von Harnack on his 70th birthday), 143–72. Edited by K. Holl. Tübingen,1921.

Knittermeyer, Hinrich. "Philosophie der praktischen Vernunft" (The philosophy of practical reason). *Zwischen den Zeiten* 7 (1929): 349–66.

——. *Die Philosophie und das Christentum* (Philosophy and Christianity). Jena, 1927. *NL* 7 A 47.

——. "Transzendentalphilosophie und Theologie: Eine kritische Erinnerung zum 22. April 1924" (Transcendental philosophy and theology: A critical memory of April 22, 1924). *Christliche Welt* 38 (1924): 220–26, 258–67, 354–61, 408–13.

Kohlbrügge, Hermann Friedrich. *Das siebente Kapitel des Briefes Pauli an die Römer in ausführlicher Umschreibung* (The seventh chapter of Paul's letter to the Romans in detailed description). Elberfeld, 1839. Reprinted as *Biblische Studien*, vol. 28. Edited by A. de Quervain. Neukirchen,1960.

Kuhlmann, Gerhardt. "Zum theologischen Problem der Existenz: Fragen an Rudolf Bultmann" (On the theological problem of existence: Questions to Rudolf Bultmann). *Zeitschrift für Theologie und Kirche*. New series 10 (1929): 28–58. Also published in *Heidegger und die Theologie* (Heidegger and theology), 33–58. Edited by G. Noller. *Theologische Bücherei* (Theological library), vol. 38. Munich, 1967.

Löwith, Karl. "Phänomenologische Ontologie und protestantische Theologie" (Phenomenological ontology and Protestant theology). *Zeitschrift für Theologie und Kirche*. New series 11 (1930):365–99. Also published in *Heidegger und die Theologie* (Heidegger and theology),

95–124. Edited by G. Noller. *Theologische Bücherei* (Theological library), vol. 38. Munich, 1967.

Lütgert, Wilhelm. *Die Religion des deutschen Idealismus und ihr Ende* (The religion of German idealism and its end). Vol. 1: *Die religiöse Krisis des deutschen Idealismus* (The religious crisis of German idealism). Gütersloh, 1923.

Luther, Martin. *Briefwechsel* (Correspondence). 19 vols. Edited by E. L. Enders. Frankfurt and Stuttgart, 1884ff.

——. "Daß diese Wort Christi 'Das ist mein leib' noch fest stehen" (1527), *WA* 23:64–283. English translation: "That These Words of Christ, 'This is my Body', etc., Still Stand Firm against the Fanatics" (1527), *LW* 37:13–150.

——. *De servo arbitrio*, *WA* 18:600–787. English translation: *The Bondage of the Will* (1525). *LW* 33:3–295.

——. *Dictata super Psalterium* (1513–16), *WA* 3 and 4. English translation: *First Lectures on the Psalms* (1513–16). *LW* 10 and 11.

——. "Ein Sermon von der Bereitung zum Sterben" (1519), *WA* 2:685–97. English translation: "A Sermon on Preparing to Die" (1519), *LW* 42:99–115.

——. "Ein Sermon von dem hochwürdigen Sakrament des heiligen wahren Leichnams Christi und von den Bruderschaften" (1519), *WA* 2:738–58. English translation: "The Blessed Sacrament of the Holy and True Body of Christ, and the Brotherhoods" (1519), *LW* 35/1:49–73.

——. "Ein Sermon von dem Sakrament der Buße" (1519), *WA* 2:714–23. English translation: "The Sacrament of Penance" (1519), *LW* 35:9–22.

——. "Ennarrationes in Psalmos" (1532), *WA* 40/2:315–470. English translation: "Commentary on Psalm 51," *LW* 12:303–410.

——. *Kommentar zum Galaterbrief*, *WA* 40/1:34–688 and 40/2:1–184. English translation: *Lectures on Galatians* (1535), *LW* 26:4–358 and 27:4–149.

——. "Operationes in Psalmos," *WA* 5:20–74. English translation: "Preface from Works on the First Twenty-two Psalms" (1519–22), "Commentary on Psalm 1" and "Commentary on Psalm 2," *LW* 14:280–349.

——. "Tessaradecas consolatoria pro laborantibus et oneratis" (1520), *WA* 6:104–34. English translation: "Fourteen Consolations for Those who Labor and are Heavy Laden" (1520), *LW* 42:121–66.

——. *Vorlesung über den Römerbrief 1515/1516.* Edited by J. Ficker. Vol. 1 of *Anfänge der reformatorischen Bibelauslegung.* Part 1: Die Glosse; Part 2: Die Scholien. Leipzig, 1925. *NL* 1 D 24. English translation: *Lectures on Romans, LW* 25. "Glosses": chaps. 1–2 trans. Walter G. Tillmanns, chaps. 3–16 trans. Jacob A. O. Preus; "Scholia": chaps. 1–2 trans. Walter G. Tillmanns, chaps. 3–15 trans. Jacob A. O. Preus.

——. *Werke: Kritische Gesamtausgabe (Weimarer Ausgabe).* Weimar, 1883ff. English translation: *Luther's Works.* Vols. 1–30 edited by Jaroslav Pelikan. Vols. 31–55 edited by Helmut Lehmann. St. Louis: Concordia; Philadelphia: Muhlenberg Press and Fortress Press, 1957–67.

Müller, Hans Michael. "*Credo, ut intelligam.* Kritische Bemerkungen zu Karl Barths Dogmatik" (I believe, that I may understand: Critical observations on Karl Barth's dogmatics). *Theologische Blätter* 7 (1928): 167–76.

——. *Erfahrung und Glaube bei Luther* (Experience and faith according to Luther). Leipzig, 1929.

Natorp, Paul. *Vorlesungen über Praktische Philosophie* (Lectures on practical philosophy). Erlangen, 1925.

Piper, Otto. *Theologie und reine Lehre: Eine dogmatische Grundlegung von Wesen und Aufgabe protestantischer Theologie* (Theology and pure doctrine: A dogmatic foundation of the essence and task of Protestant theology). Tübingen, 1926. *NL* 3 B 56.

Pontoppidan, Erik. *Der helle Glaubensspiegel und die Kraft der Wahrheit* (The clear mirror of faith and the power of truth). Copenhagen and Leipzig, 1727.

Przywara, Erich. "Drei Richtungen der Phänomenologie" (Three trends in phenomenology). *Stimmen der Zeit* 115 (1928): 252–64.

——. *Religionsbegründung: Max Scheler–J. H. Newman* (Religious foundations: Max Scheler and J. H. Newman). Freiburg in Breisgau, 1923.

——. *Religionsphilosophie katholischer Theologie* (The philosophy of religion of Catholic theology). Sonderausgabe aus dem *Handbuch der Philosophie* (Special edition of the handbook of philosophy). Munich/Berlin, 1927. *NL* 7 B 20.

——. *Ringen der Gegenwart: Gesammelte Aufsätze 1922–1927* (The struggles of the present: Collected essays 1922–1927). 2 vols. Augsburg, 1929. *NL* 6 B 35.

Riehl, Alois. *Der philosophische Kritizismus und seine Bedeutung für die positive Wissenschaft.* 2 vols. Leipzig, 1876–87. English translation: *The*

Principles of the Critical Philosophy: Introduction to the Theory of Science and Metaphysics. Translated by Arthur Fairbanks. London: K. Paul, Trench, Trubner, & Co., Ltd., 1894.

Scheler, Max. *Der Formalismus in der Ethik und die materiale Wertethik: Neuer Versuch der Grundlegung eines ethischen Personalismus.* Halle, 1921. *NL* 4.42. English translation: *Formalism in Ethics and Non-Formal Ethics of Values: A New Attempt toward the Foundation of an Ethical Personalism.* Translated by Manfred S. Frings and Roger L. Funk. Northwestern University Press, 1973.

———. *Vom Ewigen im Menschen.* Vol. 1, *Religiöse Erneuerung.* Leipzig, 1921. English translation: *On the Eternal in Man.* Translated by Bernard Noble. London: SCM Press, 1960; New York: Harper, 1961 [Archon Books edition, 1972].

Schmidt, Traugott. *Der Leib Christi: Eine Untersuchung zum urchristlichen Gemeindegedanken* (The body of Christ: An investigation into early Christian understandings of the community of faith). Leipzig/Erlangen, 1919.

Schumann, Friedrich Karl. *Der Gottesgedanke und der Zerfall der Moderne* (The idea of God and the decline of modernity). Tübingen, 1929.

Seeberg, Erich. *Luthers Theologie: Motive und Ideen* (Luther's theology: Themes and ideas). Vol. 1, *Die Gottesanschauung* (Vol. 1: The view of God). Göttingen, 1929.

Seeberg, Reinhold. *Christliche Dogmatik* (Christian dogmatics). Vol. 1, *Religionsphilosophisch-apologetische und erkenntnistheoretische Grundlegung* (Foundations in the philosophy of religion, apologetics, and epistemology). Erlangen and Leipzig, 1924. Vol. 2, *Die spezielle christliche Dogmatik* (The uniquely Christian dogmatics). Erlangen and Leipzig, 1925.

———. "Gewissen" (Conscience). *Die Religion in Geschichte und Gegenwart* (second series) 2 (1928): 1164–1169.

———. *Lehrbuch der Dogmengeschichte.* Vol. 3, *Dogmengeschichte des Mittelalters.* Leipzig, 1913. *NL* 2 C 4.44. English translation: *Textbook of the History of Doctrines.* 2 vols. in 1. Translated by Charles E. Hay. Grand Rapids: Baker Book House, 1956.

Stoker, Hendrik Gerhardus. *Das Gewissen. Erscheinungsformen und Theorien* (The conscience: Forms of appearance and theories). Vol. 2 of *Schriften zur Philosophie und Soziologie* (Writings on philosopy and sociology). Bonn, 1925.

Thomas Aquinas. *De ente et essentia.* Edited by L. Baur. Münster, 1926. English translation: *On Being and Essence.* Translated by Armand Maurer. 2d rev. ed. Toronto: Pontifical Institute of Medieval Studies, 1991.

Tillich, Paul. *Religiöse Verwirklichung* (Religious fulfillment). Berlin, 1930. Chapters 1, 2, 3, 7, and 8 translated in *The Protestant Era.* London: Nisbet & Co., 1951; chapters 5 and 6 translated in *The Interpretation of History.* New York: Charles Scribner's Sons, 1936.

Windelband, Wilhelm. *Die Geschichte der neueren Philosophie in ihrem Zusammenhange mit der allgemeinen Kultur und den besonderen Wissenschaften* (The history of recent philosophy in its connection with general culture and specific sciences). 2 vols. Leipzig, 1922. *NL* 7 A 93.

Winkler, Robert. *Phänomenologie und Religion: Ein Beitrag zu den Prinzipienfragen der Religionsphilosophie* (Phenomenology and religion: An article on the principal questions of the philosophy of religion). Tübingen, 1921.

2. Literature Consulted by the Editors

Adorno, Theodor W. *Negative Dialectics.* Translated by E. B. Ashton. New York: Seabury Press, 1973.

Althaus, Paul. "Theologie des Glaubens" (Theology of faith). *Zeitschrift für Systematische Theologie* 2 (1924): 281–323. Also published in his *Theologische Aufsätze* (Theological essays), vol. 1, 74–118. Gütersloh, 1929.

Althaus, Paul, Gerhard Kittel, and Hermann Strathmann. "Adolf Schlatter und Wilhelm Lütgert zum Gedächtnis" (In memory of Adlolf Schlatter and Wilhelm Lütgert). Vol. 40, no. 1 of *Beiträge zur Förderung christlicher Theologie* (Contributions to the advancement of Christian theology). Gütersloh, 1938.

Anselm of Canterbury. *Cantuariensis archiepiskopi opera omnia* (Complete works of the Archbishop of Canterbury), vol. 1, part 7. Edited by Franciscus Salesius Schmitt. 1938. English translation: *Anselm of Canterbury,* 4 vols. Edited and translated by Jasper Hopkins and Herbert Richardson. Toronto and New York: Edwin Mellen Press, 1974–76.

Asmussen, Hans. "Finitum capax infiniti" (The finite is capable of the infinite). *Zwischen den Zeiten* 5 (1927): 70–81.

Augustine, Saint. *Schriften gegen die Pelagianer,* vol. 1. Edited by A. Kunzelmann and A. Zumkeller. Würzburg, 1971. English translation: *Saint Augustine: Anti-Pelagian Works.* Vol. 5 of *Nicene and Post-Nicene Fathers.*

Edited by Philip Schaff. New York: The Christian Literature Company, 1887.

Barth, Karl. *Credo: Die Hauptprobleme der Dogmatik dargestellt im Anschluß an das Apostolische Glaubensbekenntnis.* Munich, 1935. English translation: *Credo.* Translated by J. Strathearn McNab. New York: Scribner, 1962; 1st ed. 1936.

———. *Fides Quaerens Intellectum: Anselms Beweis der Existenz Gottes im Zusammenhang seines theologischen Programms* (1931). Also published in his *Gesamtausgabe,* vol. 2 (1931). Edited by Eberhard Jüngel and I. U. Dalferth. Zürich, 1981. English translation: *Anselm: Fides Quaerens Intellectum.* London: SCM Press; Richmond: John Knox Press, 1960 [Pittsburgh: Pickwick Press, 1985].

———. "Kirche und Theologie." *Zwischen den Zeiten* 4 (1926): 18–40. English translation: "Church and Theology." In *Theology and Church: Shorter Writings, 1920–1928,* 286–306. London: SCM Press, 1962.

———. *Die Kirchliche Dogmatik.* 4 vols. Munich and Zürich, 1932ff. English translation: *Church Dogmatics.* 4 vols. Edinburgh: T. & T. Clark, 1936–69.

———. "Die Theologie und der heutige Mensch" (Theology and contemporary humanity). *Zwischen den Zeiten* 8 (1930): 374–96.

Barth, Karl, and Eduard Thurneysen. "Briefwechsel 2: 1921–1930" (Correspondence 2: 1921–1930). In Karl Barth, *Gesamtausgabe* (Collected works), 5 (1921–1930). Edited by E. Thurneysen. Zürich, 1974. English translation: Excerpts in *Revolutionary Theology in the Making.* Edited by James D. Smart. London: Epworth Press, 1964.

Die Bekenntnisschriften der evangelisch-lutherischen Kirche. Edited and published in the anniversary year of the Augsburg Confession, 1930. Göttingen, 1930 [1952]. *NL* 2 C 3. English translation: *The Book of Concord: The Confessions of the Evangelical Lutheran Church.* Edited and translated by Theodore G. Tappert, in collaboration with Jaroslav Pelikan, Robert H. Fischer, and Arthur C. Piepkorn. Philadelphia: Fortress Press, 1959.

Bethge, Eberhard. *Dietrich Bonhoeffer. Theologe - Christ - Zeitgenosse. Eine Biographie.* Munich, 1986. English translation: *Dietrich Bonhoeffer: Man of Vision. Man of Courage.* Abridged from the third German edition. Translated by Eric Mosbacher, Peter and Betty Rose, Frank Clarke, and William Glen-Doepel, under the editorship of Edwin H. Robertson. New York: Harper & Row; London: Collins, 1970.

Bonhoeffer, Dietrich. *Akt und Sein: Transzendentalphilosophie und Ontologie in der systematischen Theologie* (Act and being: Transcendental philosophy and ontology in systematic theology). Vol. 34 of *Beiträge zur Förderung christlicher Theologie* (Contributions to the advancement of Christian theology). Gütersloh, 1931; also Vol. 5 of *Theologische Bücherei* (Theological library). Edited by E. Wolf. Munich, 1956, 1976. English translation: *Act and Being*. Translated from the 1956 German edition by Bernard Noble. Introduction by Ernst Wolf. London: William Collins Sons, 1962; New York: Harper and Row, 1961. (Reprinted by New York: Octagon Books, 1983.)

———. "Christologie." *GS* 3:166–242. English translation: *Christ the Center*. A new translation by Edwin H. Robertson. London: Collins; San Francisco: Harper & Row, 1978. [U. K. Title: *Christology*].

———. "Concerning the Christian Idea of God" (1931). *GS* 3:100–109. [Written by Bonhoeffer in English.]

———. *The Cost of Discipleship*. Translated by Reginald H. Fuller, revised by Irmgard Booth. New York: Macmillan, 1963.

———. *Dietrich Bonhoeffer Werke*. 16 vols. Edited by E. Bethge, et al. Munich, 1986–. English translation: *Dietrich Bonhoeffer Works*. 16 vols. Edited by Wayne Whitson Floyd, Jr. Minneapolis: Fortress Press, 1996–.

1: *Sanctorum Communio: Eine dogmatische Untersuchung zur Soziologie der Kirche* (The communion of saints: A theological inquiry into the sociology of the church). Edited by J. von Soosten. Munich: Christian Kaiser Verlag, 1986.

2: *Akt und Sein: Transzendentalphilosophie und Ontologie in der systematischen Theologie* (Act and being: Transcendental philosophy and ontology in systematic theology). Edited by Hans-Richard Reuter. Munich: Christian Kaiser Verlag, 1988.

5: *Gemeinsames Leben. Das Gebetbuch der Bibel*. Edited by G. L. Müller and A. Schönherr. Munich, 1987. English translation: *Life Together*. Edited by Geffrey B. Kelly. Translated by Daniel W. Bloesch. *The Prayerbook of the Bible*. Edited by Geffrey B. Kelly. Translated by James Burtness. Minneapolis: Fortress Press, 1996.

9: *Jugend und Studium 1918–1927*. Edited by H. Pfeifer, with Clifford Green and C.-J. Kaltenborn. Munich: Christian Kaiser Verlag, 1986.

———. *Ethics*. Translated by Neville Horton Smith. New York: Macmillan, 1965.

———. *Gesammelte Schriften* (Collected works). 6 vols. Edited by E. Bethge. Munich, 1958–74.

———. "Man [*sic*] in Contemporary Philosophy and Theology," *NRS* 50–67 (*GS* 3:62–84).

———. *No Rusty Swords: Letters, Lectures and Notes. 1928–1936. From the Collected Works of Dietrich Bonhoeffer*, vol. 1. Edited and Introduced by Edwin H. Robertson. Translated by Edwin H. Robertson and John Bowden. London: Collins; New York: Harper and Row, 1965.

———. *Predigten – Auslegungen – Meditationen: 1925–1945* (Sermons, exegeses, meditations). 2 vols. Edited by O. Dudzus. Munich, 1984– .

———. *Sanctorum Communio*. Munich: Christian Kaiser Verlag, 1960. English translation: *The Communion of Saints*. Translated by Ronald Gregor Smith, et al. London: Collins, 1963; New York: Harper and Row, 1964 [U. K. Title: *Sanctorum Communio: A Dogmatic Inquiry into the Sociology of the Church*].

———. *Schöpfung und Fall. Versuchung*. Munich, 1968. English translation: *Creation and Fall / Temptation*. Translated by John C. Fletcher and Kathleen Downham. New York: Macmillan, 1966.

———. "The Theology of Crisis and its Attitude Toward Philosophy and Science." *NRS* 361–72 (*GS* 3:110–26). [Written by Bonhoeffer in English.]

———. *Widerstand und Ergebung: Briefe und Aufzeichnungen aus der Haft*. New edition edited by Eberhard Bethge. Munich, 1985. English translation: *Letters and Papers from Prison*. 4th ed. Translated by Reginald H. Fuller, revised by Frank Clarke et al. Additional material translated by John Bowden for the enlarged edition. London: SCM, 1971; New York: Macmillan, 1972.

Brenz, J. *De maiestate Domini nostri Iesu Christi* (The majesty of our Lord Jesus Christ). Tübingen, 1562.

Brunner, Emil. *Das Gebot und die Ordnungen: Entwurf einer protestantisch-theologischen Ethik*. Tübingen, 1932. English translation: *The Divine Imperative*. Translated by Olive Wyon. Philadelphia: Westminster Press, 1947.

Bultmann, Rudolf. *Jesus and the Word*. Translated by Louise Pettibone Smith. New York: Scribner, 1958.

Denzinger, Heinrich, and Adolfus Schönmetzer. *Enchiridion symbolorum*. Freiburg, 1976. English translation: *The Sources of Catholic Dogma*. Translated by Roy J. Deferrari. St. Louis: Herder, 1957.

Derrida, Jacques. *Writing and Difference.* Translated, with an Introduction and Additional Notes, by Alan Bass. Chicago: The University of Chicago Press, 1978.

Descartes, René. *Discours de la Méthode: Von der Methode des richtigen Vernunftgebrauchs und der wissenschaftlichen Forschung.* Translated and edited by L. Gäbe. Vol. 261 of *Philosophische Bibliothek.* Hamburg, 1960. English translation: "Discourse on the Method of Rightly Conducting the Reason." In *The Philosophical Works of Descartes,* 81–130. Translated by Elizabeth S. Haldane and G. R. T. Ross. Cambridge: Cambridge University Press, 1975.

Diels, Hermann, and Walther Kranz, eds. *Fragmente der Vorsokratiker,* vol. 1. Zürich and Berlin, 1964. English translation: *Ancilla to the Pre-Socratic Philosophers.* Translated by Kathleen Freeman. Oxford: Basil Blackwell, 1962.

Diem, Hermann. "Credo ut intelligam: Ein Wort zu Hans Michael Müllers Kritik an Karl Barths Dogmatik" (I believe, that I may understand: A word on Hans Michael Müller's critique of Karl Barth's *Dogmatics*). *Zwischen den Zeiten* 6 (1928): 517–28.

Dilthey, Wilhelm. "Ideen über eine beschreibende und zergliedernde Psychologie" (1894) (Ideas for a descriptive and analytic psychology). In his *Gesammelte Schriften,* 5/1, 139–240. Leipzig and Berlin,1924.

Disputatio de originali peccato et libero arbitrio inter Matthias Flacium et Vict. Strigelium (Disputation on original sin and freedom of the will between Matthias Flacius and Victorinus Strigel) (1560), 1563.

Gertz, Bernhard. *Glaubenswelt als Analogie: Die theologische Analogie-Lehre Erich Przywaras und ihr Ort in der Auseinandersetzung um die analogia fidei* (The world of faith as analogy: The theological teaching of analogy in Erich Przywara and its place in the debate about the analogy of faith). Düsseldorf, 1969.

Goethe, Johann Wolfgang von. *Werke.* Hamburg Edition, 14 vols. Edited by E. Trunz. Munich, 1975. English translation: *Goethe's Collected Works,* vol. 2. *Faust I & II.* Edited and translated by Stuart Atkins. Cambridge, Ma.: Suhrkamp and Insel, 1984.

Gogarten, Friedrich. "Ethik des Gewissens oder Ethik der Gnade?" (Ethic of conscience or ethic of grace?). *Zwischen den Zeiten* 1 (1923):10–29.

Grisebach, Eberhard. "Brunners Verteidigung der Theologie" (Brunner's defense of theology). *Zwischen den Zeiten* 7 (1929):90–106.

———. "Philosophie und Theologie: Fragen, Antworten und Thesen zum Abschluß der Vorlesung 'Grundprobleme der Ethik', Jena, Sommer Semester, 1928" (Philosophy and theology: Questions, answers, and theses to conclude the lectures on 'Fundamental problems of ethics'). *Theologische Blätter* 7 (1928):222–24.

Hegel, Georg Wilhelm Friedrich. *Phenomenology of Spirit*. Translated by A. V. Miller. Oxford: Oxford University Press, 1977.

———. *The Philosophy of History*. Translated by J. Sibree. New York: Dover Publications, Inc., 1956.

———. *Vorlesungen über die Philosophie des Geistes* (Lectures on the philosophy of spirit). Hamburg, 1994.

———. *Werke in Zwanzig Bänden* (Works in twenty volumes). Theorie-Werkausgabe (Scholars work edition). Frankfurt, 1969ff.

Heidegger, Martin. "Letter on Humanism." In *Basic Writings*, 193–242. Edited by David Farrell Krell. New York: Harper & Row, 1977.

Herrmann, Wilhelm. *Der Verkehr des Christen mit Gott: Im Anschluß an Luther dargestellt*. Stuttgart and Berlin, 1908. English translation: *The Communion of the Christian with God: Described on the Basis of Luther's statements*. Edited by R. T. Voelkel. Philadelphia: Fortress Press, 1971.

Kant, Immanuel. *Critique of Pure Reason*. Translated by Norman Kemp Smith. New York: St. Martin's Press, 1933.

———. *Religion within the Limits of Reason Alone*. Translated by Theodore M. Green and Hoyt H. Hudson. New York: Harper, 1960.

———. *Werke in zehn Bänden*. Edited by W. Weischedel. Darmstadt, 1968. English translation: *The Cambridge Edition of the Works of Immanuel Kant*. Cambridge: Cambridge University Press, 1992f.

Key, Ellen Karolina Sofia. *Das Jahrhundert des Kindes*. Berlin, 1905. English translation: *The Century of the Child*. New York: Arno Press, 1972 [London and New York: G. P. Putnam's Sons, 1909].

Kierkegaard, Søren. *The Concept of Anxiety : A Simple Psychologically Orienting Deliberation on the Dogmatic Issue of Hereditary Sin*. Vol. 12 of *Kierkegaard's Writings*. Edited and translated with introduction and notes by Reidar Thomte, in collaboration with Albert B. Anderson. Princeton, N.J. : Princeton University Press, 1980.

———. *Concluding Unscientific Postscript*. Vol. 12 of *Kierkegaard's Writings*. Edited and translated with introduction and notes by Howard V. Hong and Edna H. Hong. Princeton, N.J. : Princeton University Press, 1992.

——. *Gesammelte Werke.* Edited by E. Hirsch. Düsseldorf and Köln,1956ff. English translation: *Kierkegaard's Writings.* Princeton, N.J.: Princeton University Press, 1978f.

Kirchner, Timotheus. *Apologia oder Verantwortung des christlichen Concordienbuchs* (Apology or responsibility of the Christian Book of Concord). Heidelberg, 1583.

Lanz, Jakob. "Aufweis(ung)/Ausweis(ung)" (Exhibition/demonstration). In *Historisches Wörterbuch der Philosophie* (Historical dictionary of philosophy), 1:647–49. Basel and Darmstadt, 1971ff.

Loemker, L. E. "Spranger, (Franz Ernst) Eduard." In *The Encyclopedia of Philosophy,* 1–2. New York: Macmillan, 1967.

Mahlmann, Theodor. "Endlich 2" (Finite 2). In *Historisches Wörterbuch der Philosophie* (Historical dictionary of philosophy) 2:487f. Basel and Darmstadt,1971ff.

Moltmann, Jürgen. *Prädestination und Perseveranz: Geschichte und Bedeutung der reformierten Lehre "de perseverantia sanctorum"* (Predestination and perseverance: The history and significance of the Reformation teaching "on the perseverance of the saints"). Neukirchen, 1961.

Müller, Julius. *Die christliche Lehre von der Sünde.* 2 vols. Breslau, 1877 [1844]. English translation: *The Christian Doctrine of Sin.* Translated by William Urwick. Edinburgh: T. & T. Clark, 1868.

Musculus, Wolfgang. *Loci communes sacrae theologiae* (Common places of sacred theology). Basilae, 1560.

Nachlaß Dietrich Bonhoeffer: Ein Verzeichnis. Archiv – Sammlung – Bibliothek (Dietrich Bonhoeffer's literary estate: a bibliographical catalogue). Edited by Dietrich Meyer and Eberhard Bethge. Munich, 1987.

New Revised Standard Version Bible. Division of Christian Education of the National Council of the Churches of Christ in the United States of America. New York, 1989.

Nietzsche, Friedrich. *The Portable Nietzsche.* Edited and translated by Walter Kaufman. New York: Viking Press, 1968.

——. *Thus Spoke Zarathustra.* Translated and with a Preface by Walter Kaufman. New York: Viking Press, 1966.

——. *Werke in drei Bänden* (Works in three volumes). Edited by K. Schlechta. Munich,1966.

Peterson, Erik. "Der Lobgesang der Engel und der mystische Lobpreis" (The hymns of the angels and mystical praise). *Zwischen den Zeiten* 3 (1925):141–53.

------. "Über die Forderung einer Theologie des Glaubens: Eine Auseinandersetzung mit Paul Althaus" (On the challenge of a theology of faith: A discussion with Paul Althaus). *Zwischen den Zeiten* 3 (1925):281–302.

------. "Was ist Theologie?" (What is theology?) (1925). Also published in his *Theologische Traktate* (Theological tracts), 9–43. Munich, 1951.

------. "Zum Gedächtnis von Max Scheler" (In memory of Max Scheler). *Theologische Blätter* 7 (1928):165–67.

------. "Zur Theorie der Mystik" (Toward a theory of mysticism). *Zeitschrift für Systematische Theologie* 2 (1924):146–66.

Plato. *Werke*. 8 vols. Translated by F. Schleiermacher, et al. Edited by G. Eigler. Darmstadt, 1970ff. English translation: *The Collected Dialogues of Plato including the Letters*. Edited by Edith Hamilton and Huntington Cairns. New York: Pantheon Books, 1961.

Przywara, Erich. "Das katholische Kirchenprinzip" (The catholic principle of the church). *Zwischen den Zeiten* 7 (1929): 277–302.

------. *Schriften* (Works), vol. 2. Einsiedeln, 1962.

Rehmke, Johannes. *Logik oder Philosophie als Wissenslehre* (Logic or philosophy as the doctrine of knowledge). Leipzig, 1918.

Ritschl, Albrecht. *Fides implicita: Eine Untersuchung über Köhlerglauben, Wissen und Glauben, Glauben und Kirche* (Implicit faith: An investigation into blind faith, knowing and believing, believing and the church). Bonn, 1890.

------. *Unterricht in der christlichen Religion* (Instruction in the Christian religion). English translation: In *The Theology of Albrecht Ritschl*. Translated by Albert Temple Swing. Together with *Instruction in the Christian Religion* by Albrecht Ritschl. Translated by permission from the fourth German edition by Alice Mead Swing. New York: Longmans, Green, 1901.

Schaeder, Erich. *Das Geistproblem der Theologie: Eine systematische Untersuchung* (The problem of the spirit in theology: A systematic inquiry). Leipzig and Erlangen, 1924.

Schelling, Friedrich Wilhelm Joseph. *Werke* (Works), vol. 2. Hauptband: *Schriften zur Naturphilosophie 1799–1801* (Writings on the philosophy of nature 1799–1801). Edited by M. Schröter. Munich, 1927.

Schleiermacher, Friedrich Daniel Ernst. *Kurze Darstellung des theologischen Studiums zum Behuf einleitender Vorlesungen*. Edited by H. Scholz. Leipzig, 1910. English translation: *Brief Outline of the Study of Theology*. Translated by Terrence N. Tice. Richmond: John Knox Press, 1970.

Seeberg, Reinhold. *Lehrbuch der Dogmengeschichte*, 4/1: *Die Lehre Luthers*. Leipzig, 1917; 4/2: *Die Fortbildung der reformatorischen Lehre und die gegenreformatorische Lehre*. Erlangen/Leipzig, 1920. English translation: *Textbook of the History of Doctrine*, 2 vols. in 1. Translated by Charles E. Hay. Grand Rapids: Baker Book House, 1956. [Note: The English translation follows a 1904 revision by the author; its organization and pagination do not correspond to those of the 1917 edition used by Bonhoeffer.]

——. *Luther und Luthertum in der neuesten katholischen Beleuchtung* (Luther and Lutheranism in the most recent Catholic examination). Leipzig, 1904.

——. "Zur Religionsphilosophie Luthers" (Luther's philosophy of religion). *Zeitschrift für Philosophie und philosophische Kritik*. Neue Folge 164 (1917):81–115.

Suarez, Francisco de. *Opera Omnia* (Complete works). 28 vols. Paris, 1856–78.

Thomas Aquinas. *On the Truth of the Catholic Faith: Summa contra Gentiles*. Translated, with an introduction and notes, by Anton C. Pegis [and others]. Garden City, N. Y.: Image Books, 1955–57.

——. *Opera Omnia* (Complete works). 7 vols. Stuttgart, 1980.

Uhl, Willo, ed. *Der Franckforter* ("Eyn deutsch Theologia") (A German theology) [Beitrage zur stilistischen Kunst der 'Theologia Deutsch' ('der Franckforter')]. Vol. 96 of *Kleine Texte für Vorlesungen und Übungen*. Bonn,1912.

Windelband, Wilhelm. *Lehrbuch der Geschichte der Philosophie*. Edited by E. Rothacker. Tübingen, 1924. English translation: *A History of Philosophy, with Especial Reference to the Formation and Development of its Problems and Conceptions*. 2 Vols. Translated by James H. Tufts. New York: Harper, 1958.

Zanchi, Jerome. *De perseverantia sanctorum* (The perseverance of the saints). In *Opera omnia* (Complete works), vol. 7. Geneva, 1619.

3. Other Literature Related to *Act and Being*

Altenähr, Albert. *Dietrich Bonhoeffer—Lehrer des Gebets: Grundlagen für eine Theologie des Gebets bei Dietrich Bonhoeffer* (Dietrich Bonhoeffer, teacher of prayer: Foundations for a theology of prayer according to Dietrich Bonhoeffer). Würzburg, 1976.

Beintker, Michael. "Kontingenz und Gegenständlichkeit: Zu Bonhoeffers Barth-Kritik in 'Akt und Sein'" (Contingency and objectivity: On Bonhoeffer's critique of Barth in 'Act and Being'). In *Die Aktualität der Theologie Dietrich Bonhoeffers* (The actuality of the theology of Dietrich Bonhoeffer), 29–54. Edited by N. Müller. Halle, 1985.

Burtness, James H. "As Though God Were Not Given: Barth, Bonhoeffer and the Finitum Capax Infiniti." *Dialog* (Minnesota) 19 (Fall 1980):249–55.

Day, Thomas. *Dietrich Bonhoeffer on Christian Community and Common Sense.* Lewiston, N.Y.: Edwin Mellen Press, 1982.

Dumas, André. *Dietrich Bonhoeffer: Theologian of Reality.* Translated by Robert McAfee Brown. New York: Macmillan, 1971.

Eisenhuth, Heinz Erich. "Rezension von D. Bonhoeffer, Akt und Sein" (Review of D. Bonhoeffer, Act and Being). *Theologische Literaturzeitung* 58 (1933):188–90.

Feil, Ernst. *The Theology of Dietrich Bonhoeffer.* Translated by H. Martin Rumscheidt. Philadelphia: Fortress Press, 1985.

Floyd, Wayne Whitson, Jr. "Bonhoeffer, Dietrich." In *The Dictionary of Existentialism.* Westport, CT: Greenwood Publishing Group, 1996.

———. "Prospecting a Critical Theology: Sociality, Epistemology and Ethics in Bonhoeffer's *Act and Being* and Adorno's *Negative Dialectics.*" An unpublished manuscript. 1983. Bonhoeffer Archive, Union Theological Seminary, New York.

———. "Revisioning Bonhoeffer for the Coming Generation: Challenges in Translating The *Dietrich Bonhoeffer Works.*" *Dialog* 34/1 (1995):32–38.

———. "The Search for an Ethical Sacrament: From Bonhoeffer to Critical Social Theory." *Modern Theology* 7, no. 2 (January 1991):175–93.

———. "Style and the Critique of Metaphysics: The Letter as Form in Bonhoeffer and Adorno." In Floyd and Marsh, *Theology and the Practice of Responsibility,* 239–51.

———. *Theology and the Dialectics of Otherness: On Reading Bonhoeffer and Adorno.* Lanham, Md.: University Press of America, 1988. Originally written as "Theology and the Dialectics of Otherness: Epistemology, Sociality and Ethics in Bonhoeffer's *Act and Being* and Adorno's *Negative Dialectics.*" Ph.D. dissertation, Emory University, 1985.

Floyd, Wayne Whitson, Jr., and Clifford J. Green. *Bonhoeffer Bibliography: Primary Sources and Secondary Literature in English.* Evanston: American Theological Library Association, 1992.

Floyd, Wayne Whitson, Jr., and Charles Marsh. *Theology and the Practice of Responsibility: Essays on Dietrich Bonhoeffer.* Valley Forge, Pa.: Trinity Press International, 1994.

Frei, Walter. "Rezension von D. Bonhoeffer, Akt und Sein" (Review of D. Bonhoeffer, Act and Being). *Theologische Zeitschrift* 13 (1957):391–92.

Green, Clifford J. *The Sociality of Christ and Humanity: Dietrich Bonhoeffer's Early Theology, 1927–1933.* Missoula, Mont.: Scholars Press, 1975.

Huber, Wolfgang. "Bonhoeffer and Modernity." In Floyd and Marsh, *Theology and the Practice of Responsibility,* 5–19.

Knittermeyer, Hinrich. "Rezension von D. Bonhoeffer, Akt und Sein" (Review of D. Bonhoeffer, Act and Being). *Zwischen den Zeiten* 11 (1933):179–83.

Krause, Gerhard. "Dietrich Bonhoeffer und Rudolf Bultmann" (Dietrich Bonhoeffer and Rudolf Bultmann). In *Zeit und Geschichte: Dankesgabe an Rudolf Bultmann zum 80. Geburtstag* (Time and history: In gratitude to Rudolf Bultmann on his 80th birthday), 439–60. Edited by E. Dinkler. Tübingen, 1964.

Lovin, Robin. *Christian Faith and Public Choices: The Social Ethics of Barth, Brunner, and Bonhoeffer.* Philadelphia: Fortress Press, 1984.

Lowe, Walter. "Bonhoeffer and Deconstruction: Toward a Theology of the Crucified Logos." In Floyd and Marsh, *Theology and the Practice of Responsibility,* 207–21.

——. "The Critique of Philosophy in Bonhoeffer's *Act and Being.*" An unpublished manuscript, 1966.

Marsh, Charles. "Bonhoeffer on Heidegger and Togetherness." *Modern Theology* 8, no. 3 (July 1992):263–83.

——. "Human Community and Divine Presence: Bonhoeffer's Theological Critique of Hegel." *Scottish Journal of Theology* 45, no. 4 (1992):427–48.

——. "The Overabundant Self and the Transcendental Tradition: Bonhoeffer Against the Self-Reflective Subject." *Journal of the American Academy of Religion* 60, no. 4 (Winter, 1992):659–72.

——. *Reclaiming Dietrich Bonhoeffer: The Promise of His Theology.* Oxford: Oxford University Press, 1994.

Mayer, Rainer. *Christuswirklichkeit: Grundlagen, Entwicklung und Konsequenzen der Theologie Dietrich Bonhoeffers* (The reality of Christ: Foundations, development and consequences of the theology of Dietrich Bonhoeffer). Vol. 2/15 of *Arbeiten zur Theologie.* Stuttgart, 1980.

——. "Theologie und Glaube: Recht und Grenze des theologischen Systems nach Dietrich Bonhoeffer" (Theology and faith: Law and the boundary of the theological system according to Dietrich Bonhoeffer). *Evangelische Theologie* 31 (1971): 51–58.

Mokrosch, Reinhold. "Das Gewissensverständnis Dietrich Bonhoeffers: Reformatorische Herkunft und politische Funktion" (Dietrich Bonhoeffer's understanding of conscience: Its origin in the reformation and its political function). In *Bonhoeffer und Luther: Zur Sozialgestalt des Luthertums in der Moderne* (Bonhoeffer and Luther: On the social form of Lutheranism in modernity), 59–92. Edited by Christian Gremmels. Internationales Bonhoeffer Forum, no. 6. Munich, 1983.

Moltmann, Jürgen. "The Lordship of Christ and Human Society." In Moltmann, Jürgen, and Jürgen Weissbach. *Two Studies in the Theology of Bonhoeffer*, 21–94. Translated by Reginald and Ilse Fuller. Introduction by R. H. Fuller. New York: Charles Scribner's and Sons, 1967.

Möser, Peter. "Gewissenspraxis und Gewissenstheorie bei Dietrich Bonhoeffer" (The theory and practice of conscience in Dietrich Bonhoeffer). Theology diss., Heidelberg, 1983.

Ott, Heinrich. *Reality and Faith: The Theological Legacy of Dietrich Bonhoeffer.* Translated by Alex A. Morrison. Philadelphia: Fortress Press, 1972.

Pangritz, Andreas. *Dietrich Bonhoeffers Forderung einer Arkandisziplin—eine unerledigte Anfrage an Kirche und Theologie* (Dietrich Bonhoeffer's demand for an arcane discipline: an unanswered question to church and theology). Cologne: Pahl-Rugenstein, 1988.

——. *Karl Barth in der Theologie Dietrich Bonhoeffers: Eine notwendige Klarstellung* (Karl Barth in the theology of Dietrich Bonhoeffer: A necessary clarification). Berlin: Alektor-Verlag, 1989.

Pannenberg, Wolfhart. "Akt und Sein im Mittelalter" (Act and being in the Middle Ages). *Kirche und Dogma* 7 (1961):197–220.

Peters, Tiemo Rainer. *Die Präsenz des Politischen in der Theologie Dietrich Bonhoeffers: Eine historische Untersuchung in systematischer Absicht* (The presence of the political in the theology of Dietrich Bonhoeffer: A historical inquiry with a systematic intention). Vol. 18 of *Gesellschaft und Theologie: Systematische Beiträge* (Society and theology: Systematic contributions). Munich and Mainz, 1976.

Picht, Georg. "Akt und Sein: Einführung in das 11. Göttinger Physiker-Theologen-Gespräch" (Act and being: Introduction to the eleventh

Göttingen discussion between physicists and theologians) (January 28–29, 1961), unpublished manuscript. Published as "Akt und Sein bei Schelling" (Act and being according to Schelling). In his *Hier und Jetzt: Philosophieren nach Auschwitz und Hiroshima* (Here and now: Philosophizing after Auschwitz and Hiroshima), 1:309–23. Stuttgart, 1980.

Rades, Jörg Alfred. "Bonhoeffer and Hegel: From *Sanctorum Communio* to the Hegel Seminar with Some Perspectives for the Later Works." University of Saint Andrews, November 1988. Photocopy, unedited manuscript. Bonhoeffer Archive, Union Theological Seminary, New York.

———. "Kierkegaard and Bonhoeffer." University of Saint Andrews. Photocopy, unedited manuscript. Bonhoeffer Archive, Union Theological Seminary, New York.

———. "Luther and Bonhoeffer." University of Saint Andrews. Photocopy, unedited manuscript. Bonhoeffer Archive, Union Theological Seminary, New York.

———. "Nietzsche and Bonhoeffer." University of Saint Andrews. Photocopy, unedited manuscript. Bonhoeffer Archive, Union Theological Seminary, New York.

Scharlemann, Robert P. "Authenticity and Encounter: Bonhoeffer's Appropriation of Ontology." In Floyd and Marsh, *Theology and the Practice of Responsibility*, 253–65.

Schollmeyer, Matthias. "Die Bedeutung von 'Grenze' und 'Begrenzung' für die Methodologie und Grundstruktur der Theologie Dietrich Bonhoeffers" (The meaning of 'limit' and 'boundary' for the methodology and fundamental structure of the theology of Dietrich Bonhoeffer). In *Die Aktualität der Theologie Dietrich Bonhoeffers* (The actuality of the theology of Dietrich Bonhoeffer), 55–79. Edited by N. Müller. Halle, 1985.

Schwarz, Joachim. "Christologie als Modell der Gesellschaft: Eine Untersuchung zu den ersten Schriften Dietrich Bonhoeffers" (Christology as model of society: An inquiry into the first writings of Dietrich Bonhoeffer). Theological dissertation, Vienna, 1968.

Sherman, Franklin. "Act and Being." In *The Place of Bonhoeffer: Problems and Possibilities in his Thought*, 83–111. Edited by Martin E. Marty. New York: Association Press, 1962.

Tödt, Ilse, ed. *Dietrich Bonhoeffers Hegel-Seminar*. From the student notes of Ferenc Lehel. Munich: Christian Kaiser, 1988.

Weinrich, Michael. *Der Wirklichkeit begegnen: Studien zu Buber, Grisebach, Gogarten, Bonhoeffer und Hirsch* (Encountering reality: Studies in Buber, Grisebach, Gogarten, Bonhoeffer, and Hirsch). Neukirchen, 1980.

Weizsäcker, Carl Friedrich von. "Gedanken eines Nichttheologen zur theologischen Entwicklung Dietrich Bonhoeffers" (Thoughts of a non-theologian on the theological development of Dietrich Bonhoeffer). In *Genf '76: Ein Bonhoeffer-Symposion*, 29–50. Edited by Hans Pfeifer. International Bonhoeffer Forum 1. Munich, 1976. Also published in Friedrich von Weizsäcker, *Der Garten des Menschlichen: Beiträge zur geschichtlichen Anthropologie* (The garden of the human: Contributions to a historical anthropology), 454–78. Munich and Vienna, 1977.

Wendel, Ernst Georg. *Studien zur Homiletik Dietrich Bonhoeffers: Predigt—Hermeneutik—Sprache* (Studies in the homiletics of Dietrich Bonhoeffer: Sermon, hermeneutic, language). Vol. 21 of *Hermeneutische Untersuchungen zur Theologie* (Hermeneutical investigations into theology). Tübingen, 1985.

Wolf, Ernst. "Foreword" to *Act and Being*. New York: Harper and Row, 1961.

INDEX OF
SCRIPTURAL REFERENCES

INDEX OF NAMES

INDEX OF SUBJECTS

EDITORS AND TRANSLATORS

WAYNE WHITSON FLOYD, JR. (M.Div., Ph.D., Emory University) is visiting professor and director of the Dietrich Bonhoeffer Center at the Lutheran Theological Seminary at Philadelphia. An Episcopal layperson, he also serves as Canon Theologian for the Episcopal Cathedral of St. Stephen in Harrisburg, PA. He is the author of *Theology and the Dialectics of Otherness: On Reading Bonhoeffer and Adorno* (University Press of America, 1988); he co-authored the *Bonhoeffer Bibliography: Primary Sources and Secondary Literature in English* (American Theological Library Association, 1992); and he co-edited *Theology and the Practice of Responsibility: Essays on Dietrich Bonhoeffer* (Trinity Press International, 1995). In addition to his other various published essays on modern Jewish and Christian thought, Dr. Floyd's articles on Bonhoeffer have appeared in *Union Seminary Quarterly Review, Dialog, The Lutheran, Modern Theology,* and *Christian Century.*

H. MARTIN RUMSCHEIDT (Ph.D., McGill University) is professor of historical theology at Atlantic School of Theology in Halifax, Nova Scotia. He is a member of the Editorial Board of the *Dietrich Bonhoeffer Works* English Edition. He has translated works by Karl Barth, Luise Schottroff, Dorothee Sölle, and Ernst Feil's *The Theology of Dietrich Bonhoeffer* (Fortress Press, 1985).